A HUNDRED ACRES
OF AMERICA

A HUNDRED ACRES
OF AMERICA

*The Geography of Jewish American
Literary History*

M ICHAEL H OBERMAN

RUTGERS UNIVERSITY PRESS
NEW BRUNSWICK, CAMDEN, AND NEWARK,
NEW JERSEY, AND LONDON

Library of Congress Cataloging-in-Publication Data

Names: Hoberman, Michael, author.
Title: A hundred acres of America : the geography of Jewish American literary history / Michael Hoberman.
Description: New Brunswick, NJ : Rutgers University Press, [2018] | Includes bibliographical references and index.
Identifiers: LCCN 2018011675 | ISBN 9780813589701 (cloth : alk. paper) | ISBN 9780813589695 (pbk. : alk. paper) | ISBN 9780813589718 (epub) | ISBN 9780813589732 (web PDF) | ISBN 9780813589725 (mobi)
Subjects: LCSH: American literature—Jewish authors—History and criticism. | Jews in literature. | Geography in literature.
Classification: LCC PS153.J4 H63 2018 | DDC 810.9/8924—dc23
LC record available at https://lccn.loc.gov/2018011675

A British Cataloging-in-Publication record for this book is available from the British Library.

∞ The paper used in this publication meets the requirements of the American National Standard for Information Sciences—Permanence of Paper for Printed Library Materials, ANSI Z39.48-1992.

www.rutgersuniversitypress.org

Manufactured in the United States of America

This book is dedicated to my wife, Janice Sorensen.
Her love, honesty, and brilliance assure me of my truest home.

CONTENTS

CONTENTS

PREFACE

Like the members of many other ethnic groups, Jews have acculturated to America not only by imbibing the ideological precepts enshrined in its founding documents but also through their relationship to its varied geographies. Several generations of Jewish American writers have earned critical attention by highlighting the joys of individual freedom, celebrating the dignities of egalitarianism, and mulling over the implications of material bounty. Few literary scholars, however, have devoted sustained attention to the centrality of place in Jewish American literature. This book offers a new reading of Jewish American literary history that not only takes the sense of place into consideration but also assigns it signal importance as an imaginative construct. The six essays that comprise its main contents address themselves to a selection of texts beginning in the mid-nineteenth century and culminating in the first decade of the twenty-first. The first four chapters concentrate on literary texts that examine a succession of historically important North American landscapes: the frontier, the city, the small town, and the suburb. The final two chapters explore Jewish American fiction that conjures the legacy of the prewar Eastern European shtetl and the contemporary experience of the Land of Israel, respectively.

The book as a whole argues that the relationship between people and land has been intrinsic to the development of Jewish American identity. Moreover, each of the essays shows how writing about places has allowed Jewish American writers to engage, challenge, and revise the evolving motifs and themes that have shaped American literature at large. Geography is one of the few constants in American life. In a nation whose people have always been divided from one another on the basis of race, class, and a range of social exclusions and affiliations, the landscape imposes a chastening proximity that precludes ethnic isolation. Jewish American writers' varied and imaginative responses to the experience of place have contributed to their development of a dynamic and multifaceted literary legacy that engages all the exhilarations and complexities of American life without relinquishing its claim to Jewish particularity.

A HUNDRED ACRES
OF AMERICA

"A NEVER FAILING SOURCE OF INTEREST TO US"

JEWISH AMERICAN LITERATURE
AND THE SENSE OF PLACE

The yard in front of the house was very green and there was a walk running down to a little green gate not distant from the house, and on each side of this walk there was a hedge of Scotch broom. . . . The long lane in front of the house had a whitewashed plank fence on each side. . . . The lane had no turning, but came to a little white gate, which opened on the public road, and across that road there was a beautiful millpond . . . [whose] mill was a never-failing source of interest to us.

— Ellen Mordecai, "Spring Farm" (1907)[1]

More than half a century after her family left its rural Virginia homestead for the bustling city of Richmond, Ellen Mordecai strained to remember what it felt like to walk out the front door of the house at Spring Farm. In the noisy atmosphere of post–Civil War Raleigh where the blind and eighty-six-year-old Miss Mordecai sat dictating her memoir to her granddaughter, a quiet lane in the verdant Virginia countryside must have felt like a fading memory. While its expansive sentences were merely trying to represent the simple act of sauntering forth through a yard, past a gate, across a road, and to the edge of a pond, Ellen Mordecai's description was in fact an act of pure and affectionate invention on a par with the most fanciful acts of the literary imagination. As exiles, her people had long since acquired the habit of assigning a special compensatory power to words to imagine places.

The passage of time has only increased their investment in that enterprise. The familiarities, enchantments, and alien qualities of American geography have had a shaping influence upon every stage in the evolution of Jewish American literature. Reflecting upon his own earliest development as a reader and writer,

Philip Roth once said that American literature's "most potent lyrical appeal" to him lay "precisely in the sounding of the names of the country's distant places, in its spaciousness, in the dialects and the landscapes that were at once so American yet so unlike [his] own."[2]

The subject of this book is the historical relationship between the Jewish American literary imagination and the sense of place. The fact that it is the first book to devote sustained attention to this topic hardly reflects a lack of appropriate subject matter. Though few critics have highlighted either their emotional force or their ubiquity, musings like Ellen Mordecai's recollection of her family's Virginia farm are rife throughout Jewish American literature. Jewish writers have never been exempt from the tendency to seek fulfillment in and impose meaning upon American landscapes, even as their doing so has often seemed problematic and tentative within the larger framing context of diaspora, contingency, and alienation that has so frequently shaped Jewish life in the modern world. "Israel is to serve humanity precisely through separation from it," scholar Arnold Eisen has written, and belonging to America or any other land besides Israel itself challenges the very notion of Jewish identity.[3] Nonetheless, Jews have been as transfixed by American places as the members of other ethnic groups have been. Whether they have been enthralled with the dynamism of its cities, inspired by the tranquility of its rural landscapes, relieved to find a haven in its suburbs, or nostalgic for its rough-hewn charms while sojourning abroad, Jews have become Americans by virtue of their relationships to the North American continent. Through close attention to a selected group of literary sources dating from the nineteenth to the twenty-first centuries, *A Hundred Acres of America* explores the ways in which Jewish subjects have engaged the long-standing American tendency to contemplate and experience geography as a crucible for the formation of cultural identity.

For Jews, whose history has been marked by a profound belief in the transformational power of the written word to fill a fluctuating world with meaning, writing about places enables both self-discovery and communal reckoning.

Given the Jews' vaunted heritage as the "People of the Book" and the "wandering" motif that has so long defined their strained passage through world history and geography, the idea that Jewish American writers would be so deeply invested in expressing their attachments to and misgivings about places makes perfect sense. As the critic Brooke Fredericksen asserts, "The idea of written-ness is the underpinning of the culture" and has often made up for an absence of geographic cohesion in Jewish life.[4] Writing about their relationships to places has been an integral means by which Jews have reckoned with their reputed lack of territorial agency in the New World. Whether they have regarded America as their Promised Land or as an extension of their exile, Jewish American writers have devised meaningful and fraught relationships to its geographic heritage in order to understand themselves more fully. The Jewish historical experience has stipulated "profound displacement," but specific places matter and warrant serious attention throughout the Jewish American canon.[5] Writing about American places has forced Jewish Americans to compare themselves to gentile Americans and to engage the topic of race. It has encouraged them to experiment with, expand upon, and alter American idioms. It has inspired them to sound and test the limits of American pluralism. It has also enabled them to exert profound, if subtle and complex, influences upon the national discourse.

Our collective failure to note the many instances in which Jewish American writers have purposefully and passionately written about places reflects long-standing assumptions about the Jewish American experience. It has come about as the result of some fairly simplistic formulations, including the notion that America is a place that Jews of yesteryear came *to* as opposed to a place that they now come *from*. While few Jewish American writers have ever unequivocally asserted their historical rootedness in the land, their reluctance to do so has had less to do with any lack of affinity on their part for American places than it does with their misgivings about making unequivocal assertions in general. Moreover, if Jewish authors have desisted from asserting strong claims to American soil, their hesitation to do so has not resulted from any lack of appreciation on their part for the importance of place. The writers whose work I have highlighted in this book accept the complex conditions that have defined their inhabitation of the North American continent. From mid-nineteenth-century travel writers who acknowledge the multiracial composition of frontier society to late twentieth-century novelists whose alienated protagonists pay the price for their physical isolation from the rest of American society, the authors represented in *A Hundred Acres of America* typically reject straightforward formulations of geographically specific cultural identities.

Jewish American literature often engages the sense of place by eliding, or at least questioning, the notion of territoriality. At its most subversive, it does invoke more proprietary elements within the American literary tradition—but often in order, as one critic puts it, to "turn this inheritance from a reassuring postcard-certified landscape into an open, mutable diasporan space."[6] In its subtler manifestations, it expresses just the sort of wistfulness that Ellen Mordecai and Philip Roth enunciate. It rarely comes free of misgivings, insecurities, or qualifications, but its reluctance to assert claims is as much the result of its literariness as it is of its Jewishness. After all, writing about places is not the same thing as staking permanent birthright claims to them. Even as Jewish Americans have constituted some of the nation's most geographically mobile inhabitants and reputedly its most stalwart aficionados of urban settings in particular, they have formed strong psychic relationships to all the places they have passed through, visited, settled in, and even just imagined. Their practice of writing about those places, as literary scholar Sarah Phillips Casteel writes, "reflects [their] desire . . . to participate in—sometimes admiringly and sometimes critically—the discourses about land and belonging."[7] Given the frequency with which the participants in so many other "minority" ethnic American literary traditions have imagined places in order to shore up their own discrete and complex cultural identities, the frequency with which Jewish American authors have attempted to formulate their relationships to the American landscape should be perfectly understandable. Writing about place has enabled them to test assumptions, challenge hegemonies, and assert agency.

Though it has been a frequently neglected and underappreciated component of literary and historical study, "the innate human desire to be connected to a place," as historian Joseph Amato has written, has been intrinsic to the shaping of American history and the development of American cultural identities.[8] Recent scholarship in the humanities has emphasized the importance of geography as a shaping force that both underlies and complicates cultural identities. This "reacquisition of the spatial dimension" bears important implications for the study of Jewish American and Jewish literature in general.[9] Against the backdrop of a pluralistic and dynamic society, the literary representation of place comprises one of the most profound reference points for gaining insight into the invention and proliferation of ethnic selves, not to mention the syncretic adjustments that follow from such a high volume of cultural convergences. *A Hundred Acres of America* suggests that Jewish writers' engagement with the classic locales of American identity-making has been a central but largely disregarded component of their acquisition and transformation of American culture. By exploring the ways in which Jewish American subjects have contemplated and experienced geography as a basis for literary historical and cultural continuity, the essays in this book challenge preconceived notions of Jews as either oppressed outsiders to or excessively complacent recipients of American privilege. The book posits the idea of homecoming as the dominant motif in Jewish American literary history.

This book's focus on place as an organizing principle for the study of Jewish American literary history also offers an alternative to the immigrant model that has so long prevailed in the field, according to which several successive generations of newcomers from Europe either lost, abandoned, or transformed their Jewish souls and evolved into American selves. While the immigrant experience has been central to the formation of Jewish American identity, like any conceptual framework, it imposes as many limits on understanding as it offers possibilities for insight. As critic Benjamin Schreier has recently argued, the immigrant model has been so thoroughly "naturalized and normalized that no one ever thinks of analyzing or mentioning it."[10] For many Jews, Old World origins were themselves exilic, oppressive, and often eminently forgettable. This book argues that a rich and complex relationship with American geography itself, and not merely the immigrant experience, constitutes a central reference point and touchstone for the development, over the course of several centuries, of a Jewish literary consciousness in the United States.

One of the most regrettable effects that the immigrant model has wrought upon the practice of Jewish American literary history has been its tendency to mark the origin of notable Jewish writing as only having occurred at the turn of the twentieth century, when the largest "wave" of immigrant Jews arrived in the United States from the Eastern European Pale of Settlement. By effectively postponing the birth of Jewish American literature to the point at which the largest numbers of Jewish immigrants arrived in the cities of a heavily industrializing United States, scholars have perhaps unwittingly acquiesced to a view that Jews who arrived in America during the seventeenth, eighteenth, and nineteenth centuries were, by definition, anomalous strangers in a strange land as opposed to active agents in the fashioning of a dynamic national culture.[11] This book does not ignore the importance of immigration and modernization as central components in the formation of Jewish American cultural identity, and more than half of its contents are addressed to works by the progeny of Ashkenazi Jews. By concentrating on how Jewish writers described and responded to a range of American geographic settings from the earliest phases of American history to the present, however, including nonurban environments during a preindustrial era, it resists the temptation to read Jewish history as external to American history until well after the Civil War. It posits Jewish history, American history, and the inhabitation of American geography from the colonial era onward as entirely contiguous entities.

In addition to its departure from the immigrant model and to its positing of an earlier point of origin for Jewish American literary history, *A Hundred Acres of America* widens the boundaries of what constitutes properly American subject matter. As much recent scholarship not only on early America but also on contemporary culture has shown, America itself cannot be properly encompassed by a viewpoint that limits its scope to the space of the North American continent south of Canada and north of Mexico. The essays in this book, whether they concern themselves with the travelogues of mid-nineteenth-century Jewish explorers in the Far West or with the fiction writing of fifth- and sixth-generation millennial Jewish youth in postindustrial urban America, examine texts whose writers are inspired by the landscapes but not constricted by the politically determined parameters of North American geography. The book's transnational focus proceeds from the first two chapters' exploration of the writing of nineteenth-century Jewish writers whose personal origins, families, trade networks, and written subject matter necessitated frequent travel to and relationships with communities on both sides of the Atlantic as well as through the Caribbean and up and down the Eastern Seaboard of North America. The book's final portions, which explore contemporary Jewish American representations of prewar Europe and contemporary Israel, address the relationship between American-born Jewish subjects (whose sense of self was a product of their identification with American geography) and their lands of ancestral origin across the ocean.

For all of its variability as a theme and negation of arbitrary borders, the subject of place necessitates that writers form relationships with physical actualities—the places themselves. The organization of *A Hundred Acres of America* reflects this circumstance. Each chapter in the book takes shape around a specific landscape category. The first half of the book explores three "classic" American geographies of the pre–World War II period—the frontier, the city, and the small town—when most Jews in America still acted upon and felt their Otherness. In regarding these three settings as they were configured in the "aspirational" phase of Jewish American history, I have explored how Jewish American authors both incorporated and responded to dominant tendencies within American literature. For instance, chapter 2 explores what I refer to as the Jewish colonial revival—a cohort of late nineteenth- and early twentieth-century amateur historians. These writers' accounts of early Jewish settlements in the cities of the Eastern Seaboard sought at once to mimic the heritage-minded predilections of the "local color" movement and to argue that dynamic cities, as opposed to unchanging rural nooks, were the birthplaces not only of Jewish American history but also of American history writ large. Writing about these sorts of places allowed Jews to engage and also critique dominant motifs concerning America's geographic origins. It enabled them to act upon their homecoming urges without entirely relinquishing their exilic perspectives.

While the book's first three chapters address the sorts of geographical settings into which Jewish Americans sought entry and acceptance during a probationary and assimilative period of their history, the final three essays in the book concern themselves with an aftermath condition in which they have often sought to extract themselves from the mainstream of American life. What the American exurb, the imaginary Eastern European shtetl, and the Land of Israel all have in common is the fact of their removal from, as opposed to their proximity to, the majority American experience. After World War II, as Jews attained the status not only of "white folks" but also of highly educated and financially secure beneficiaries of American plenitude, their relationship to American geography, like their relationship to the American social conditions that influence that geography, evolved dramatically. No longer preoccupied by their eagerness to fit in, Jewish American writers of the contemporary period, whose birth or at least adulthood postdated the anxiety-filled era during which Jews were outsiders trying to gain entry, instead grappled with the troubling facts that accompanied, or tainted, their achievement of American success. Especially as members of other, and particularly nonwhite minority, groups have sought to dramatize their experiences of oppression and their attempts to assert agency through their attention to the meaning of place, Jewish American beneficiaries of white skin privilege have found themselves at a loss for how to see themselves positively reflected in the landscapes whose bounty they have inherited. Their attempts to cope with this problem have resulted in a literature that is profoundly American in its idioms and themes but sometimes darkly alienated from America itself.

If critics have thus far either not noticed or ignored the extent to which writers in the Jewish American literary tradition have not only considered but also devoted their full attention to exploring the meaning of place, it may be because the quiet and seemingly unchanging facts of geography so often appear to provide little more than a backdrop to the more dramatic stories that shape people's lives. From dynamic narratives that describe the transformation of Jewish immigrants into Americans, to verbally stupendous accounts of social triumph and downfall among assimilated Jews, to stylistically innovative reinventions of Jewish identity in the postmodern idiom, Jewish American literature has already provided more than enough excitement and stylistic energy to keep scholars busy. "Pulses race and pound in debates over ethnic history and gender history," the historian Patricia Nelson Limerick wrote in 1996, but for many scholars, the study of place "is where one goes for a nap."[12] Region and place are far more fraught arenas than sentimental formulations and simplifying mythologies would have us believe, however. America has been a zone of cultural encounters for the last several centuries, and place has been its main convergence point. The tranquil and virtually unpeopled image of a pleasant Virginia farmstead that Ellen Mordecai conjured in her memoir represented only one facet of a far more complex and, frankly, disturbing reality about the history of American locales.

In her book *Mordecai: An Early American Family*, biographer Emily Bingham points out that the Mordecai family's occupancy of Spring Farm in 1819 bore significant racial implications. The Mordecais had risen to social prominence during the first two decades of the nineteenth century because of the innovative school for young women that they had founded and run in Warrenton, North Carolina. When they decided to close the school and move to the farm on the outskirts of Richmond (in part in order to be closer to an organized Jewish community in that city), their action had its most dramatic effect upon the several slaves who were "bought . . . sold, and . . . sent to Richmond to be hired out."[13] Moreover, from "the hedge of Scotch broom" to the "whitewashed plank fence" that stood on either side of what was undoubtedly a lovely lane that marked the approach to the Mordecai family's new house, the landscape's most noticeable and pleasant characteristics—the very ones whose features Ellen Mordecai had so lovingly attempted to recapture in her memoir—had been the products of forced labor performed by enslaved African Americans.

Jewish American writers may well have promulgated a range of subtle and even subversive critiques of the pioneering and proprietary mythologies that have shaped so much of the discourse on American places since well before the Civil War. That being said, the work of many of these writers has also, as Sarah Casteel points out, been "implicated in the dynamics of settlement and conquest."

They are complicit in the very acts by which so many American places have been precluded from being the oases of tranquility and peace we like to imagine and reminisce upon.[14] A literary tradition that continues to bear such a significant influence upon the culture at large cannot help but partake in the nation's most troubling transgressions, even if its adherents have sometimes believed or wished themselves to be outsiders to it. I say this on the basis of firsthand experience as well as upon scholarly authority. My background as an educated and politically liberal product of late twentieth-century urban Jewish American culture has done little to inoculate me against the power of truth-obscuring romantic mythologies. From my earliest frog-catching adventures as a day-camper on Staten Island to my family's proprietorship of a five-acre homestead in western Massachusetts, enthrallment with the American landscape and admiration for the reputedly intrepid settlers who populate its history have been the most consistent and powerful shaping forces in my imaginative life. Against the backdrop of an imagined Promised Land, it has always been perilously easy to repress and abstract the conflicts and contingencies that define us both as Jews and as human beings.

1

"IN THIS VESTIBULE OF GOD'S HOLY TEMPLE"

THE FRONTIER ACCOUNTS OF SOLOMON CARVALHO
AND ISRAEL JOSEPH BENJAMIN, 1857–1862

"LET IT STORM ELSEWHERE": JEWISH TEXTS DOMESTICATING THE FAR WEST

Solomon Nunes Carvalho realized how deep into the wilderness he had traveled when he met an Indian hunter on the banks of the Arkansas River. The nephew of a cantor and the son of one of Reform Judaism's American founders, Carvalho watched in horror as the man borrowed his knife, used it to extract the liver from a freshly killed antelope, and then ate the organ raw. In the book he later wrote about his experience as the daguerreotypist for John C. Frémont's expedition across the Rocky Mountains from 1853 to 1854, Carvalho confessed to having at first "considered the Indian little better than a cannibal," recalling that as he accepted the bloody knife back, he "turned from [the hunter] in disgust." Days afterward, however, Carvalho had "got bravely over it" and was not only devouring buffalo steaks and venison in the company of his Cheyenne hosts but also "magically" polishing the tribal women's brass bracelets with the quicksilver he had brought to make daguerreotypes.[1]

Carvalho's willingness to forgo the rules of kashrut eventually proved to be essential to his physical survival. It also indicated his awareness that life in the wilderness neither freed him from social obligations nor relieved him of the responsibility to act upon the conscientious and tactful impulses he had acquired as a Charleston-born Jew of Sephardic parentage. Sharing enthusiastically in the Cheyennes' repast, even at the expense of his own dietary principles, he demonstrated his respect for the preexisting, historically informed protocols that had shaped his and his coreligionists' negotiated existence in the diaspora. Carvalho's temporary abandonment of Jewish dietary laws did not stipulate the abandonment of all laws. He seems to have understood that while frontiers and

9

borderlands may appear to some of their newest inhabitants to be lawless places where ordinary social codes do not bind on human interactions, successful passage through such places demands a high degree of cultural sensitivity and collaborative improvisation.

Rather than announcing his own accomplishments as a master of the frontier environment in his 1857 book, *Incidents of Travel and Adventure in the Far West*, Carvalho emphasized the complex social interactions that shaped his experiences in the wilderness. "In the heyday of imperialist expansion and acquisition," as Rachel Rubinstein points out, Carvalho's representations of the Native Americans he met on the prairie, the Mormons he later encountered in Utah, and the polyglot members of Frémont's expeditionary party were "curious, absorptive, willing to suspend judgment, self-mocking, and self-effacing."[2] No matter how wild and remote the immediate physical surroundings were, he understood and welcomed the presence of human order wherever he encountered it.

Carvalho's emphasis on the social component of the Frémont expedition set his approach apart from the dominant strain in nineteenth-century treatments of the frontier experience, which eagerly embraced the notion that escape from more densely populated areas offered an expansionist future free from the behavioral restraints imposed by historically inscribed societal compacts. James Fenimore Cooper's Hawkeye described the contempt he felt toward his tradition-bound English colonist brethren: "My people have many ways, of which, as an honest man, I can't approve."[3] The dominant mode in mid-nineteenth-century American depictions of such places was mythological, not historical, in its conception. Accordingly, as Richard Slotkin explains, "the complexities of social and historical experience [were] simplified and compressed into the action of individuals."[4] As Huckleberry Finn would announce in 1884, "the territory" was the place he planned to "light out for" in flight from his aunt's and others' attempts to "sivilize" him into acquiescence with its outmoded rules of engagement. According to this same individualistic formulation, in instances in which its remoteness enforced a state of depravity, the wilderness inspired people to act on their basest, most ancient instincts.

The defining element in dominant nineteenth-century American representations of the frontier experience was dialectical: the novelty of its geographical separation inspired its inhabitants' tendencies either to abandon the legacy of preexisting social arrangements altogether or to revert to a state that enforced primitive hierarchies. The two Jewish authors who are the subject of this chapter generally ignored this dialectical condition. Within a wider milieu that often ascribed to the wilderness the transcendent power not only to erase history but also to rejuvenate (or corrupt) individuals, their books about the Far West diminished the significance of single persons and engaged the highly contingent and often peculiar historical implications that were entailed by the collective settlement of new places. They did their best to domesticate its wildest prospects through the expression of humanistic, and sometimes theological, sentiments, and in so doing, they created a decentering counternarrative to the notion of the United States as a quintessential "'frontier' settler nation" dominated by rampant individuals.[5]

Solomon Carvalho's attempt to write about the Far West yielded an account that emphasized its author's eagerness to act in quiet and highly personalized accordance with diasporic expectations, but it did not comprise the only representation of a Jewish perspective on the antebellum American West. Five years after his *Incidents of Travel and Adventure in the Far West* was published, another self-consciously Jewish author, the Romanian-born Israel Joseph Benjamin (1818–1864), published *Three Years in America* (1862), a book that, in an even more deliberate fashion, also read the geography of the western wilderness through the lens of the diaspora. Writing in German for the edification of an assimilated German-Jewish audience (the book was published in Hanover), its author devoted considerable time to surveying the region's growing Jewish congregations, particularly in California. While Carvalho's book, in keeping with its title, concentrated in episodic fashion on "incidents" that occurred in the company of specific people and highlighted its author's singular "adventures" in particular places, Benjamin wrote in a more reportorial mode, attempting to comprehend all of the Far West as one of several logical, even prophetically anticipated, destinations for Jewish settlement. As an outsider to the United States who was nonetheless enthusiastic about its prospects as a place where Jews might retain their traditions under the protection of a beneficent nation-state, Benjamin described the Far West as an extension of, rather than a departure from, an emancipated Europe and a prosperous diaspora. "Let it storm elsewhere," he wrote, invoking several biblical prophecies, including Micah's famous meditation on the peace to be had by every man under his "vine and fig tree."[6]

The Legacy of the "Finishing Up Country": Reckoning the History of Western History

As Dalia Kandiyoti points out, since the United States itself was "founded on the erasure of the story of conquest and empire," it is no wonder that "the fiction of available land as a basis of national feeling" would come to "define the mission of the 'classic' American author."[7] The literary record of the North American frontier in the nineteenth century included significant evidence of a collective desire to forget or at least dismiss the importance of history. Owing to their ideological fixation with the notion of new beginnings, their sense that they were discovering and settling "virgin land," and their widespread belief in the nation's "Manifest Destiny" to occupy the space between the Atlantic and the Pacific oceans, many writers of the period who sought to represent the settlement of the West described it as a vast territory whose most distinguishing features erased the capacity for memory.[8] Well into the nineteenth century, the literature of the American frontier had often sought, for both ideological reasons and the purposes of pure entertainment, to maintain the idea of the individual's triumph over history. The legacy of the past could be eliminated through the conquest of land that, according to the collective imagination, was all but empty of any significant human trace. Frontiersmen were depicted, and sometimes portrayed themselves, as bigger, bolder, louder, and freer than their more civilized counterparts along the seaboard and inland waterways.[9] Frontier communities were represented as "at best tributary and derivative and of little serious interest" from a cultural standpoint.[10]

As the section of the United States whose depiction and place in the collective imagination has been the most frequently influenced by the power of myth, the West has long constituted the nation's idea of what one mid-nineteenth-century writer, Thomas Bangs Thorpe, referred to in his mock tall tale "The Big Bear of Arkansas" as a "finishing up country."[11] With its vast open spaces and its gargantuan landscape features, the West's very scale seemed to invite the nineteenth-century authors who wrote about it in detail to assert its symbolic capacity to transcend all earlier geographies. But while the looming presence of myth has been intrinsic to the life of the West and caused "the proportions of most recorded western history" to be "strangely inconsistent with the visible realities of western life," as Earl Pomeroy has put it, we are well advised to remember that the study of western history does not offer an "escape from modern troubles" but a direct confrontation with them.[12] Thanks in large part to the generation of western scholars who have chronicled the region's history as, among other things, an urbanized, multilingual, and racially diverse arena, we understand that what the myth has long configured as a spatial expanse whose vastness and evident distance from the rest of the world rendered time irrelevant was experienced by actual people "as a place—as many complicated environments occupied by natives who considered their homelands to be the center, not the edge" of existence.[13]

Within the Jewish experience of the diaspora, the notion of an easily delineated difference between core and periphery hardly ever applied, and the frontier was more of a social arena than an avenue of escape from human interaction. With no consistent or definable geographic center shaping the conditions of their portable identity, Jews had learned to experience life as a constant "dialectic between tent and house, nomadism and agriculture, wilderness and Canaan, wandering and settlement, Diaspora and State."[14] Given their unique ancestry and religious orientation, Solomon Carvalho's and Israel Joseph Benjamin's descriptions of the time they spent in the American wilderness emphasized the forms of social order and contiguity that they found there, however fleeting they may have been. Though Jews, of all peoples, may seem to have had the most to gain by turning their backs on a history that for them had been full of cruelty and collective suffering, the idea of a brand-new beginning in a potentially lawless environment could only have suggested still greater dangers to them than anything they had previously experienced. As Barbara Mann explains, because Jews have always been "a displaced people," they have been all the more willing and able to "turn space into place"—in other words, to domesticate liminal sites.[15]

For a range of reasons, the denial of history has rarely suited Jews, whose only alignments with the "finishing up country" have been figments of an apocalyptic Christian imagination that once configured Native Americans as members of the Lost Tribes of Israel in order to project an imminent Armageddon.[16] The American West in the nineteenth century was no more a "finishing up" country for Jews (or any number of other "minority" populations) than New England had been for Puritans in the seventeenth. If anything, its settlement did not vanquish historical patterns; it reified, extended, and complicated them. For writers like Carvalho and Benjamin, the West was "a magnetic new epicenter" that "dramatized what might be called the continentalization of the American and the American Jewish experience."[17] The earliest Jews to travel to the Far West were not escapees from civilization or order but people who sought stability where they could find it and were also willing and able to be agents of that stability in the midst of an ever-shifting and dynamic social geographical milieu. "If Jewish history is . . . a story of confrontation at the margin," Bryan Stone writes, "then Jews in peripheral places, where confrontation with non-Jews is commonplace and unavoidable, become central to the Jewish experience."[18] In a world in which travel writing in general offered people of European ancestry "a sense of ownership, entitlement and familiarity with respect to the different parts of the world that were being explored, invaded, invested in, and colonized,"[19] Jewish writers like Carvalho and Benjamin could be especially sensitized to the efficacy of adaptive, as opposed to disruptive, behavior.

Owing in large part to their sustained attention to the geography of the Far West, Carvalho's and Benjamin's travel accounts comprise the most telling indices of this domesticating tendency within the nineteenth-century Jewish American canon. By openly proclaiming his own limited ability to describe the vast landscape he experienced on his journey, Solomon Carvalho produced a memoir of his 1853–1854 trip across the Rockies that diverged notably from the dominant pattern of hyperbolic and self-aggrandizing frontier literary reminiscences that had been written by or ghostwritten for such men as Jim Bridger and Kit Carson. His book also reverted to an age-old pattern according to which Jews avoided investing excessive claims upon the importance of an exilic geography. Instead of supplying an account of his triumph over the wilderness, Carvalho posited an alternative, chastening view of the Far West's grand landscape features as humbling presences that seemed at times to have been inspired by his reading of the Hebrew Bible. Israel Joseph Benjamin's 1862 account of his travel through the Far West on the eve of the Civil War offered a self-consciously prophetic investigation of American geography as a font of potential Jewish and, indeed, civilization-wide renewal—or downfall. Benjamin's version of the Far West was invested with and overdetermined by such an excess of prophetic historical meaning that the individual describing it had by necessity to relinquish all hubristic claims upon its transformational power to release him from the legacies of the past or the obligations of the present. For Carvalho and Benjamin alike, the awe-inspiring geography of the frontier precluded the repression of a haunted past or the launching of an autonomous self. Instead of inviting them to forget their ties, either to their fellow Jews or to the gentile society that surrounded them, the landscape of the Far West presented itself as a touchstone to historical memory, edifying companionship, and the promise of sustained contact with the outside world.

"TO PROVE THE CORRECTNESS AND AUTHENTICITY OF
MY STATEMENTS": SOLOMON NUNES CARVALHO'S
INCIDENTS OF TRAVEL AND ADVENTURE IN THE FAR WEST

Solomon Nunes Carvalho was thirty-eight years old and an accomplished portrait artist and daguerreotypist when he accepted John C. Frémont's invitation to join his exploratory party on August 22, 1853.[20] The group was about to undertake a midwinter crossing of the Far West from Kansas to California. The dangerous expedition's charge (which Frémont was funding out of his own pocket) was to map out a potential route for the transcontinental railroad. The party's achievement of safe passage through the worst imaginable conditions in the Rocky Mountains, the Great Basin, and the Sierra Nevada would ascertain the viability of Frémont's proposed route for the train's crossing.[21] While Frémont was an old hand at wilderness exploration and had gained his entire reputation as a public figure by virtue of his leadership of trips like this one, Carvalho was an urbane and coddled scion of the Jewish merchant class, entirely unschooled in the art of outdoor survival. By the year of his birth in 1815, several generations of Solomon Nunes Carvalho's family had established a pattern of seeking an orderly existence in waypoints of civilization. Refugees from the Inquisition, they made their homes first in Amsterdam and then in London, where Carvalho's grandfather and namesake had been born in 1743. Solomon's father, David Carvalho, had spent eight years in Barbados before leaving that island for the bustling Jewish community of Charleston in 1811, where he was one of the founders of the New World's first Reform congregation. While he never referred overtly to his Judaic heritage in the course of his narrative,[22] Carvalho's representation of the Far West reflected this diasporic perspective. Having spent most of his youth in Philadelphia and Baltimore, by the mid-1850s he had established daguerreotype studios in those cities as well as in Charleston and New York. Despite his urban upbringing and the fact that he was "accustomed to the luxuries that were part of his heritage as a Jewish grandee,"[23] Carvalho also possessed a plucky (and, to his intermittent detriment, reckless) spirit.

He did not hesitate to accept Frémont's invitation, and he left his home in New York to join the party in September 1853. Within two weeks of departing New York, he was on the Missouri-Kansas border, where final preparations for the expedition were under way. For the duration of his time along the exploratory trail, from September 1853 to June 1854, Carvalho kept track of the places he saw and the people he met. Like many other would-be chroniclers of the wonders of the Far West, however, Carvalho faced a considerable challenge in doing so: How might he render an accurate *and* credible written description of extraordinary places and adventurous occurrences whose sheer scale exceeded anything known in Europe or the eastern United States? Highly sensitive to the difficulty of the task that faced him as he sought to present an account of his travels that would highlight, as opposed to gloss over or ignore, the Far West's contiguity with known landscapes, Carvalho produced a work that was self-consciously and consistently attentive to its origin as an act of literary invention. It was, as Robert Shlaer suggests, "not a journal . . . not a narrative . . . [but] exactly what it claimed to be in the title, incidents."[24] The somewhat unconventional history of its composition no doubt contributed to its eventual shape. Because Frémont had expressly forbidden any member of his party to keep a journal of the expedition's proceedings, Carvalho only managed to cobble an actual book together by stringing together the long letters he had written to his wife during the course of his travels. Its most distinguishing aspect, as Rachel Rubinstein points out, was the fact that it was "a travel narrative that in many ways circumvent[ed] the triumphalist conventions of the Euroamerican narrative of discovery, adventure, and conquest."[25]

Instead of resorting to the dominant and popular frontier tropes of hyperbole and bluster, Carvalho attempted to resolve the credibility dilemma by soberly embracing his appointed role as the chronicler of the expedition's progress (he was, in fact, the only member of the party ever to produce a full-length account of its journey; Frémont himself was preoccupied with other matters and never prepared any sort of final report[26]). As Carvalho conceived of it, the trip was to derive all of its interest and legitimacy from its production of a thorough record of its progress and achievements. The raw material of experience would be transformed, thanks not only to the words he wrote in his account but also to the photographs he had been hired to take en route to California, into a cultivated and artful textual record of human observation and accomplishment in the midst of the wilderness. Moreover, by concentrating so much of his attention on the complex social interactions that had influenced the journey's progress at each of its junctures (including his extended sojourn among Utah's Mormons), Carvalho knew that he was writing against the tide of individualistic frontier literature. By virtue of its consistent attention to the framing cultural and social contexts within which the Frémont expedition had been undertaken, the account that Carvalho wrote and published of the trip presented a profound testament to an emergent Jewish American literary perspective on the geography of the American West. His book's uniquely Jewish contribution took shape as it decentered the era's dominant motif of individualistic triumphalism. As Sarah Phillips Casteel has recently written, Jewish American writers "unsettle[d]" such "myths by exposing them to the profoundly historicist orientation of Jewish diasporic consciousness."[27]

POETIC PROSPECTS: CARVALHO'S EVOCATION
OF THE EMERSONIAN SUBLIME

Solomon Nunes Carvalho's *Incidents of Travel and Adventure in the Far West* domesticated its subject matter. The author described every extremity in geographical and climatic conditions he had encountered in effusive and often stilted terms. An early morning view of the prairie in what is now central Kansas offered a case in point. The passage's self-consciously programmatic language and its invocation of an entirely derivative romantic nomenclature would have been worthy of William Cullen Bryant, among others. With its particular attention to the changing sky, the description's rich visual configurations also replicated the emotive and symbolically fraught landscape paintings of Thomas Cole:

> At the dawn of the day I was up; I found the weather perfectly clear; and in breathless expectation of seeing the sun rise, I saddled my pony, determined to ride away from the camp.... Gradually the eastern horizon assumed a warmer hue, while some floating clouds along its edge, developed their form against the luminous heavens. The dark grey morning tints were superseded by hues of the most brilliant and gorgeous colors, which almost imperceptibly softened, as the glorious orb of day commenced his diurnal course, and illumined the vault above; a slight rustling of the long grass, caused by a deliciously pleasant zephyr, which made it move in gentle undulation, was all that disturbed the mysterious silence that prevailed.[28]

By the time he had set out with Frémont in 1853, Carvalho had already established himself as a painter of some renown, so his framing of the scene along such deliberately coloristic, visually expressive, and spiritually elevated lines was in part a function of his own artistic vision, not to mention his susceptibility to the era's prevailing romantic ethos. He had received his early training as a painter from Philadelphia's Thomas Sully (1783–1872), and in the years preceding his taking up the work of a daguerreotypist, his own work showed a strong tendency to evoke abstract and spiritual associations through his use of color.[29] In his capacity as a professional photographer who had also made paintings for a living, Carvalho brought a framing perspective to bear upon the vast prairie landscapes he was now encountering for the first time in his life.

Carvalho had not merely stumbled upon this prospect, after all. By announcing to the reader that he had risen from bed that morning "determined to ride away from the camp," he revealed that his domesticating, artistic impulse had driven him to view the prairie sunrise. In the resulting rendering of the western landscape, geographical description served a strictly spiritual and ideological purpose and sought to inspire the elevation of the human soul. In Carvalho's rendering, the physical experience of the frontier proffered a supple stillness, a symbolically evocative encounter whose meaning could only be appreciated and derived as a profoundly and poetically exquisite aesthetic experience. Art and artistic representation were central components in Carvalho's attempt to frame his understanding of the western frontier's role in American life. He could not so much as describe its subtlest features without energetic resort to the visionary language of the arts. For all of its dangerous and physically intimidating potential, the prairie itself was a canvas of sorts, not to mention a font of inspiration for those who would seek to engage the revivifying power of divinity to restore and rejuvenate humanity. In the letters home that would eventually form the basis for his book, he engaged a painterly vocabulary. The book itself, which he composed without access to the daguerreotypes over which he had labored so hard, attempted to render a verbal record that could compensate for their absence.

The prairie's wildest aspects served the wider interests of those who sought heights of refinement as opposed to an escape from such urbane figurations and concerns. Having described the outward scene of the prairie sunrise, Carvalho went on in his account to narrate the sequence of personal revelations that affected him in its immediate aftermath. "My heart beat with fervent anxiety," he wrote, "and whilst I felt happy, and free from the usual care and trouble, I still could not master the nervous debility which seized me while surveying the grand and majestic works of nature. Was it fear? no, it was the conviction of my own insignificance, in the midst of the stupendous creation; the undulating grass seemed to carry my thoughts on its rolling surface, into an impenetrable future; glorious in inconceivable beauty, extended over me, the ethereal tent of heaven, my eye losing its power of distant vision, seemed to reach down only to the verdant sea before me."[30] If the landscape itself was of any importance within such a vision, it was owing to its powers to inspire the hope for a renewal of the human spirit. Rather than constituting the central subject of Carvalho's narrative account on its own alien terms or elevating him personally, the sweeping view occasioned an aesthetic flight of fancy and a personal revelation in which the land and the wind that traversed it spoke the language of the writer's longing but diminished soul. The writer freely acknowledged the distance that lay between him and the "stupendous," "impenetrable," and "inconceivable" meanings embodied by the endless prospect. The story he told about his encounter with that prospect had to make up for the fact that he could not supply his audience with a visual reproduction of it. Verbal memory was a wanting substitute for visual art.

In a sense, the Kansas prairie was Carvalho's version of Ralph Waldo Emerson's "bare common." As in Emerson's "transparent eyeball" passage in *Nature*, time spent in such places reminded the writer of an in-dwelling divinity whose recognition was entirely a function of his human-ness. Not surprisingly, the literary conventions of the era had insinuated themselves into Carvalho's rendering of the American wilderness, further domesticating its otherwise untouchable and indifferent aspect. At the end of a particularly dangerous arduous ascent in southwestern Colorado, Carvalho recounted, he and Frémont looked about at the surrounding "panorama of unspeakable sublimity" that had been "spread before" them. As "continuous chains of mountains reared their snowy peaks far away in the distance," the writer took note of the "awful sublimity" of the scene. As Carvalho laid it out, everything in the scene spoke to the idea of landscape as artifice, as a species of visual, even painterly, revelation. Both its "panoramic" and "unspeakable" aspects had to have appealed to and challenged a man who earned his living as an artist and was now undertaking to write a book about what he had once glimpsed and even been able to reproduce in photographic form.

In its strident religiosity, the language of the subsequent passage did more than mimic the romantic conventions of the era, however. By emphasizing God's diminution of the human sphere, it also approximated a synagogue liturgy. To all appearances, Carvalho cribbed his words directly from Emerson's most famous utterance: "Standing as it were in this vestibule of God's holy Temple," Carvalho intoned, "I forgot I was of this mundane sphere; the divine part of man elevated itself, undisturbed by the influences of the world."[31] While much of the force of his landscape descriptions derived from an obviously Emersonian strain to his thinking, however, the daguerreotypist framed his own transcendent experiences as indicative not of his *own* divinity but of all of humanity's higher purpose. Ironically, Emerson had resorted to an imperious figuration in order to depict his achievement of egolessness. The moment of transcendence that the Concord Sage experienced on the twilit Boston Common had prompted his famous announcement, "I am part and parcel of God." Carvalho's pronouncement, while similar in form, was less assertive in its content, moving as it did from its initial first-person announcement that the speaker had lost track of his origins in "the mundane sphere" to its third-person reference to "the divine part of man." The descriptions of the geography of the Far West in Carvalho's *Incidents* conferred a redemptory quality upon the wilderness, but the basis of this redemption was not its power to renew *him* as an individual. Instead, he spoke of the "elevation" of nature's divine potential to uplift all humans to their highest possible state. Though he had borrowed some of Emerson's language, the views he expressed both of God's inconceivability and of humanity's potential as an instrument of His divinity bore a closer resemblance to the humbling sentiments contained in the kaddish prayer than they did to the triumphalist ones that the Transcendentalists were in the habit of promulgating.[32]

"STRICT PRINCIPLES OF MORALITY AND VIRTUE":
CARVALHO'S SOJOURN IN SALT LAKE CITY

The Pathfinder's 1853–1854 expedition fell short of success. One of the officers, the "mild and amiable" assistant engineer Oliver Fuller, perished of starvation just as the party was on the verge of reaching the Mormon settlement of Parowan (Utah). The explorers were repeatedly beset by a lack of fodder and inhibited by inclement weather that blocked their passage through the snow-choked mountains. Stalled and demoralized by such conditions and having been forewarned that the remaining territories to be passed through on the way to California would be no less formidable than the space through which he had just barely survived passage, Carvalho himself chose upon reaching Salt Lake City not to accompany Frémont and the rest of his party on the final leg of the journey to California. The winter he spent in the newly established Mormon enclave presented the author with a unique opportunity to depict the efforts of a society in the making as opposed to limiting himself to recording the experiences of a single expeditionary party traversing the wilderness. Carvalho made acquaintance with a number of recent Mormon emigrants, including Brigham Young himself. The several chapters of *Incidents* that were devoted to his extended description of Salt Lake City and the expanding Mormon settlement that had so recently taken shape there served the wider purpose of demonstrating the suitability of even the wildest appearing landscapes to cultivation, permanent habitation, and the establishment of institutions.

Carvalho arrived in Salt Lake on March 1, 1854, having traveled the three hundred miles from the southern Utah Mormon settlement of Parowan in ten days, still in the company of Frémont and the rest of the expeditionary party. Having just barely survived the crossing of the Rockies, both the daguerreotypist and his friend, the engineer Frederick Wilhelm von Egloffstein, waved Frémont on as he set off to travel the rest of the way, across the desert and the Sierra Nevada to California. For their own part, the two men quickly found themselves guests of the Mormon leadership, which had already established a permanent and fast-growing settlement in Salt Lake, less than seven years after their initial arrival there in July 1847. Carvalho offered an overview of the new city in *Incidents*. His description of the place emphasized its founders' considerable accomplishments and projected an impressive future over a landscape that had seen scant evidence of any settled human presence. What was striking in Carvalho's description of Salt Lake was how it balanced its attention to the civilizing impositions of humanity with its frequent remarks concerning the surrounding, and still quite wild, landscape in which the city was being built. As a description of the frontier landscape, Carvalho's rendering of the area around Salt Lake resonated with his book's recurrent and defining references to the wilderness not as a refuge from civilization and its institutions but as an extension of them. The people who mapped out and were in the midst of building such a place seemed eager to replicate the advanced achievements that had shaped life in the settlements from whence they had come.

By the time of his sojourn there, Salt Lake had boasted several "principal business streets" running "north and south." Its inhabitants had planted cottonwood saplings on the sides of these streets, set up sidewalks, and "appropriated an acre and a quarter of ground" ("for gardening purposes") to each dwelling. Moreover, the city had already built a "governor's residence" (as Carvalho made sure to point out, Brigham Young required an especially large home to accommodate his nineteen wives and thirty-three children), a courthouse, post office, and theater. Its famous temple was under construction during Carvalho's ten weeks of residence. These landmarks of human accomplishment had not been torn out of or sloppily erected upon the ground, however. Intermingled within his enumeration of the city's growing structures were passages devoted to describing "a delicious stream of water" that ran along the main thoroughfare, "murmuring rivulets" that paralleled each of the side streets, the "range of high mountains" that formed the eastern edge of the settlement, and the River Jordan, which passed through the Mormon settlement on its way to emptying into the Great Salt Lake itself.[33] Salt Lake approximated the writer's highest ideals of civilization and nature in balance with one another. Notwithstanding Carvalho's considerable misgivings concerning their practice of polygamy (he devoted several pages of *Incidents* to moralizing on the subject), the city's carefully planned and executed settlement by the Mormons offered proof positive that life in a border region did not necessitate the abandonment of the principles that governed communal existence in the east.

"CARVALHO NO KILL BUFFALO": ESTABLISHING HUMILITY

At the time that Carvalho began Frémont's expedition, by his own admission, he "had never saddled a horse" himself.[34] Whether he did so in order to enhance the readability of his narrative or to highlight the achievements of his book's ostensible protagonist, Carvalho frequently drew attention to his own shortcomings as an outdoorsman. That he had even survived the ordeal of the winter's passage through the Rockies was nothing short of miraculous. His attempt to catch his own mule in camp made for comical fodder. "Watch me while I tramp through the frozen snow," he instructed his readers, in pursuit of an animal who is clearly capable of outsmarting him. "At the moment I think I have him securely," Carvalho wrote, "he dashes away at full gallop, pulling me after him through the snow."[35] Carvalho was no more effectual as an ax-wielder. In a letter to his wife that he embroidered into his narrative, he wrote about the day it was his turn to fetch a load of firewood to camp. Lacking the physical strength or the know-how to fell trees, he straggled back to camp with "several decayed limbs" in tow—enough to supply his comrades "with kindling wood for the night."[36] Weeks later, upon his arrival in Parowan, he had become so weakened and emaciated that his Mormon rescuers "mistook him for an Indian."[37] *Incidents* was rife with episodes and descriptions whose purpose it was to highlight Carvalho's diminutive stature. He was, as he put it, a subject "truly to be pitied," whose presence offered his Mormon hosts an opportunity "for the exercise of the finer feelings of nature."[38]

Carvalho faced the challenge of writing about the Far West by crafting a humble and candid account of the time he spent there. Extended descriptions of many bouts with illness and hunger that he had experienced along the way from Kansas to California occupied a significant portion of his narrative. While he described the most stirring geographical features he experienced with considerable enthusiasm, he made no triumphant claims for himself on the basis of his having survived, much less conquered, them. For him, the vastness of the Far West did not reflect the purported greatness of men who were barely able to live through their encounters with it. It stipulated a humbling experience and a deeper appreciation of the pleasures of contact and communion with other humans. Not the least of its influences upon human endeavors was its evident indifference to their truth claims. Because the dominant tendency in the literature of the frontier was exaggeration, both of the landscape's enormity and of the courageousness of the men who traveled through and surmounted its greatest dangers, writers like Carvalho who wished to be believed or who wanted their words to be perceived as thoughtful as opposed merely to entertaining faced a difficult task. He could not but have been aware of the reputation that western explorers had acquired for hyperbole. His description of "Peg-leg" Smith, whom he met on the route between Salt Lake City and Los Angeles as "a weather-beaten old chap" who "tells some improbable tales" was a case in point.[39]

Carvalho gained a memorable insight into the importance of modesty, not to mention the companionship of his fellow party members, at an early phase of the expedition, when he participated in his first ever buffalo hunt on the Kansas prairie and inadvertently shot and killed a male buffalo (buffalo hunters generally killed females, whose bodies offered significantly more meat). He had been a reluctant hunter, having had no intention of joining the hunt until one of the Indians in the group, noting his evident plans to remain in camp that day, had challenged him by asking, "What for you no hunt buffalo?" Whether he had been shamed into going along or was genuinely eager to do so, he prepared quickly for the hunt and, within three hours of departing camp, found himself chasing "at least 6000 buffaloes" across the wide expanse of open country. Carvalho's narrative account of the hunt conveyed the thrill he experienced upon encountering the "grazing," "playfully gambolling," and slumbering herd "on their verdant carpet," which he described as "a sight well worth traveling a thousand miles to see." Later on, in the heat of the chase, he became entirely separated from the rest of the party but pressed on to fire his rifle at a male buffalo's "vital part." Carvalho described the animal's dying look as having haunted him with a sense of having "uselessly shot him down."[40]

With no compass to consult (he had inadvertently left it in camp that morning), he summited a small hill in order to get his bearings. After an hour or so of riding in the direction of the hills from which he and the rest of the party had come that morning, he was fortunate to cross the path of one of the Indians in the expeditionary party who was out searching for his tomahawk pipe. The two made their way to camp, where the once kosher Charlestonian Jew was appointed the task of carving the liver out of a buffalo cow. Notwithstanding the lesson he had learned in his earlier encounter with the Cheyenne hunter who favored raw antelope liver, to extract a buffalo's liver was beyond Carvalho's ability. All that remained for him to do was to recount his adventure on the buffalo hunt to the rest of the party, but this act would prove to be the most humbling of the day's several humbling events. When Carvalho recounted his killing of the bull, Captain Wolff, the leader of the party of Delaware scouts whom Carvalho had previously "cured" of a near-fatal indigestion, looked at him "with a most quizzical and incredulous smile, and emphatically remarked . . . 'Carvalho no kill buffalo.'"

No amount of insistence was sufficient to convince Captain Wolff or any of the other Indians in the expeditionary party that Carvalho had slain the buffalo. The Delawares' logic in reaching such a conclusion was incontrovertible. As Captain Wolff put it to the daguerreotypist, "When Capt. Wolff kill buffalo, he cut out the tongue. Indian shoot buffalo, bring home tongue. Carvalho no bring buffalo tongue; he no kill buffalo."[41] In the broader scheme of things, the author of *Incidents* seems to have understood well enough that *not knowing* the proper protocols and practices of buffalo hunting had been his downfall. Lacking the ability to distinguish a cow from a bull, failing to maintain an awareness of where the rest of the party had gone, being drawn into a useless and recklessly "heroic" chase after a lone buffalo, and not knowing that one needed substantial and communally corroborative proof of, not mere words about, one's hunting accomplishments in order to be believed were detrimental to Carvalho's case. It is a testament to the unusual degree of self-reflexivity and studied humility that we find in *Incidents* that its writer offered such a candid view of his shortcomings, especially on the subject of his credibility. By telling the story about his having failed to remove the buffalo's tongue, he owned that he might as well have cut out his own.

"A Journey That No Israelite Had as Yet Made":
I. J. Benjamin's *Three Years in America, 1859–1862*

In starkest contrast to Solomon Carvalho's self-appointed role as a modest spokesperson for no one but himself, Israel Joseph Benjamin, the Romanian-born Polish Jewish traveler who published an account of his extended visit to North America, and especially the Far West in 1862, offered himself as a prophetic voice of Jewish redemption. *Three Years in America*, as Moses Rischin notes, was "the first wide-ranging account of America to be written by a Jewish traveler" and for a Jewish audience.[42] Carvalho, whose emphasis on his account's veri-fiability necessitated concentration on the physical experiences associated with his having narrowly survived passage through a forbidding landscape, avoided making undue and patently unrealistic projections into that landscape's future. Perhaps because he had not been subject to the same sorts of physical trials that Carvalho had faced in joining the Frémont party and participating in the mid-winter traverse of the Rockies, Benjamin evidently felt freer to invest the land-scapes he encountered with greater meaning.

Benjamin conceived of himself as an emissary to the American West from the Jews of the Old World. As a mere chronicle of travel through the Far West on the eve of the Civil War, *Three Years in America* offered relatively little that other books of its type had not already presented to their readers. Benjamin himself traveled most of the way in relative luxury and comfort, and he incurred little personal danger. As a projection of a Jewish future onto the western American landscape, on the other hand, I. J. Benjamin's book was without precedent or equal. Despite its "vein of messianic mid nineteenth century nationalism" and its rhetorical echoes of the prevailing expansionist impulse, the work, according to Rischin, was "akin to mission, not manifest destiny" because its author "ascribed almost redemptory properties to his fellow Jews," as opposed to Americans in general. In California, Benjamin suggested, the Jews were "destined at last to ful-fill their providential role . . . of bringing all the peoples of the world together."[43]

By the time he arrived in San Francisco, Benjamin had already written one travel account, which recounted the time he spent visiting Jewish communities throughout Eastern Europe, North Africa, the Middle East, and Asia. *Five Years of Travel in the Orient, 1846–1851* chronicled his tour of such places as Constan-tinople, Egypt, Palestine, Syria, Babylon, Persia, India, and Afghanistan.[44] In the broadest scheme, these were the lands of the Jewish past. In traveling not only to North America but, more specifically, to its westernmost parts, Benjamin was deliberately venturing into the entirely speculative territory of the Jewish future. While aspects of *Three Years* were contrived, misinformed, and compromised by the author's blustery rhetoric, its central premise was remarkably prescient, even if inadvertently so. "The historical significance of the Jewish people," he wrote, "did not end with the downfall of their state." Rather, as he saw it, after

nearly two thousand years of life in the diaspora, Jews were facing a new opportunity to "plant the seed of civilization in [the] virgin soil" of the "young country beyond the ocean."[45] That Benjamin had chosen to spend so much time in
California and other parts of the Northwest was the result as much of happen-
stance as it was of his specific interest in documenting the Jewish experience
in the Far West. Had he been more politically minded and less eager to frame
his view of America in deliberately geographic terms, his arrival in 1859 would
most certainly have drawn him in the direction of investigating and documenting the crisis over slavery and the lead up to secession and civil war. What made
I. J. Benjamin unique among Jewish authors of his time, however, was his particular interest in the relationship between Jews and land. While it fell short of
constituting a socially or politically incisive view of antebellum Jewish life on
the western frontier or anywhere else, *Three Years in America* was remarkable
all the same for its unprecedented interest in investigating the relationship
between Jews and geographical space in North America.

While the book's most memorable passages offered thorough descriptions of
mountain ranges, rivers, seaways, deserts, and settlements, the occasional lyricism of these sections occurred within the wider context of the author's attempt
to frame a scientifically informed survey. Benjamin derived much of his material directly from almanacs that would have been of great interest and importance to an author who viewed his primary mission as of supplying data. As
Benjamin remarked in his foreword, his earlier work on Jewish life in the Orient had received the acknowledgment and approval of none other than "such
coryphaei of German science as . . . Alexander von Humboldt and Carl Ritter."[46]
In the service of his larger objective of surveying the American landscape, Benjamin was an enthusiastic "borrower" of other people's materials. Embedded in
a several-chapters-long narration of the author's travels through present-day
Oregon, Washington, and British Columbia, for instance, Benjamin presented a
lengthy description of "Prospecting for Gold in the Cascade Mountains," complete with a harrowing and stirring account of an ascent up Mt. St. Helens (rendered in the first person). Benjamin had taken the account, verbatim, from the
similarly titled "Gold Hunting in the Cascade Mountains," which was published
in 1861 in Vancouver (Washington) by an unknown author who had taken the
pseudonym "Loo-Wit Lat-Kla" (the local Native American name for Mt. St. Helens). Because he meant it to serve as an extension of his scientific predilections,
which seem to have operated on the principle that the amassing of raw data was
of more importance than any claim to personal accomplishment or authorial
expertise, his habit of incorporating the work of his predecessors in the field
looked less like plagiarism than compositional haste.[47]

GAZING AT THE MOUNTAINS OF CALIFORNIA:
BENJAMIN'S EVOCATIONS OF A JEWISH SUBLIME

Whether the observations included in I. J. Benjamin's account derived from his own firsthand experiences with the geographical features of the Far West that he had actually seen or from his extensive borrowings from other sources on the subject of the western landscape, his book consistently emphasized the central-ity of landscape as an organizing principle both for conceiving his own place in the world and for glimpsing the collective Jewish future. The author's fondest and most spiritually elevated descriptions seem mostly to have been inspired by the time he spent in California. Recounting his journey eastward after his several-months-long sojourn there, he recalled the feeling of wistfulness he had as he crested the Sierra Nevada range. Poised at the edge of two worlds, he paused and looked backward. "Before us lay the broad Carson Valley," he wrote; "behind us the Sierra Nevada mountains towered to the heavens." Whether he was inspired by the grandeur of the mountainous scene or touched by a feeling of regret at having left the coastal paradise of California, Benjamin used the occasion of his entry into Nevada to wax eloquently about the place that, at other points in his book, he portrayed as the land of Jewish redemption, among other things. "Greatly moved and with the most religious of feelings I gazed at the mountains of California," he wrote, hinting both backward at his training as a committed and observant Jew and forward toward the attitude of spiritual exaltation that would soon define John Muir's and other conservationists' writing about the "Range of Light."

"In this land I had spent an important period of my life, a period which I, as long as I breathe, will think back upon with a feeling of satisfaction," Benjamin continued, as he assigned both great personal and collective redemptory signifi-cance to the "fairyland" or "land of fable" that he had just left behind:

> I had succeeded, at least it seemed to me, in performing the task that I had set for myself; I had journeyed in all directions through the land that many would give part of their lives to see; with my own feet I had walked upon the land that many will never see in spite of all their longing because of poverty, family circumstances, or other reasons, and which, therefore, appears to them like a paradise than an angel with a flaming sword forbids them to enter. With my own eyes, I have seen the charms of this land, the charms that Europeans try to imagine—in vain.[48]

Like Carvalho, Benjamin equated grand scenery with Jewishly articulated bibli-cal themes and motifs even as he invoked the post-Enlightenment Protestant notion that God expressed His greatness through the inspiring beneficence of natural wonders. The influence of American expansionism seems also to have

shaped his depiction of the Far Western landscape. Foreigner that he was, it had
evidently taken little time for him to acquire and promulgate the idea that land
was equivalent to destiny. By the same token, the description of his ascent of
the Sierras that preceded his Muir-esque reference to the "religious feeling" that
accompanied his backward glance at the California mountains was also a vehicle
for his deliberately Jewish inflections of the romantic sublime.

Benjamin identified the scenery on the western slopes of the Sierras as "in
the highest degree romantic." As the party ascended, they saw "canyons [that]
were more than a thousand feet deep" and "firs two to three hundred feet high."
They heard "the beautiful song of the nightingale and the howling of ani-
mals." The author's experience of the pristine and remote mountains of California by night also inspired him to look heavenward. "The stars twinkled brightly
in an unclouded sky," he wrote, noting that this view was complemented by the
sight of the "silver snow glitter[ing] across to us from the mountains" that lay
in the distance. The prospect, which he readily identified as a "romantic spectacle," had set the entire party "trembling" with excitement. Stirred as he was
by the dangers he associated with the remoteness of the place (at several points,
Benjamin had mentioned the party's having fired its weapons to warn any concealed enemies that they were passing through the mountains), Benjamin seems
to have been no less moved than Solomon Carvalho had been by the comparative
enormity and aesthetic richness of its natural landscapes. By virtue of his stilted
literary language, at least, the scientifically motivated author of *Three Years in
America* was an enthusiastic purveyor of romantic conventions. He applied a
similarly fanciful sensibility to his description of the Nevada landscape where,
as he put it, "one can easily imagine that one is in the Sahara Desert." There, as
"hills of sand rise and sink according to the wind," the party with whom he was
traveling experienced such an extreme thirst that his recollection of it evoked
two biblical allusions in short succession. "Like the prophet Jonah, [they] looked
in vain for the gourd that gave him shadow and water," he asserted, before com-
paring the members of the group to the "deer [who] pants for fresh water."[49]
Later on, as his party experienced a brief exposure to a cooling mountain wind in
another part of the Sahara-like Great Basin, Benjamin referred to the episode as
"evidence of the wisdom of the All-Bountiful Who has placed the snow-covered
mountains near the desert."[50]

"INDUSTRY, PERSISTENCE, AND CONTENTMENT":
PROJECTIONS OF AN URBAN FUTURE

Benjamin's interest in Jews and Jewish affairs comprised only part of his motivation as the author of *Three Years*. As he readily acknowledged, like a "botanist who roams a mountainous region looking for a particular plant many not
turn his eyes away from the multitude of other flowers that he sees,"[51] he too

had been unable not to attend to a range of other interests that followed from his central curiosity about American geography. He was certain, for instance, that the Atlantic and Pacific coasts would soon be linked to one another by rail and wished to explore the drive toward and implications of that eventuality as they affected people within and beyond America itself. He wanted to know more about the buried mineral reserves that were being dug up throughout the Far West. The political development of the new states and territories interested him as well, and he devoted extensive portions of his description of San Francisco, Sacramento, and other California towns to discussing elections, civic leaders, and the relationship between national affairs and the burgeoning communities along the Pacific coast. Benjamin's interest in the geography of American destiny was not restricted to California. He devoted an extensive portion of *Three Years* to a detailed, if largely cribbed, survey of the geography, community life, and economic prospects of Oregon, Washington, and British Columbia.

While they did not escape Benjamin's occasional censure, Jews played an important part in the development of these new communities by virtue of their being the world's foremost proponents of modernization. In spite of their being of a "most stingy temperament" and having gotten no farther in their communal endeavors than establishing a consecrated burial ground, by his estimation, at least he could say that "all the Jews" in Oregon were identifiably "well-to-do."[52] By the same token, the Jews in another northwestern community—Victoria, British Columbia—had truly distinguished themselves not only for their having achieved financial stability but also because of their vision. In Benjamin's opinion, they had been entirely responsible for the "beginnings of the city." While a great number of gold prospectors had "streamed" in and out of the place at the beginning stages of its development, only the Jews had, as he put it, "held their ground [and] set up tents for residence and booths for shops." The Jews, as the forerunning agents of the modern era, had realized what the itinerants who had been struck by gold fever had failed to notice: owing to its location "between the Sandwich Islands, California, and China," Victoria "had a great commercial future."[53] Not that the Jews had acted out of pure selfishness in choosing to settle in a commercially promising location. As Benjamin pointed out, "In their compassion and their charitable disposition towards the poor," they had also "remained true to the fundamental character of the Jew."[54]

In Benjamin's survey of life in the Far West, no single development warranted as high praise as the establishment of cities along just such lines. For that matter, though he was no less apt to pursue heights of lyricism in his descriptions of sweeping wild landscapes than many of his late romantic contemporaries, the description he supplied of the coming of a great city, as in his overview of the San Francisco Bay area, was matchless for its attempt at eloquence. Inspired by the likes of "Gibbon, Hume, and Prescott," Benjamin looked at San Francisco in its developing stages and saw the "indications of [its] future greatness." What could be more inspiring, given his emphasis on the progress of humanity from the "barbarous customs and usages" that he associated with the "dark woods" in which the primitive Indians dwelt? "Before the rays of civilization," he wrote, "the clipper makes the slow-sailing ship unnecessary" as the "sail of the white merchant takes the place of the Indian's paddle." Eager to celebrate the transformation of the once primitive backcountry into a modern city, the author of *Three Years* built his paean to the growth of San Francisco on a succession of poetic parallel structures that were meant to emphasize a notion of progress toward civilization—first, the "firmly fastened tent" replaced the "original hut," then the "friendly dwelling" occupied the space that had once been marked by the "smoking fire-place of the native." As Moses Rischin points out, Benjamin's California was a "ready and vital extension rather than a remote colonial appendage of a far-distant, older America."[55] Where "cane, bark and brushwood" had once represented the extent of architectural achievement, "timber, brick, and sandstone" were now ubiquitous. The chief virtues of the natural world were the plentitude of its resources and its overall suppleness to human intervention. Thus as Benjamin put it, "The busy hands of man and his intelligence have changed the threatening face of nature itself into a picture which the visitor greets with a smile and which leaves a pleasant memory in the minds of those who go their way."[56]

For all of the state's promise as the landscape of the American future, however, the rapid growth and prosperity that Benjamin associated with California also posed a potential threat to the achievement of a stable urban society. California presented this visitor from the Old World with a curious dilemma. Owing to its resource richness and temperate climate, it was indeed a "land of promise." At the same time, the enticements commensurate with flush times and the constant influx of fortune-seeking itinerants who bore no interest beyond their own financial gain were poised to turn it into a land of "painful disillusionment."[57] He noted that the "many thousands" of lost souls who were flocking to the state in search of easy money had already "lost all energy for further striving." In keeping with his natural tendency as a geographer to resort to landscape imagery, he suggested that San Francisco itself had been built on "quicksand" and that the "splendid castles-in-the-air" they had erected would soon be replaced with "the ashes of the fires that have wasted them."[58] As always, the state of the land itself was indicative both of human attainments and of human failings. Too many people were intent upon chasing illusions that "beckon[ed] . . . in a golden glitter in the misty distance." If the current course was not reversed, he feared, the promise would vanish, leaving only a chaotic amalgam of self-absorbed people hurrying to "push their neighbors aside" with little care for the welfare of their fellow strivers.

I. J. Benjamin's departure from California, which constituted the concluding chapter of the first volume of *Three Years in America*, reached its height of prophetic eloquence as the author looked outward toward the Pacific from the tentative perch he had assumed in the "Mountain of Love" cemetery. Next to the ocean itself, which marked the geographical limit of human progress and the end of American westward expansion, it was possible for "every man [to] rejoice in peace." Oddly enough, in a book that made barely any mention of the coming crisis of the Civil War, he marked his time in the cemetery as the proper occasion for remarking upon the tumultuous affairs to the eastward, "the struggle for freedom against slavery."[59] He unleashed a torrent of biblical prophecies that might have been worthy of a seventeenth-century Puritan bent on delivering a forceful jeremiad. Benjamin evidently felt sufficiently inspired by the contrast between the quietness of the ocean-facing burial ground, and especially the enormous force that the waters themselves manifested, to announce God's intentions for the chastisement—but also the eventual improvement of humanity. Citing the Book of Joel, he noted that the earth would soon be as full of "the knowledge of the Lord" as the sea was filled with water. This, in turn, would bring about Isaiah's prophecy concerning the transformation of swords into plowshares and Micah's pronouncement regarding the coming peace when "they shall sit every man under his vine and under his fig tree," fully unafraid.[60]

Benjamin's account presents us with a rare instance, particularly in the context of the diaspora, of a self-styled Jewish geographer. At times, the author seems to have been bent upon establishing the notion that Judaism and the North American continent were linked to one another by destiny. Thus at an early juncture in the book, this emissary from Old World Judaism asserted his "love of this land" and the even odder notion, given that he had no intention of settling permanently in America, that "we," meaning Americans, were "the most enlightened people" on earth. While the author of *Three Years* did not hesitate to pronounce his sympathies with the Union and his admiration for the democratic principles with which he associated its perseverance, his central and stated purpose in coming to America had been to experience and describe the land itself, and especially its farthest reaches, through the lens of his knowledge of other lands. It was the settlement of those portions, those newly admitted territories that were "advancing towards a great and splendid future," as he put it, that constituted his primary subject matter and motivated his production of a book that would offer "treatment at the hands of a traveler."[61]

GEOGRAPHY, JEWISH RENEWAL, AND THE CRISIS OF THE REPUBLIC

Where the native-born but admitted newcomer to western life Carvalho represented himself as unequal to the task of narrating his experience of the Far West and lucky to have survived his harrowing adventures in the wilderness, Benjamin portrayed himself as having sauntered forth with the utmost confidence in his ability to render an accurate description of an enormous swath of territory. What united the efforts of both authors was their evident eagerness to assign a surfeit of transcendent meaning to the landscape of the American frontier from the standpoint of Jewish experience and worldview. Their respective Jewish frameworks differed somewhat. While Carvalho never announced a religious affiliation, and his book did not offer the slightest evidence of any interest on his part in surveying the conditions of Jewish life in the Far West, *Incidents* was rife with landscape descriptions that evinced his association between the grandeur of the scenery he encountered and the language of the Torah and Jewish liturgy. Benjamin's attentiveness to Jewish settlement patterns throughout the West suggested a more obviously programmatic interest on his part in linking the geography of North America to a Jewish collective destiny, but the primary means by which both he and Carvalho demonstrated a Jewish sensibility vis-à-vis the Far West was in their shared tendency to write about the spaces and places they encountered there as entirely contiguous with, as opposed to exceptions to, the progress of urbanization and civilization as they knew it.

The authors of both *Incidents* and *Three Years* presented readers with two central motifs for landscape description. In the first scenario, the remotest, even the most desolate portions of the American wilderness constituted grounds upon which the human spirit, in accordance with both Jewish precept and the prevailing romantic sentiment of the era, might be elevated to its highest spiritual potential. In the second, places like Salt Lake and San Francisco presented themselves as the most promising grounds upon which civilization itself might renew its ethical promise and rekindle its ties to the traditional precepts of monotheistic religion. Landscape and geography were integral to both of these motifs because they comprised the touchstones and starting points for both writers' articulation of their moral principles, whether those principles were Jewish or non-Jewish in origin. In both instances, land not only inspired the writers' thinking on such matters but also shaped the language in which they formulated it. The starting point for both books appears to have been their respective authors' sense that their audiences, evidently comprised either of John C. Frémont admirers in the United States or of German-speaking Jews in Europe, were curious for more information regarding the progress of settlement of the American Far West, especially within the context of the conflict over slavery and the future of the Union. Therefore, they couched their most salient thoughts concerning the mounting crisis in American affairs in the language of travel and of landscape description. Political and religious sentiments alike were occasioned by the firsthand experience of frontier life. What made America noteworthy, after all, not only for Jews but also for all people who maintained any sense of an Old World inheritance, was its abundance of open space that, in turn, was evidently inviting all comers to redeem the failures of that inheritance. Simply stated, for mid-nineteenth-century readers on both sides of the Atlantic, the most novel feature of American life was the nation's expansion into this landscape of the future.

Since attention to the westward expansion of the American republic constituted the most important catalyst for debates over slavery, it is no surprise that
such troubled times would produce the nineteenth century's two most sustained
Jewish treatments of American geography. To any number of observers, the viability of such a republic—which was proving to be the world's most welcoming,
or at least the most tolerant, environment within which Jews could live—seemed
to hang in the balance as Lincoln's election precipitated the secession of eleven
Southern states between November 1860 and May 1861. Both authors' sense
of the impending crisis over the future of the Union and the maintenance of
the principles of human freedom had been informed by the question of how the
land was to be settled. That being said, their production of Far Western travel
accounts at the exact point at which the nation was poised to sacrifice hundreds
of thousands of lives as a direct result of its failure to answer that question was
tragically ironic.

As Carvalho's and Benjamin's books attempted to show, the frontier could
not be configured or represented as the sole preserve of willful or intrepid individuals, and it was not a spatial vacuum or a world apart in which the rules
that governed human existence and cooperation in more settled areas no longer
applied. Both men wrote against the grain of popular conceptions of the Far
West as a savage no man's land that awaited the violence-bearing and taming
dominance of lone heroes. Carvalho and Benjamin depicted the frontier as an
inspiring canvas upon which to project a humbly religious, possibly even Jewishly informed, view of human limitation. They viewed it as an arena in which a
new rank of cultured emissaries would either reassert the highest attainments of
human ingenuity and culture or fail catastrophically at the attempt.

COLONIAL REVIVAL IN THE IMMIGRANT CITY

THE INVENTION OF JEWISH AMERICAN URBAN HISTORY, 1870–1910

"We Cannot Understand the Present without a Study of the Past": Staking a Jewish Claim to the Early American Urban Landscape

When the pogroms of the 1880s launched the migration of Eastern European Jews to America, New York City was already home to eighty thousand Jews. Like other major cities in the United States, New York had borne a Jewish imprint from its founding. In 1888, Isaac Markens, a German Jewish businessman and the author of a book entitled *The Hebrews in America*,[1] noted that "the first Hebrew burial ground" in New York had been established in 1681 "on a high hill" just off what was then the King's Highway.[2] As the new Jewish immigrant tide swelled, it was important for the city's "native" Anglo population and newly arrived Eastern European Jews to know not only that previous generations of Jews had experienced "marvelous prosperity and steady progress" there but also that they had been shaping the city's streetscapes since they had "first reached Manhattan Island."[3] Inspired by a wider interest in early American history that peaked in the aftermath of the nation's centennial and in the face of the immigrant influx, a group of Sephardic and German Jews fashioned a literary colonial revival of their own—one that was distinctly Jewish in its subject matter and urban in its material focus. Markens and his fellow revivalists asserted unequivocally that from a Jewish perspective, to borrow a phrase from Deborah Dash Moore, the city had been "their American starting place, their version of Plymouth Rock."[4] These writers' efforts to assert a Jewish historical claim to the nation's urban landscapes underlay their unique contribution to Jewish American literary history.

In the face of the rampant industrialism, urban expansion, and massive immigrant influxes that were taking shape just ahead of the turn of the twentieth century, established elites sought to stoke revivifying memories of an earlier, more recognizable, and homogeneous America by preserving and assigning ideological significance to the remnants of the nation's colonial past. The gentile version of this revival recreated the "colonial setting" in various domestic and public venues, as Susan Williams explains, in order to present "a new national narrative of restrained progress from a traditional 'homespun' past."[5] Its recuperative and curatorial mission coincided in literature with the regionally identified local color movement, many of whose practitioners, in accordance with the Protestant norm, typically "scorned cities."[6] From the local colorists' perspective, "the rustic," as Dalia Kandiyoti writes, "was a refuge from the alien nations now populating" the nation's expanding urban core.[7]

Unlike the mainstream local color movement, however, the Jewish colonial revival could only take shape as Jews asserted long-standing claims to the geographical spaces of America's colonial-era port cities, the literal grounds upon which the nation had been established. At the heart of this enterprise lay the work of outlining Jewish contributions to the initial growth of the very same cities whose expanding residential neighborhoods were now filling up with what Emma Lazarus, herself a descendant of Jews who had settled in North America before the Revolutionary War, famously referred to as the "wretched refuse" of the Old World's "teeming shore." Beginning in the 1870s and culminating in the first decades of the twentieth century, these authors endeavored to assert the Jews' early and influential presence in the New World, especially in the cities that had been built during the colonial era along the Atlantic Seaboard. As Max Kohler, a lawyer, historian, and the editor of a book entitled *The Settlement of the Jews in America* (1893), wrote, "We cannot understand the present without a study of the past." Kohler and his fellow Jewish colonial revivalists did not hesitate to attach their "study of the past" to the urgent needs of their own age.[8] Knowing that they could make their most convincing claims to American identity on the basis of their ability to establish early Jewish involvement in the development of America's oldest cities, these writers went out of their way to emphasize the urban origins of American democracy itself as they argued their case for the nation's continued absorption of Jewish immigrants.

In their efforts to substantiate so drastic a claim, the Jewish colonial revivalists tried to establish two parallel cases through a combination of painstaking research and forceful (though entirely genteel) rhetoric. These writers needed to remind their readers of the integral role that the commercial and civic activities that took place in cities had played in the founding of America, for gentiles as well as for Jews. They needed to argue that the American experiment had been urban at its inception. In the face of growing doubts as to the cultural legitimacy of urban life and modernization, these writers made the case that the very principles upon which the nation had been built and which were increasingly associated in the public mind with the notion of "frontier democracy" had, in fact, first been hatched in the colonial ports of the Atlantic Seaboard. As they did so, they had at the same time to delineate the history of Jewish involvement in these endeavors and show that Jews had not been mere witnesses to them but fully committed participants in the colonial era's greatest achievements.

The founding of the American Jewish Historical Society (AJHS) in 1892 as the nation's first deliberately ethnic-specific historical organization institutionalized the growing interest in staking a Jewish claim to the development of the nation's urban landscapes.[9] Among its other contributions to this effort, the AJHS's establishment of a journal of American Jewish history comprised an important stage in the adaptation of Jewish history to American norms and the modernization of the practice. As Max Kohler put it, Jews could no longer be "content . . . with stopping at a period two thousand years" in the past.[10] The significance of this endeavor was magnified in various locales inclusive of but also outside New York owing to the publication of several Jewish urban histories during the decades between 1880 and 1910.[11] As an outgrowth of their distinctly Jewish variation on the theme of colonial revival and because they sought to edify and assuage multiple audiences for divergent and sometimes contradictory purposes, the books that these writers produced were historiographical but also literary curiosities. On the one hand, the Jewish revivalists went out of their way to hew closely to the documentary record as they found it and to avoid any imputation of the sort of sentimentality, bias, and wistfulness that often defined the work of regional and ethnic local colorists whose own recuperation of history constituted much of the era's most popular literary fare. Owing to their deliberate and consistent attention to the preexisting written record of Jewish life in early America, the books produced by the Jewish revivalists read often enough like the straightforward historical narratives they purported to be. At the same time, the Jewish urban histories of the turn-of-the-century period constituted overtly ideological and politically outspoken literature, both on the subject of longstanding Jewish loyalty to America (and Enlightenment ideals upon which it had been founded) and on the immigrant question itself. Their authors frequently, and often quite floridly, announced their advocacy of Jewish rights. Unlike the mainstream colonial revivalists, whose fear of a "mongrelizing" American future motivated an underlying resistance to the encroaching forces of immigration and modernity, Jewish revivalists assumed a stance on the subject of immigration that, despite its frequently condescending attitude toward the immigrants and their alien qualities, was bold in its attempts to argue on their behalf. Because the "uneasy, ambivalent gaze"[12] with which assimilated Jewish American writers viewed the Eastern European Jews evoked equal parts condescension and fellow feeling, the products of the Jewish colonial revival were multitextured.

The creation of such works entailed a certain level of ideological grandiosity and literary drama. Freely ranging between the deserts of the Middle East in the biblical era and the wildernesses of North America in the seventeenth, eighteenth, and early nineteenth centuries, they outlined narrative versions of Jewish American history that began in the Israelite kingdoms; recounted the experience of the Inquisition, among other dark chapters in postbiblical Jewish history; and culminated with the earliest of arrivals of Jews in the port cities of North America. Like Emma Lazarus's 1867 poem on the Jewish cemetery in Newport, the revivalists' sought in their urban histories to "bridge the gap between their modern Jewish lives and the Jewish ancient tradition."[13] Often enough, they went so far as to resort to the nativist rhetoric of the mainstream in their demeaning characterizations of the newly arrived Russian Jews whose presence had, because it made them feel "embarrassingly visible," inspired their works in the first place.[14] On the other hand, their books eagerly sought, on the basis of the case they were making for their own Sephardic and German ancestors' long-standing presence in America, to convince a non-Jewish readership that, wherever they came from and however foreign they seemed to be in the present, these recently arrived Jews could be counted upon to become thoroughly Americanized owing both to the glorious legacy of world Jewish history and to the example provided by their immediate American forerunners' historical contributions to the rise and improvement of the nation's cities. In the face of a racializing anti-immigrant sentiment that demonized all things "foreign" and "backward," the Jewish colonial revivalists presented the Jews as "a regenerated, or at least regenerate-able race."[15] Their urban histories asserted America's role not as a merely compliant and incidental refuge for Jews from throughout the world but as their predestined homeland.

CONFIGURING A USABLE JEWISH PAST IN URBAN AMERICA: THE INFLUENCE OF THE COLONIAL REVIVAL AND LOCAL COLOR MOVEMENTS

The Jewish colonial revival applied a counterintuitive approach to the search for a usable American past. Jews had nothing to gain by following their gentile compatriots' pattern of attaching a surplus of meaning to a long-dead Jeffersonian ideal whose ideological heyday had certainly passed well before the Civil War. As far back into American history as they wished to reach for illustrative examples of regionalized or agrarian Jews, they could only point to a mere handful of such people, most of whom had been Southern Jews identified with the disloyal and discredited Confederacy. Instead of relinquishing the nation's legacy as a transoceanic extension of the European metropolis, the commemorators of early Jewish American history saw the advantages of identifying themselves, and the rest of the nation by extension, with the European-based commercial, civic, and religious endeavors that had inspired and eventually ensured the building of its greatest cities. They were, in effect, asserting the centrality of the urban experience and landscape to the most sacrosanct period of American history—the era during which European settlers first crossed the Atlantic and sought to establish their enterprise as culturally distinct from and superior to the Old World. The revivalists' claims for the vital importance of cities to this vaunted endeavor were entirely plausible because so many of the pivotal events and personages associated in the American imagination with the establishment and rise of the republic had, in fact, occurred in its largest settlements. Likewise, their claims that Jews had played a significant role during the earliest phases of American history could be supported if and when the development of the oldest cities was taken into account.

The books that the Jewish colonial revivalists wrote and published during the turn-of-the-century period were fraught documents. Their authors exuded a sort of confident authority that followed from their sense that the historical record itself was sufficient to bear out their claims of Jewish participation in the nation's founding and loyalty to the principles with which other latter-day supporters of the colonial legacy were eager to uphold. At the same time, they were well aware that the growing influx of large numbers of linguistically, religiously, and culturally alien Eastern European Jews could easily endanger their own precarious legitimacy as bona fide Americans and, for that matter, their sometimes contingent claims to whiteness. The Russian Jews reminded the rest of America that Judaism itself, particularly in its more orthodox practice, bore little resemblance to the worship of the more established American immigrant groups. While assimilated Jews could and did make the case that they had been blending into American society since the colonial era, they were well aware that the Lower East Side ghetto, as Barbara Mann writes, was quickly becoming "a cultural arena in which to test and shape American Jewish identity."[16] The Jewish neighborhood enclaves on the Lower East Side of Manhattan "offered visual representation of Jews and Judaism as quintessentially urban, foreign, poor, and exotic."[17] In an age that was becoming increasingly obsessed with racial categorization, Eastern European Jews were subject to being "perceived as a 'foreign race' with its own peculiar physiognomy."[18] For that matter, though the Jewish claim to American urban history had a relatively solid footing in the facts, Americans' misgivings regarding the rising tide of industrialism, urbanization, and immigration were only increasing as time passed. Jewish Americans' urban heritage cut both ways. As Lila Corwin Berman has recently written, it "reflected both the possibility of Jews' acceptance in modernizing nations and, also, the ongoing suspicion with which . . . leaders and citizens regarded Jews and modern cities."[19]

Late nineteenth-century Americans' misgivings about city life reflected their fears of cultural displacement. Henry James spoke for many when he wrote famously about his feeling of alarmed estrangement as he walked through Manhattan's Lower East Jewish ghetto, where "the complexity of fire escapes with which each house-front bristle[d]" replicated "a little world of bars and perches and swings for human squirrels and monkeys."[20] Between 1870 and 1900, as the nation's urban population grew from 26 percent to 40 percent, its foreign-born population doubled in size and proportion, from 5 percent to 10 percent of the total population. Nativism had been a mainstay on the national political scene since well before the Civil War, as the arrival of German and especially Irish immigrants was perceived as a threat to an Anglo-Protestant dominance that had long been taken for granted. Nonetheless, the post–Civil War expansion of the nation's cities, and especially of New York City, accompanied as it was by the arrival of so many speakers of foreign tongues, inspired latter-day nativists to argue that the land of the Knickerbockers had been transformed into an unrecognizable bedlam. Among others, Jacob Riis, himself a first-generation immigrant from Denmark, drew a close association between the attenuation of historical memory, the waning of cultural order, and the transformation of the urban environment. In *How the Other Half Lives*, his 1890 tract on the New York City ghettoes, he made a point of invoking the memory of the city's Dutch founders, who, as he suggested, would have been "shocked" at the sight of the "promiscuous crowd[s]" who now inhabited the site of their original settlement. "The proud aristocracy of Manhattan in the early days," as Riis explained, could not have anticipated the arrival and settlement of so many constituents of life's "other half."[21]

While Riis and other prophets of social change argued for the physical refurbishment of the nation's urban slums and for the rapid assimilation of its foreign hordes to Protestant American norms, the colonial revival promulgated nostalgic views of a mythical colonial past in hopes of reasserting nativist dominance. When the nation celebrated its centennial in Philadelphia in 1876, members of the nation's "proud aristocracy" exercised their nostalgic impulse as they visited that city's stylized reconstruction of the "New England Farmer's Home and Modern Kitchen." While the actual city of Philadelphia, like New York, Boston, and other seaboard cities, had long since evolved into an immigrant-filled and industrialized environment, those who wished to experience the tranquilities of "Ye Olden Time" had only to attend the Centennial Exhibition (or read about it in the national press) in order to catch reviving glimpses of such items as a grand hearth, a 165-year-old candle mold from Maine, an antique kitchen cupboard, and a goat's cream churn.[22] To those who felt discomfited by the transformation of the nation's oldest cities, the revival offered material reassurance that the spirit of the Anglo-American ancestors lived on. Since the cities themselves had long since been physically transformed into modern environments, revivalists had for the most part to content themselves with decontextualized versions of the past, often in the form of enclosed exhibits, as opposed to inhabited landscapes. Moreover, as the Philadelphia centennial exhibit's reconstruction of a New England farm kitchen demonstrated, the revival generally ceded its claims

to the urban environment in order to concentrate its imaginative energy on con-
figuring rural settings, which continued to be associated in the public mind with
authentically "native" American values.

This ideologically motivated preference for the rural atmosphere also inspired
a contemplative cohort of fiction writers to fashion a literary movement whose
goal it was to encourage the wistful appreciation of the nation's vernacular
heritage. Local color fiction usually depicted remote places like northern New
England and the upland South as holdouts of historical continuity and as places
where, as one of the movement's most famous practitioners, Sarah Orne Jewett, put it, "inward force does not waste itself upon those petty excitements of
every day that belong to cities," but instead life's "primal fires break through the
granite dust in which our souls are buried."[23] Jewish colonial revivalists were no
less committed to reviving their readers' sense of connection to the American
past, but the landscapes they sought to reclaim as they did so were not outlying areas but the central districts of the nation's oldest cities. Moreover, their
attitude toward immigration itself was profoundly ambivalent. For all the supe-
riority that assimilated Jews may have felt toward the latest contingent of Jewish
arrivals from overseas, and for all their revulsion toward the urban ghettoes in
which these "foreigners" were gathering, the kinship that assimilated Jews felt
toward them was undeniable. Thanks in part to the historically grounded connection that their books had been able to forge between Jews and the history of
American cities, this affinity fueled the revivalists' efforts to stake an early Jewish
claim to the American urban landscape instead of disavowing their connection
to it. Their work echoed the ideological interests of the local color movement
while arguing at the same time that the older America had urban as well as rural
origins and offshoots. Its motivations and its content alike resonated with the
era's dominant schools of regionalist and urban-realist fiction.

Local color fiction did not entirely restrict itself to rural or even Anglo settings. Because it was a profoundly "decentralized" literature that nearly always
favored the periphery over the core, however, its practitioners typically avoided
elite or establishment settings.[24] The genre's "color" aspect referred in large part
to its authors' frequent recourse to idiosyncratic vernacular dialects and unconventional or "off-center" places as cultural backdrops.[25] Attention to pockets of
lively ethnic difference and folklife shielded readers from and offered potentially edifying alternatives to the ravages of modernity. Whether they were being
brought to the bayous of Creole (and largely Catholic) Louisiana, the windy and
predominantly Scandinavian prairies of the upper Midwest, or, for that matter, the noisy Jewish neighborhoods of the Lower East Side, local color audiences were encouraged to look for traces of an authentic American experience
in inaccessible places among unlikely people. Against the backdrop of an ethnic
streetscape, local color writing and urban realism converged.

The most prominent Jewish practitioner of urban local color, Abraham Cahan, set his works in the Jewish ghetto of lower Manhattan and thereby distinguished himself by "establish[ing] a 'foreign' ghetto as an American *topos*."[26] Despite the apparent contrast to the "serene residential outpost[s]" where the assimilated Jews now lived, "the congested streets of downtown Manhattan" where the Russian Jews dwelt did not constitute a foreign land in Cahan's depiction.[27] Writers like Cahan found ways to claim such places as authentically American on the basis of their residents' fervent—sometimes blinding—desire to *become* American. They represented their microcosmic local environments as quintessentially American by virtue of their inhabitants' inspiring embodiment of forward-thinking and pluralistic American ideological principles. Although Cahan was ostensibly describing the diverse cultural origins of the Jewish residents of the Lower East Side in the following passage from *Yekl*, he may as well have been talking about America itself, a country that was, indeed, made up of "people with all sorts of antecedents, tastes, habits, inclinations, and speaking all sorts of subdialects of the same jargon."[28] That Cahan himself employed the dignified and staid tones of urban realist fiction in order to depict this Babel was significant. As Murray Baumgarten suggests, Jewish writers like Cahan "took possession of New York as they wrote about their experiences in English."[29] In attending to the latter task, he was following closely in the footsteps of the Jewish colonial revivalists, albeit inadvertently.

The shared Jewishness of the ghetto local colorists and the cohort of assimilated writers who comprised the Jewish colonial revival were hardly sufficient to label them as participants in a "common literary tradition," however.[30] For their part, the amalgam of historians, attorneys, clergymen, and philanthropists whose work comprised the Jewish colonial revival had misgivings about claiming the ghetto environment as the latter-day consummation of American possibility. Though they shared Cahan's goal of legitimizing the presence of latter-day Jewish immigrants in an industrialized United States, their means for doing so more closely resembled the practices of the regionalist local colorists by virtue of its emphasis on the proximity that long-standing rootedness in place afforded them to the material facts, as opposed merely to the symbolic mantle, of American history. Wherever it was pertinent to do so, they devoted energy to investing actual locations, such as the sites of the nation's founding synagogues, with transcendent historical meaning. In the urban histories that they produced, the Jewish colonial revivalists also organized their materials in close accord with historically significant episodes or eras in American history, such as the discovery of the New World and the Revolutionary War. The sum total of their efforts to show that a small number of Jews had been present in and active shapers of these places at these times comprised their central contribution to the evolving geography of Jewish American literary history, but that literary history had divergent origins and followed varied trajectories. The revivalists' antecedents were more romantic than realist in their inspiration and aesthetic predilections. In literary historical terms, the Jewish colonial revival bore the influence of Emerson and Longfellow as opposed to that of Howells and Crane.

While they were historical in their original conception, the ideological innovations that the Jewish colonial revivalists' articulated evinced a distinctly literary sensibility through the rhetorical energy they invested in outlining three distinct narratives of early Jewish American life. To begin with, and in keeping with their need to render a picture of early America as an extension of an urbanizing Europe, they each endeavored to describe the early history of Jewish migration to North America as having been of a piece with the wider commercially inspired cosmopolitanism that had launched the colonization efforts of the Dutch and English in the New World. The Jewish revivalists' basis for a Jewish claim to early American cities and for the centrality of urban history to American history was also an outgrowth of their efforts to describe the earliest phases of settlement in places like New York, Newport, Philadelphia, and Charleston as having been commercial, as opposed to strictly religious in their inception. The revivalists cited their most profound evidence for this claim as they broached the topic of the Revolutionary War, which would never have occurred had it not been for the colonists' commercially based objection to what they perceived as the economically repressive measures of the British authorities.

When the same authors arrived at the next phase of American history, they found ample evidence to support their claims for the Jews' full-fledged participation in the material growth of the early republic. Concentrating on the sorts of stories that featured Jews as "patriots, soldiers, and citizens," the revivalists outlined the development of the seaboard cities as commercial spheres, banking centers, and hotbeds of mixed religious and civic activity. Charles Daly, a Jewish-history enthusiast who also happened to be the chief justice of the New York Court of Common Appeals and the president of the American Geographical Society, had unequivocally asserted as much, pointing out that "the Jews who dwelt upon this island [Manhattan] for more than two centuries . . . have, as an integral part of our population, exercised a very material influence upon the commercial development and prosperity of this city."[31] Urban life was the backdrop against which the nation's most important financial, civic, and educational institutions were being built, and the revivalists highlighted the Jews' regular and generous contributions to their development during the early republic and antebellum periods.

"The Cosmopolitan Character of Its Population":
Establishing the Metropolitan Origins of Colonial America

Henry Samuel Morais's *The Jews of Philadelphia* (1894) was the longest and most painstakingly compiled of the Jewish urban histories. It not only recounted the most important episodes of Jewish and American history to have occurred in connection with the city of Philadelphia but also gave attention to such varied subjects as the development of Jewish publishing in the city, religious education, social clubs, cemeteries, and benevolent societies—all going back to the eighteenth century. The second of its extensive halves (the book in its entirety consisted of 592 pages) offered detailed listings of prominent Jewish personages in business, the professions, the arts, and politics, among other subjects. Morais readily noted that out of the "small element" of Jews who resided in the United States (a population whose size he estimated to be six hundred thousand), the Philadelphia contingent constituted "even a smaller fraction."[32] While his book was almost ledger-like in its attention to street-level detail, Morais could not have been more wide-ranging in his attention to the geographically distant origins of its subjects, as well as the widespread influences that they would eventually assert. What he found to be most remarkable about the Jewish experience in the United States was "the cosmopolitan character of its population."[33] Like a number of the other Jewish urban histories, *The Jews of Philadelphia* laid the groundwork for its locale-centered approach by casting a wide net at the outset and recounting the large-scale historical changes that had inspired Jews to go to Philadelphia in the first place. His historical view of this one city was meant to serve a larger ideological purpose, showing its readers how "a few stragglers" from all over the world served as "forerunner[s] of an influx" whose results included the "up-building of the Republic" and in "setting aloft the principles of human liberty and the brotherhood of mankind."

Morais's starting point, accordingly, was "the enforced exile from Portugal and Spain," which resulted in Jewish migrations to "the sunny land of the Alps and the Appenines" and religiously tolerant Holland. He was not the first writer to hint at a strong circumstantial link between the Inquisition and the discovery of the Americas,[34] but in his attention to the momentousness of this strange convergence of "untoward" and "fortuitous" elements, he went out of his way to emphasize a more or less causal relationship that explained that convergence. "The discovery of America," Morais pointed out, coincided with "the dawn of an enlightenment of which no European nation could boast." His suggestion was that the Inquisition itself had been the culmination of a period during which "the iron clutch of despotism," "the enslavement of the masses," and "the crushing of free thought and free speech" inspired not only Jews but also Europeans in general to seek shelter and betterment in America. "To whom could the occasion" of the four hundredth anniversary of Columbus's expedition "appeal with greater significance" than "the Jew," who had been driven out of Spain on the very eve of its having set sail? Like Emma Lazarus, the Philadelphia historian combined "the history of Jews as perennial exiles and the history of America as immigrant asylum."[35] Indeed, as Morais pointed out, three "members of the stock of Abraham the Hebrew" had been part of Columbus's crew. One of them, the *converso* Rodrigo Sanchez "had the honor of seeing land immediately after it was espied by Rodrigo Trianna, and prior to the cry, '*Tierra! Tierra!*'" As Morais recounted these events, it was almost as if these Sephardim had been anticipating the landfall that was about to usher in the age of their redemption.

The renaissance of hope and freedom to people throughout the western world, in other words, had been made necessary by conditions and circumstances whose primary sufferers had been Jews but whose broader effects had traumatized, but eventually inspired and even redeemed, Europe itself. These events and trends that "were so momentous in the annals of the world, and of humanity" and would eventually lead to the establishment of the United States and of Philadelphia, in other words, had long ago linked the fate of America to the fate of the Jews. When Morais referred to the "cosmopolitan character" of his city's Jewish population, his implication was that the diversity of its origins was only one aspect of its of worldliness. The city itself had been established as an extension of a sort of pan-European cosmopolitanism, whose urban origins in places like Genoa, Amsterdam, and London, in turn, accounted for the uniqueness of America itself. Morais was not alone in proposing this set of associations.

In his summary of the early Jewish presence in New York, for instance, Isaac Markens had offered a similar implication, noting that "the formation of the West India Company of Amsterdam" had been the impetus, first, for the founding of the Dutch colonies in Brazil and, shortly afterward, for the settlement of New Amsterdam itself. After all, the circumstances that had inspired Jewish merchants to set sail for the New World had been the very same ones that had instigated the transatlantic European commercial expansion. Jews had been at the center of Europe's development as a modernizing, metropolitan society, and the growth of that society had been the force that underlay the earliest settlement of America. Samuel Oppenheimer, the author of *The Early History of the Jews in New York* (1909) made similar references in his account to various Jewish New World ventures having had specifically metropolitan points of origin. Besides his detailed attention to Amsterdam's history as New Amsterdam's municipal precursor and instigator, his account mentioned another colonization scheme that began as an extension of another European metropolis: "Jews were allowed by the English to go from London to Barbados," he pointed out, in the process of explaining the multiple origins of North America's earliest Jewish settlers.[36]

The metropolitan origins both of America itself and of its earliest Jews accounted, as all of the Jewish colonial revivalists pointed out, for the rapidity with which the New World's European inhabitants were able to establish successful and free societies wherever they went. As Morais and his fellow Jewish colonial revivalists reviewed the history of Jewish settlement in the Americas, which began with the movement to Brazil of small numbers of Sephardic merchants in the mid-seventeenth century, they gave frequent attention to the urban origins of their commercial enterprises. They also drew close associations between the growth in influence of urban-based mercantile activity and the sort of social advancement from which Jews benefitted. Max Kohler (1871–1934), an immigration attorney, amateur historian, and the editor of the 1893 version of Judge Charles Daly's *The Settlement of the Hebrews in North America*, stated this point matter-of-factly in connection with the history of New Amsterdam. In his introduction to Daly's book, Kohler addressed himself to the question of whether Roger Williams's Rhode Island or Peter Stuyvesant's New Amsterdam was more tolerant of Jewish settlers. Neither society, he pointed out, had granted Jews the same rights accorded the members of other religious groups. The only operative factor that pertained in these instances was the conduct of business, and the conduct of business, in turn, had been a direct outgrowth of northwestern Europe's burgeoning metropolitanism. "It required the leveling and humanizing influences of Commerce," Kohler wrote, "to bring about religious toleration" in the colonies. When the eagerness to trade prevailed over the impulse to restrict, expansiveness was the result. "The commercial instinct of the Dutch," which manifested itself as transatlantic urbanism, defeated "old-time prejudice and intolerance."[37] Isaac Markens recounted an episode from 1700 that also highlighted the prevalence of this sort of expansive thinking. As a group of New York merchants "combined together to 'traverse'" the local agent of the English government in his attempt to pay his soldiers their weekly pay by lowering the exchange rate, only the intercession of "one Dutch merchant and two or three Jews" had made it possible for the official to avoid disaster.[38]

The revivalists were aware that the Jews who made their way across the Atlantic in the seventeenth and eighteenth centuries had not made the journey without first having had the experience of having lived in a pluralistic, dynamic, and rapidly urbanizing milieu. The greatest case that could be made in their favor was that the Jews advanced the cause of civilization wherever they went, in part because they represented such a diversity of geographical origins. They came, as Barnett Elzas wrote with reference to Charleston, "from everywhere—from England, Germany, Holland, Denmark, France, Russia, Poland, Curacao, Jamaica, St. Eustatius, San Domingo, New York, and Philadelphia."[39] A single individual's personal history frequently embodied this principle. As Morais recounted the story of Jacob Raphael Cohen, who became the "minister" of Philadelphia's Mikveh Israel upon the death of Gershom Seixas, he pointed out that Cohen "was, it is said, a native of the Barbary State, but came from London, England . . . to Quebec, thence to Montreal, where he became the first minister of the Spanish and Portuguese Congregation" in 1778. Cohen "subsequently repaired to New York City" but eventually settled in Philadelphia.[40]

One of the most direct sources of evidence for the claim of Jewish cosmopolitanism was embodied by the urban landscape itself, which in the colonial era had represented the transoceanic reach of European commercialism, in whose initial successes Jews had played no small part. In early America, the most noticeable physical marker of civilization, as people of European origin would have configured it, was architecture. Natives and visitors alike who wished to take stock of North America's growing urban centers were drawn to the sight of the Atlantic Seaboard's developing skylines and streetscapes. It was therefore important for late nineteenth and early twentieth century readers to know, for instance, that in New York during the latter decades of the seventeenth century, Asser Levy "acquired, evidently with an eye to business, a title to a house on 'Hoogh Straat,' the first house within the city gates, which had been for some time used as an inn, and was the resort of the country people entering the town from Long Island."[41] In Isaac Markens' view, at least, the centrality of Levy's physical locale lent the burgeoning colonial settlement an aura of urbanism, and it also showed how a Jew could prove to be integral to that urbanism in the eyes of those just arriving in the city's outskirts.

By the same token, since New York in the seventeenth and eighteenth centuries also represented the point in space where European commerce converged with the North American hinterland, Markens also described the business conducted by Hayman Levy, "who owned most of the houses on Duke Street, now Beaver Street." As the author of *The Hebrews in America* put it, Levy's "principal business was in furs, which he traded largely with the Indians," and he was not only "beloved by the Red man but was 'actually worshipped by them [sic].'"[42] That Markens depicted Hayman Levy in the vein of a James Fenimore Cooper protagonist was of a piece with his and his fellow revivalists' privileging of a distinctly American romantic-era sensibility. So too was his close attention to the specificities of geographical provenance an echo of the local color ethos. Eager to remind his readers that the atmosphere of New York had been always been enhanced by Jewish mercantile activity, Markens was particularly given to identifying the exact locations of these long since departed Jewish businesses, from Emanuel Abrahams's "Indian goods" outpost in Stone Street, to Maurice Josephson's clothing store "at Slip Market," to Judah Hays's "Broadcloths, velvets, linens and sundry other goods too tedious to mention," which had been located "at the corner of Stone and Broad Streets."[43]

Though it bore no comparison in scale to the scene presented by London, Amsterdam, or just about any other European city, the most salient feature of the urban skyline in colonial North America had been its array of church spires and steeples. As the turn-of-the-century commemorators of colonial Jewry went about establishing their claims for its cultural vibrancy and economic contributions to a nascent urban America, they devoted considerable attention to telling the story of the establishment and describing the construction of its first synagogues. Several more recent historians have noted that the outward appearance of these buildings was deliberately adapted to existing architectural trends and patterns, but the mere fact of their existence in an overwhelmingly Protestant milieu was a testament to the pluralistic aspect of English colonial endeavors. As Deborah Dash Moore points out, "Synagogues acknowledged a Jewish urban presence" in a city "and invited Christians to reflect on their own faith and willingness to accommodate non-Christian believers." In the eighteenth century, the material existence of genteel synagogues in places like New York, Newport, and Philadelphia—not to mention the conduct of worship within their walls—"were expressions of [Jewish] urban prosperity and willingness to establish roots."[44] The history of their design and construction, in addition to the collective memory of the liturgical activities that they had hosted, provided the Jewish colonial revivalists with further evidence for their arguments concerning the metropolitan origins of America's oldest urban districts.

According to the account that Isaac Markens gave in *The Hebrews in America*, gentile visitors to Shearith Israel such as "Disisoway, the author of 'Earliest Churches in New York,'" were enthralled by the sight of "the venerable Rabbi reading out of the Book of Law, his splendid robes of office, the long flowing beard, the men with their silk scarves, the women latticed in the galleries and the whole congregation chanting aloud in Hebrew."[45] The fact that such exotically appearing Jewish worship had been on display at the heart of America's oldest cities during the founding era was indicative of those cities' having been founded as extensions of Europe's culturally mixed and religiously heterogeneous metropolitan ventures. Samuel Morais's picture of Philadelphia's Mikveh Israel's dedication and establishment was no less colorful. The author of *The Jews of Philadelphia* went out of his way to highlight not only the most aesthetically pleasing aspects of Jewish worship during the colonial and Revolutionary War eras but also the extent to which those who witnessed it considered themselves to have been the beneficiaries of Jewish worldliness. The presence of Jews at the exact moment when and in the exact places where the United States was becoming itself constituted powerful proof of the nation's cosmopolitanism. "The dedication ceremonies" for Mikveh Israel, Morais wrote, "were of a very imposing character," as he recounted *hazzan* Gershom Seixas's prayers in behalf of the newly formed United States government and its officials.[46]

By the middle of the eighteenth century, American urban landscapes had begun to replicate the sorts of genteel features that could be found on display in English cities. Newport's synagogue, which was built in 1763, was a case in point. "This venerable edifice," as Markens described it in 1888, was "built in old-fashioned style" and was "lighted by seventeen windows on the front and sides, and fine chandeliers . . . suspended from the ceilings."[47] His attention to the

synagogue's most ancient and exotic features was reminiscent of Henry Wadsworth Longfellow's 1852 depiction of Newport's Jewish cemetery, which also
emphasized the city's colonial-era Jews as having been of "strange/Of foreign
accent, and of different climes."[48] Borrowing from another historian, as both
Simon Wolf and Isaac Markens had done in their accounts of early American
Jewish history, Philadelphian Samuel Morais went on to enumerate the most
curious features included in "Dr. Mease's" 1830 "curious description of [Mikveh
Israel's] sacred shrine"—which included not only the traditional "Ark and Altar"
but also the building's "Egyptian columns copied from the Temple at Tentyra."[49]
As Barnett Elzas described the building and dedication of Kahal Kadosh Beth
Elohim, the synagogue that served Charleston's Jewish population, he borrowed
a description that he found included in the city's 1883 *Yearbook*. The author had
hearkened back to "Friday, the 14th day of September, 1792 [as] the day appointed
for the ceremony of laying the corner stones for the sacred edifice." The formal-
ity of the *Yearbook*'s language matched the ritualized grandiosity of the occasion,
notwithstanding the fact that the "solemn and imposing ceremony" in question
had taken place nearly ninety years earlier. Before going on to describe the place-
ment of the eight marble stones whose purpose it was to mark the corners both
of the building itself and of the sweeping porch that ushered visitors and congregants alike into its grandeur, Elzas's source explained that "the Congregation
[had] assembled in the Old Synagogue, and after Divine service proceeded in
procession to the spot where the new building was to be erected."[50] As Deborah
Dash Moore writes, for those who participated in and witnessed them, these
sorts of dedication services fulfilled a self-reflexive and commemorative function that displayed "Jews' desire to recount their own history in the United States,
despite its relative brevity."[51] One hundred years after these events had taken
place, Jewish colonial revivalists who recounted them did so in order to substantiate their claims regarding the cosmopolitan and pluralistic origins of America's
oldest cities.

COMMERCIALISM AT THE CORE: DOCUMENTING JEWISH
PARTICIPATION IN THE REVOLUTIONARY WAR

While the entirety of North America's "wilderness empire" was a sphere of contention during the conflict between the United States and Great Britain, the war
itself began in and was inspired by events that took place in its seaboard cities and
settlements. Disagreements that inspired political agitation and became a pretext
for rioting were the products of what several historians have since described as
a late eighteenth-century version of "urban mobilization" and unrest.[52] In the
prewar atmosphere of "heightened political awareness" that led in turn to "mass
meetings, petition signings, tea protests, boycotts, bonfires, and riots," Jews were
admittedly minor players. While the Jewish American colonial revivalists could

hardly argue that Jewish merchants had been the instigators or fomenters of this unrest, however, their descriptions of life in the colonial ports in the years leading up to the outbreak of hostilities often emphasized the degree to which Jews, as risk-taking venture capitalists, were subject (and frequently objected) to the exact same restrictive trade and taxation policies that other colonial merchants repudiated. Colonial-era Jews bore few expectations regarding their "rights" as British taxpayers to parliamentary representation, but the turn-of-the-century historians who sought to revive the memory of their activities in places like Newport, New York, and Philadelphia sought, found, and highlighted evidence that proved their sympathy to the cause of nonimportation, for instance. Likewise, even though only a handful of Jews spoke or acted forthrightly on political matters during the Revolutionary War itself, the colonial revivalists gathered and presented the facts regarding their military service and financial contributions to the American war effort. As Henry Morais boldly asserted, "Hebrews had no small share in the events of the Revolution."[53] Writing in 1895, Simon Wolf was also confident that he possessed "sufficient data . . . to prove conclusively that comparatively recent settlers and few in number as they were," the Jews "furnished, as usual in all struggles for liberty and freedom, more than their proportion of supporters to the colonial cause."[54]

Nowhere had the Jews' role as vanguards of urban capitalism been more apparent than it was in Newport, whose commerce, according to Isaac Markens, had "exceeded that of New York" and allowed for their "remarkable prosperity" during the decades leading up to the outbreak of war.[55] According to the remarkable comparison that Markens invoked in his account of Newport's postwar decline, Jews had figured as the city's primary movers and shakers, commercially speaking. "As their forefathers had been compelled to flee from Spain to more tolerant countries in Europe many years before," he wrote, "so now the refugees and their families, warned by the opening of hostilities at Lexington and the appearance of a British fleet in Newport harbor, hastened to escape the ravages of war." The flight of the city's Jews, by his reckoning, ushered in "the decline of Newport's commercial supremacy." His venturing of the refugee comparison in the first place suggested that he was equating the absence of Jews with commercial failure, which in turn spelled the death of a once great American city. On the other hand, as Markens went on to explain, the evacuation of the Newport Jews who, "before their dispersion, occupied residences on . . . the Mall" (the row of well-appointed mansions that lent the city its prewar grandeur) would eventually contribute significantly to the growth of the cities to which they fled (again, the implied parallel with post-Inquisitional Spain and Portugal could not have been far from his mind).

Active Jewish participation in the prewar mercantile economy had also been an important factor in Philadelphia, where anti-British sentiment ran high enough to inspire dozens of the city's merchants to sign a nonimportation petition, "the

adoption of which," as Simon Wolf wrote, constituted "the first organized move-
ment in the agitation which eventually led to the independence of the colonies."[56]
As Hyman Polock Rosenbach wrote in his book *Jews in Philadelphia Prior to 1800*,
David Franks, along with Benjamin Levy, Samson Levy, Joseph Jacobs, Hyman
Levy Jr., Moses Mordecai, and Michael and Barnard Gratz, "entered into an
agreement with other merchants not to import any goods until the repeal of the
Stamp Act."[57] Rosenbach pointed out that Philadelphia was also the one city to
see its Jewish population grow as a result of the Revolutionary War. As the "Jews
of the city of New York, being strong Whigs, were driven out by the occupation of
the British army," many of them came south, "where they increased the number
of the Congregation."[58] Writing eleven years after Rosenbach, Henry Morais was
still more forthright and rhetorically florid in his account of the Philadelphia
Jews' eager participation in the nonimportation campaign as well as in subsequent developments that eventually lead to the waging of the Revolution and
eventual establishment of an American republic. Through their actions during
this period, Philadelphia's Jews had earned "a prominent rank" and "heightened
the respect for their coreligionists, and by their deeds earned—if they did not
all receive—the gratitude of the nation."[59] As if to underscore the symbolic significance of the Jews' role as integral contributors to Philadelphia's resistance
movement, Morais referred to the fact that the nonimportation agreement, with
their names indicated among those of "the merchants and other citizens" of
the city was "a famous document" that could "be seen to this day in Independence Hall."[60]

Morais's and the other urban colonial revivalists' point about Jewish contributions to the movement for American independence were reinforced by the
evidence they found and presented that bore on Haym Solomon's (as well as
other Jewish merchants' and brokers') residence in Philadelphia, a fortuitous circumstance of proximity that in turn had occasioned his financial generosity to
the cause. Once again, the starting point for Solomon's rise had been his activities as a banker both in New York and in Philadelphia. His loaning of "extraor-
dinarily large sums towards the cause of the American colonists in their struggle
for independence" had earned for him "a golden page in the history of the United
States" and, as Simon Wolf put it in his book on Jewish American patriots, the
reputation of a "munificent and patriotic individual in Philadelphia."[61] Isaac
Markens noted Solomon's charity toward the city's most impoverished citizens
during their time of need. Aware that they had been "deprived of the use of any
circulating medium by the act of withdrawal of Continental money," Solomon
"caused $2000 in specie to be distributed among the poor" of the city.[62] As Beth
Wenger notes, five years after the publication of Markens's book, in 1893, Haym
Solomon's descendants undertook an effort to have the United States government issue a medal to commemorate their ancestor's momentous deeds. Their

effort to do so "was a conscious effort," Wenger writes, "to place Jews at the center of an emerging public memory of the American Revolution."[63]

It is worth noting that in describing the material contributions made by Solomon and other Philadelphia Jews to the American war effort, Henry Morais was careful to identify the men in question with particular street addresses—after all, his book was an attempt to reinscribe a Jewish presence onto the urban landscape. As James Madison had once written to his friend Edmund Randolph, Solomon was "our little friend in Front Street." Other Revolutionary War–era Philadelphia Jews who had contributed in some way both to the city's growth and to its stature as an experiment in republican virtue included Michael and Barnard Gratz, located at "107 Sassafras Street," who "traded with the Indians, and supplied the government with 'Indian goods,'" as well as Michael's son Simon, who "was among the founders of the Pennsylvania Academy of Fine Arts" and also exercised a material claim on the city's glorious history by virtue of his having "bought the property on the south side of Market Street adjoining Seventh Street on the west side, wherein Thomas Jefferson had apartments, and where he had written the Declaration of Independence."[64]

Aside from highlighting the roles that Jewish merchants had played either as willing (or at least compliant) agents of economic resistance to British rule or as active contributors to the American cause in the various seaboard cities in which they had settled, the Jewish colonial revivalists of the turn-of-the-century period were also eager to document Jewish participation in the armed conflict of the Revolutionary War. Approximately two hundred Jews are believed to have served either in the Continental Army or in the various state militias, and the revivalists went to great lengths to enumerate every instance they could find of Jews under arms. Barnett Elzas had perhaps the easiest time of attending to this task, as Charleston fielded by far the highest concentration and largest contingent of Jewish soldiers during the war. This circumstance existed in part owing to that city's practice of requiring able-bodied men from each area of town to "enroll themselves in the district in which they lived."[65] The men who served in the Lushington Company were residents of an area that "extended on King Street, from Broad Street to Charles Town Neck." Since "King Street was . . . the principal business street and most of the Jews had their stores there," the Lushington Company attracted more Jews than any other unit in any of the American cities. While the Jewish membership in this group had never been large enough to warrant the nickname that subsequent historians assigned to it ("the Jew Company"), Elzas's attention to its history was indicative all the same of his and the other revivalists' larger efforts both to enumerate Jewish contributions to the patriotic cause and to demarcate the Jewish imprint upon the urban landscapes of early America.

STALWARTS OF PROSPERITY: JEWISH MERCHANTS
AND BENEFACTORS IN THE EARLY REPUBLIC

As Laura Leibman writes, the outcome of the Revolutionary War may have boosted morale in the formerly British colonies of North America, but "in the short term," the fighting itself had been "highly destructive to the economy of the Atlantic Rim."[66] Notwithstanding the triumph of the newly born United States, the conflict exacted a heavy toll upon the commercial fortunes and, in some cases, the architectural infrastructure of the nation's most important cities. In the earliest stages of the war, as well as in the years leading up to the outbreak of hostilities, Boston—the hotbed of mercantile resistance to British trade policies—had sustained the worst damage. When the British evacuated Boston in 1776, they went south to New York, which they easily wrested from American control. New England's only other major port, Newport, fell to the British in 1778. Philadelphia, the city to which a great many of the New York Jews fled, fell in 1778. The southern ports did not fare much better. Though they were both strongholds of American sentiment, Savannah and Charleston were lost to British control in late 1779 and early 1780, respectively. When the turn-of-the-century Jewish colonial revivalists reviewed the history of those cities in the aftermath of the war, they went out of their way to address the Jews' role in reconstituting, rebuilding, and expanding upon the commerce and civic life of these seaboard cities whose inhabitants had absorbed the war's most punishing blows. Having made the case that the cities had been the birthplace of the Revolution, they went on to highlight the facts attendant upon those same cities having been integral to the postwar recovery as well as to the establishment of the nascent United States.

New York, much of which was destroyed by fire in 1776, lost much of its Jewish population during the war. Nonetheless, upon the departure of the British in 1783, the city quickly reclaimed its status as a leading commercial center, and the Jewish merchants who returned there, as well as the ones who arrived there for the first time, played no small part in this recovery. As Isaac Markens wrote in *The Hebrews in America*, Hayman Levy, who had "met with severe losses during the great fire . . . when most of his property was swept away," went on to become "one of the most upright and enterprising merchants in New York." The Hendricks family had also contributed conspicuously to the city's rise from the ashes of the war years. Uriah Hendricks, who had come to New York from Amsterdam and lived until the turn of the nineteenth century, was the founder of a veritable dynasty of ironmongers, copper mill owners, and merchants. As Markens described it, the Hendricks family's various metal manufacturing endeavors constituted the "oldest Hebrew business concern in the United States in any branch," and their stature as leading merchants both within and beyond New York itself was unquestionable.

Hyman Polock Rosenbach's account of pre-1800 Philadelphia enumerated the philanthropic activities and commercially beneficial enterprises of several other Jews in that city. Samuel Hays "was one of the original subscribers to the old Chestnut Theater, in 1792." Moses Levy, who "stood high in his profession" as a "well-known lawyer" at 311 Chestnut Street, served as "Recorder of the city from 1802 to 1808, and subsequently President Judge of the District Court."[67] "For many years," wrote Isaac Markens, "the Hebrews of Philadelphia have occupied an honorable place in the community."[68] During the early decades of the nineteenth century, the more prominent among them on his list included the ship-owners and dry goods salesmen John and Samuel Moss and "Leon J. Levy, who occupied a large establishment on Chestnut Street."[69] Bankers in the postwar period included Hyman Marks and Robert and Isaac Philips.[70] One of the city's most prominent businessmen and admired personalities during the first half of the nineteenth century was Abraham Hart, who became known for his "uprightness and integrity, during his business career of more than a quarter of a century" (he ran "the leading book house of the United States").[71] Of still greater note, as Markens described them, were the children of Michael Gratz, who included Simon and Rebecca, the latter of whose beauty and charm were sufficient to "immortalize [her] as the heroine of Scott's *Ivanhoe.*" Her literary fame notwithstanding, Rebecca Gratz's greatest claim to the admiration of her fellow Philadelphians would undoubtedly have been the fact that she was "prominently identified in the organization of numerous charitable and benevolent associations" that benefitted the city at large.[72]

When it came to memorializing the postwar contributions of Jews to the development of the early republic's cities, Barnett Elzas was by far the most literarily enterprising and expansive of the Jewish colonial revivalists. Though he readily admitted that "nothing very remarkable" occurred during the period immediately preceding 1800 in Charleston, he understood and acknowledged that, at least in terms of sheer numbers, the city whose history he was chronicling had actually been on the verge of experiencing its greatest period of Jewish growth at that exact point, when it boasted "the largest Jewish population in America." Jews who, as he put it, "had suffered in common with their neighbors [during the war] . . . had to begin the battle of life over again."[73] As the United States embarked upon its first full century of history, Charleston's Jews "were to be found in every branch of trade and commerce." Moreover, "their influence, not only as merchants, but in the arts and professions," was "considerable."[74] After providing a seven-page-long list of every Jew who was known to have lived in South Carolina between 1800 and 1824, Elzas went on to highlight the careers of the more prominent figures among them. His enumeration included political officials and civil servants, portrait painters, physicians, notaries, clerks of court, schoolmasters, and military officers, among others. For the opening decades of the nineteenth century, which the historian once again referred to as a "zenith," "the record of the Jews of South Carolina commercially, professionally, politically, and socially," was "in truth a remarkable record."[75] Elzas sought to place the city into the wider perspective afforded by a comparative look at modern Jewish history, at least within the Anglo-American world.

Taken together, the revivalists' accounts of post-Revolutionary New York, Philadelphia, and Charleston established those cities as exemplars of Jewish modernization. In each instance, the Jewish citizens whose reputations and accounts the colonial revivalists celebrated had prioritized both commercial expansion and civic duty. One of the primary tasks undertaken by the revivalists had been to narrate the development of *Jewish* communities, including the philanthropic activities that had led to the establishment and construction of actual synagogues. Within the wider ideological context created by immigrant influx during the turn of the twentieth century, however, readers of these books required particular edification on the subject of Jewish loyalty to national and civic institutions. The arrival of increasing numbers of newcomers from the culturally alien portions of Eastern Europe multiplied the Jewish population of these and other American cities, threatening both to engulf the assimilated Jews and to renew suspicions as to their ability and willingness to adapt to American ways. The revivalists' attention to the record of early Jewish contributions to the civic development of the nation's first cities was a fitting antidote to this dual dilemma.

By highlighting instances of Jewish participation in the foundation of the vital institutions and enterprises of the early republic, the work of the revivalists addressed two central constituencies—the one comprised by the newcomers themselves, who needed to be reminded of how much work had been done ahead of time to establish a Jewish claim to America, and the one comprised by those non-Jewish skeptics who doubted the commensurability of Jewish life with American life. With particular regard to this second constituency, the argument that America itself had been ushered into existence as an extension and through the development of metropolitan institutions was a key component. "We may be proud and rejoice," Max Kohler wrote in his preface to Daly's *The Settlement of the Jews in North America*, "that Jews were interested co-workers in the discovery, settlement, and development of our land." The time had come, he continued, for Jews "to acquaint ourselves as well as our Christian neighbors with those incidents in our national history."[76] In the era of local color fiction, which placed emphasis on the importance of establishing physical claims to American geography as a basis for American belonging, Kohler's reference to the "land" and to the actions that early Jews had taken to demonstrate their commitment to it was more than incidental.

"PROBLEMS OF THE PRESENT MAY OFTEN BE SOLVED BY A STUDY
OF PAST EXPERIENCES": APPLYING EARLY JEWISH AMERICAN
HISTORY TO THE TURN-OF-THE-CENTURY IMMIGRANT CRISIS

When assimilated Sephardic and German Jews first confronted the issue of Eastern European Jewish immigration at the turn of the 1880s, their reactions toward
the prospect of newcomers' arrival and settlement tended to be guarded and even
xenophobic at times. "In their cultural and class arrogance," writes Gerald Sorin,
assimilated Jews hesitated to embrace their coreligionists.[77] They were eager not
to jeopardize their own still fairly precarious status as provisional Americans,
"anxious that [their] non-Jewish neighbors distinguish between [their] western-
ized habits and the ghetto-oriented approach of the Eastern European members
of [their] faith."[78] Within fewer than ten years, however, as the anti-Semitic policies of the Russian regime worsened (and in the face of other world Jewish crises
like the Dreyfus Affair), a growing number of prominent American Jews, including Simon Wolf himself, chose to argue, often quite effectively, on behalf of the
Eastern European Jews' right to settle in the United States. As they rounded their
urban histories to their conclusions, these privileged Jews took the extraordinary
step of applying their knowledge of and claims for Jewish participation in early
American history as bases for their proimmigrant stance.

By necessity, they had to be careful to distance their own Americanized
practice of Judaism from the orthodoxy of the Eastern Europeans, and they
also went out of their way to contrast their enlightened American republican-
ism from the "imported" forms of labor radicalism popular among the Russian
Jews. As Michael Kramer writes with regard to Emma Lazarus, whose somewhat ambivalent advocacy on behalf of the newcomers mirrored the view taken
of them by the Jewish colonial revivalists, "these were her people, [but] then again
they were not."[79] Nonetheless, the final chapters of their books sought to make
a claim for the assimilability of the Eastern Europeans. Fully appreciative of the
fact that Jews had long been in the habit of "us[ing] the urban milieu to express
themselves as Jews and as Americans," they took advantage of the opportunity to
build a case for city life as the starting point for Jewish acculturation to American
life. They offered statistical evidence for the size and effectiveness of city-based
Jewish charities whose work was intended to assure the transformation of new
immigrants into full-fledged Americans through education, job training, and
even resettlement projects that moved small numbers of newly arrived Jews to
rural areas where they could become farmers. They also cited the immigrant
origins of the nation itself, urging legislators and citizens alike to recall their own
ancestors' relatively recent arrival from Europe in many of the same cities that
were now being condemned and avoided for their allegedly alien quality. On
the basis of their own experiences in the nation's major cities, from the colonial

era and into the first two-thirds of the nineteenth century, they "proclaimed the compatibility of Jewish and American values."[80]

When Max Kohler argued for the importance of studying early American Jewish contributions to the establishment of the United States and its most important cities, he did so in large part because he was a lawyer whose job it was to argue for the rights and needs of the tens of thousands of Eastern European Jewish immigrants who were arriving and attempting to settle in those same cities. In his introduction to Charles Daly's *The Settlement of the Jews in North America*, he pointed out that when the book had first been published in 1873, the nation was at "about the middle of the German Jewish migration to America." "Since then," he continued, "other and more numerous classes of Jews have arrived here, while their predecessors have multiplied and thrived." Like his fellow revivalists, he could easily find and did in fact produce plenty of evidence that Jews had what it took to achieve material success in the United States. Physical survival was not as important, however, as what he referred to as "the intellectual development of the body of American Jews." Kohler understood that his most important task would be to establish not just the adaptability of the Jews but also their unique and even natural affinity for American culture and ideals. From the arrival of the first Sephardim in the seventeenth century, through the successive waves of Ashkenazi immigration dating back to the eighteenth century, to the present-day movement from Eastern Europe, Jews had shown that their commitment to America was an extension of their commitment to the ideological principles on which it had been founded. "Inasmuch as the great majority of the most prosperous Hebrew merchants of to-day landed on these shores under conditions not dissimilar to the later comers," Isaac Markens wrote, "it is reasonable to expect that the latter will experience equal progression."[81]

Simon Wolf, also an attorney and one of the most outspoken proponents, at least by the 1890s, of the continued support of Eastern European Jewish migration to the United States followed a similar logic. He understood that his "review of the subject of American Jewish citizenship necessarily involve[d] a consideration of the recent accretions to the Jewish population in this country through the immigration of those of expatriated Russian Jews."[82] As his editor, Louis Edward Levy, put it, Wolf was concentrating "the light of historical truth" on the subject of Jewish settlement in America. Wolf would show that, "like their ancestors and brethren of the Old [World]," Jews in America had been "unfailing in their devotion to their country's cause." In the past, Jews had "been counted in the van of the country's progress and in the forefront of its defense," and on the basis of the evidence that Wolf had marshaled in order to demonstrate these points, he would succeed in enlightening an ignorant (and often disturbingly hostile) public on the subject of Jewish loyalty in the present and future.[83]

That works like these were being written at this particular juncture in the first place was the outgrowth of the immigration crisis. Why else, considering the fact that Jews had in fact been present in North America since 1654 and that many of the families whose ancestors came during the first two hundred years of settlement, had Jews taken so long to prepare historical accounts of their presence in the cities in which they had been dwelling for so many successive generations? The outpouring of scholarship on Jewish American urban history that occurred during the turn of the twentieth century came about as a direct response to the rising tension both within Jewish circles (as assimilated Jews encountered the more recent arrivals) and within the wider American milieu (as assimilated Jews felt increasingly threatened by the prejudices that the arrival of the Eastern European Jews had begun to exacerbate toward them on the part of other "native" Americans). The numbers alone told a startling story. As Henry Morais pointed out in connection with Philadelphia, while the Russian Jewish population of that city had been two thousand in 1881 (the year before the czar's most punishing edicts were issued), by the time his book was published in 1895, that number had risen to twenty-five thousand and was increasing by approximately two thousand more per year.[84]

No antidote to "ill-founded prejudices" could be more convincing, as Morais announced at the outset of his book on Philadelphia's Jews, than his coreligionists' record of "activity in our local centre" and "active participation in works of great interest" around the city.[85] Once the case had been made for the Jews of earlier eras having been "true and loyal to American institutions" (one of the most important of which was the city itself), readers could be counted upon to extrapolate the imminent success of the newcomers. After a brief period of acculturation administered by philanthropically minded uptown Jews, the newer Jewish arrivals would blend properly, in accordance with a precedent that, as the revivalists' books showed, dated back to the mid-seventeenth century. According to Morais's formulation, as the members of "an ancient race" that had introduced the world to monotheism, Jews could be counted upon to uphold a common set of core moral principles that were entirely commensurate with modern American values. "For no other people has the promise of Columbian epoch been more completely fulfilled than for the Jews," wrote the historian.[86]

According to Simon Wolf, the earliest migrations of Abraham and his stock constituted a "prologue to the history of civilization," and the later migrations of the Jews as a people, especially to cities, represented its logical continuation. According to Wolf's exegesis, Abraham's movement was significant because, unlike countless other episodes in ancient and modern history of people from one place forcing themselves upon and exploiting the limited resources of people from another place, it was a peaceful, even generous movement. "We find him earnestly pleading the cause of his adopted countrymen, notwithstanding their great wickedness," Wolf wrote. Like the earliest movement of the father of the Hebrews, the Jews who had come to America had acted in a similar fashion, contributing to its betterment, particularly through their assistance in the development of its first cities. The generosity and responsible behavior of Jewish immigrants had distinguished them from the mass of migrants throughout history. They had followed in the civilizing footsteps of their patriarchal figure who, "in general," the historian wrote, "figure[d] on the horizon as in all respects not only a typical but a model immigrant"[87] and, for that matter, city-dweller.

In proposing that America's origins lay in the founding of its cities and in insisting that Jews had played an instrumental role in the growth and development of those cities, the Jewish colonial revivalists articulated a version of American history and identity that departed dramatically from the dominant narrative of the nation's rural agrarian and Anglo-Protestant heritage. An argument that sought to refute nativist rhetoric by claiming the centrality of cities within the early American milieu went against the American grain even as it was attempting to assert its adherents' American credentials. As Deborah Dash Moore writes, cities had a natural appeal to Jews (and other cultural outliers) because they "allowed diverse minority groups to elaborate their own subcultures by affording them enough space" to do so.[88] Despite the objections and misgivings that nativists would continue to level at America's newest, as well as its oldest Jewish inhabitants, the nation as a whole was already launched upon a future in which the patterns of urban life would play a major role in shaping social, economic, and cultural life. The citizens to whom George Washington himself had once referred to as "the children of the stock of Abraham" had been affecting that transformation all along.

lived in "triple-digit" communities (i.e., communities whose Jewish population ranged between 100 and 999) whose overall populations were under sixty thousand.[3] A full quarter of the nation's total Jewish population resided in cities and towns with fewer than one hundred thousand inhabitants.[4] Even as increasing numbers of Jews moved to small towns, however, the nation at large viewed this same era as a period of rural decline. With urbanization occurring at an ever-accelerating rate and small farmers losing their footing in the national economy, little towns were often represented in the popular imagination as isolated places that had long since descended into stasis and provinciality. In the age of Zona Gale's *Friendship Village* and H. L. Mencken's "The Sahara of the Bozart," depictions of small-town life tended to be either warmly nostalgic or harshly condemnatory. Both points of view shared a common attitude of despair—the small-town mentality was either a hopelessly inaccessible remnant of the receding past or a closed-minded attitude of ignorance that refused to die. Edna Ferber and her fellow small-town Jews saw things differently. Avoiding recourse to rose-colored idealizations and stinging polemics alike, Jewish writers who depicted the small-town environment viewed it as a shifting arena that existed in a dynamic relationship with the emergent urban America that surrounded it. In keeping with their wider understanding that America itself was too complex to be comprehended by polarities, Jewish writers described their small-town experiences without abstracting them from the dominant trends that were shaping their assimilation into the modernizing milieu of the middle class.[5] They challenged notions of small-town obsolescence. Embracing their role as agents of transformation, they articulated a unique claim to a changing rural landscape.

By virtue of her small-town origins, Edna Ferber's story also challenged the notion that Jews were strangers in America. To "those concerned about the nature of American society," as social historian Lee Shai Weissbach explains, small towns constituted "the nation's heart and soul."[6] The Jews who called such places home in the early decades of the twentieth century defied more than one set of norms. Some of their ancestors had first arrived during the nineteenth century and earlier, but even the relative latecomers played a role in shaping the culture of the heartland. As Jews, they may or may not have been fully accepted as part of their respective small towns' social fabric. But merely fitting in or achieving stasis within a milieu that was itself undergoing dynamic changes had not been their goal in the first place. The period that Weissbach refers to as the "classic era" of small-town Jewish life in America was hardly an agrarian age but rather a period of rapid transformation during which "American Jewry, like American non-Jewry, continu[ed] to move inexorably towards its white-collar destiny."[7] Jews who settled in small towns were agents of their communities' economic and social advancement. As Adam Mendelsohn puts it, they "linked remote villages to a larger world of commerce."[8] In small towns across the Midwest and prairie states, in the deepest South and in northern Maine, throughout the Rockies, along the Pacific Coast, and in the formerly homogenously Anglo-Protestant nooks of the Eastern Seaboard, Jewish merchants, farmers, and professionals participated in and sometimes fomented the modernization, not to mention the ethnic diversification, of rural America.

As writers like Edna Ferber depicted their families' existence in small towns, they showed that, as one contributor to *Commentary* magazine would write in 1960, "there is much that the Jew can receive from the American rural tradition."[9] Their experiences in small towns and the literature that they produced out of those experiences were indicative of more than merely assimilative behavior, however. Jewish American writing about small-town life in the early and middle decades of the twentieth century was often a testament to the wider transformations that the nation as a whole was undergoing. Rural Jews did not think of their American identity as a stable entity but as a work in progress shaped by changing conditions.[10] Even when they idealized the conditions of rural life that had attracted their families in the first place, first-person accounts by small-town Jewish Americans challenged dominant mythologies about the nation's pristinely agrarian and culturally homogenous heritage and also emphasized the susceptibility of village life to historical and demographic changes.[11] Edna Ferber and other early to mid-twentieth-century Jewish American writers who spent their formative years in small towns coined a literature that claimed rural geography by emphasizing its contiguity with the rest of the nation's eclectic and urbanizing trajectory. While their previous experiences as "religious aliens and petty capitalists" in Europe bore some rudimentary resemblance to the lives they were now shaping in the American countryside, as Ewa Morawska explains, Jews' newfound ease of passage between urban and rural commercial environments meant that they now "belonged to the dominant economic group" in the small American towns in which they had settled.[12] The stories they told demonstrated how closely linked the small town was to the larger city, even in the face of a popular mind-set that conceptualized of the two environments as diametric opposites.[13] As Ferber put it in her autobiography, her job was to learn how she had gotten from "that faintly improbable sounding town called Kalamazoo" to "a penthouse apartment on top of a roof on Park Avenue, New York."[14]

Decades ahead of Edna Ferber's attempt to answer this question, a lesser-known Jewish writer set about describing his small-town experience against the backdrop of an increasingly urbanizing society. Joseph Leiser (1873–1940), a third-generation Jew from upstate New York, produced a young adult novel that described the lives of rural-dwelling Jews as an integral phase in their development as Americans. Like Edna Ferber, Joseph Leiser, who was a product of Canandaigua, New York, commemorated the small-town environment from the point of view of a child who had grown up in it. Even as his novel, *Canaway and the Lustigs* (1909), celebrated the advantages that rural life conferred upon young people, however, it made no pretense of arguing that Jewish Americans would be better off choosing to settle permanently in small towns, much less cutting their ties to the cities from which so many of them had come. As long as the residents of places like Canaway, Leiser's fictional version of his actual hometown, could build and maintain vital connections to the outside world, they could support Jewish life. In the absence of such lifelines, however, and especially as youngsters approached adulthood, Leiser's novel suggested, such an existence was unsustainable over the long term for Jewish families who wished to live as modern-day Americans. Nonetheless, small-town Jews like Leiser were uniquely positioned to comprehend the complicated dynamic that united these seemingly disparate geographies. By virtue of their externality and frequent passage between rural and urban environments, they were people who could be said to have "walked alone on the country roads and city streets of America."[15] They knew that the space between the two places was not nearly as vast as it often appeared to be.

Neither Joseph Leiser nor Edna Ferber would have reveled in the uniqueness of their respective birthplaces if their goals had been to highlight these town's ordinariness any more than they would have played up their Jewish origins if they had wished to be taken as fully assimilated products of a homogeneous Anglo America. For her part, Ferber went out of her way to emphasize "the Soul and Spirit of America," which she assumed to be "very disconcerting to the European visitor."[16] As if to underscore the role that its small towns played in shaping this "electric element," she was pleased to note that "Kalamazoo" was actually "an Indian name meaning boiling pot." "In America," she wrote, "all town names beginning with the letter K . . . are considered comic and used to be a surefire laugh in the days of vaudeville."[17] Whether or not such places deserved to be thought of as comical on the basis of their names, Ferber would not cede to the prevailing view of them as sleepy holdovers from a departed age. Rather, her description of Kalamazoo, as well as her depictions of the other small midwestern towns in which she had spent her formative years, highlighted idiosyncrasy as opposed to predictability, liveliness as opposed to quietude. Her narratives, as Lori Harrison-Kahan puts it, "tend[ed] to unsettle rather than stabilize" the American settings in which they took place.[18]

Both Leiser and Ferber also made it clear that the presence of Jews had contributed to the diversification and growth of such environments. Jewish shopkeepers and their families played a pivotal role in ensuring that the residents of small towns gained and maintained access to the nation's expanding consumer culture.[19] A case in point had been Ferber's Chicago-born mother, who "had never lived in a small town" as a child "and had not learned to change her gait and garb to suit its more provincial standards."[20] Julia Neumann Ferber distinguished herself by wearing "the first short skirt in Appleton, Wisconsin." Years earlier, when she and her husband left their former home in Chicago so that Jacob Ferber could open a dry goods store in Kalamazoo, the newly married Julia marched downtown dressed in "a large 'picture' hat with a sweeping plume, and a flowing cape whose hood was lined with red satin." She was shortly "followed by an assorted rabble of small boys, idlers, and the curious generally" who mistook "the very respectable young bride" for a member of the burlesque troupe that was visiting town.[21] Notwithstanding their inability to distinguish a stylish urbanite from a visiting showgirl, the people of Kalamazoo as Ferber depicted them were grateful and ready for the opportunity to experience such novelties. Her autobiography argued that they were better off for having done so. So too were the residents of Leiser's Canaway. "In those days," as Herman Lustig, the novel's protagonist, explained to his sons, he had done a brisk business because "there were few stores, and it was difficult for farmers to get to town."[22] As one 1952 commentator would write, immigrant and city-bred Jews had introduced "vitality to small town life."[23]

Neither Leiser nor Ferber was blind to the darkness and deprivations of small-town life. Leiser did not hesitate to describe the cruel harassment suffered by Canaway's lone Hebrew teacher (notably, a first-generation "greenhorn" who spoke English with a markedly foreign accent) at the hands of the town's mischievous boys. Writing thirty years later, on the eve of World War II, Ferber addressed anti-Semitism bluntly, in large part by drawing a stark contrast between the two midwestern towns in which she had spent most of her childhood and adolescence. In between the more positive experiences that she and her family underwent first in Kalamazoo and later in Appleton, she described her family's time in Ottumwa, Iowa, whose residents' "brutality and ignorance" toward her Jewish family (and each other), as she put it, "must be held accountable for anything in me that is hostile toward the world in which I live."[24] Years later, however, upon revisiting Ottumwa around 1930, she saw those formative years in a different light. "The cool clean Iowa air cleansed them," she reflected, and she was newly able to view them "not as bitter corroding years, but as astringent strengthening years."[25]

The cruelty that she had experienced as a child in Ottumwa who, over the course of seven years, as she put it, "never went out on the street without being subject to some form of devilment"[26] had a lingering effect on her, but she did not conclude from that experience that small-town America was intrinsically anti-Semitic.[27] In Ottumwa, Ferber wrote, "business was bad, the town was poor, [and] its people were frightened, resentful and stupid."[28] She also noted, however, that as a future writer she would eventually draw benefits from her girlhood habit of watching the daily parade of townspeople go past her house. "There I sat at my ease," she wrote in A Peculiar Treasure, "an intent and obnoxious little student of the human race, fascinated, God knows why, as I saw this cross section of America go shuffling by in a little Iowa town."[29] The seven years she spent in Ottumwa had equipped her to appreciate "all the elements of courage, vitality, humor, sordid tragedy, [and] high tragedy"[30] that would later form the basis for her literary successes. The benightedness of the town's residents may first have caused her to feel a "ghastly inferiority," but in the end, it was she who had become "rich and famous" and had "lived to see entire nations behaving precisely like the idle frustrated bums perched on the drugstore railing" who had made her so miserable as a child.[31]

GLOBALIZING THE SMALL-TOWN ENVIRONMENT: JEWISH REVISIONS OF AN AGRARIAN MYTH

Notwithstanding the efforts of authors like Joseph Leiser and Edna Ferber to describe rural America's dynamic potential, by the late 1930s and early 1940s, the small-minded habitués of drugstore railings had been the subjects of mainstream American literature for several decades. Retrospective accounts of small-town life frequently took a dim view of it as an unchanging, intractable environment.[32] In the aftermath of the Civil War, regionalism and local color fiction attempted to capture the last remnants of a rapidly vanishing (if highly mythologized) rural atmosphere that writers believed could still be glimpsed in relatively remote places like northern New England, Appalachia, and the upper Midwest. While broad variations could be found within this body of literature, especially as time passed and as social conditions shifted with the growth of industry and a massive influx of immigrants, the overall tenor within literary representations of small-town America was often wistful, if not downright elegiac. From Hamlin Garland's mournful accounts of practically deserted "Middle Border" farming communities to Sarah Orne Jewett's images of a Maine coastline that vanished from view like a distant dream as the narrator recounted her departure from it, the earliest phases of this rural-focused literature were marked by an overriding view that small-town America represented a dying world and an unrecoverable past. Its representations forced readers to make impossible choices. Small towns were either "agrarian peaceable kingdoms" or hopelessly stagnant hotbeds of provincialism.[33]

Perhaps no other work of American literature during this period would cast such a darkening shadow over the mantle of small-town existence as Sherwood Anderson's collection of loosely connected stories, *Winesburg, Ohio* (1919). Anderson's book punctured the "myth of community" that had so long been cherished by Americans and instead equated small-town life with deprivation and eclipse.[34] Whether it influenced subsequent literary treatments of rural America or merely epitomized the motif, *Winesburg*'s salient qualities—its sadly retrospective view, its relentless depiction of gloom and stasis, its formal emphasis on fragmentation as a means of replicating the isolation felt by rural dwellers—were reflective of a perspective that dominated literary depictions of small-town settings in pre–World War II America. As Anthony Channell Hilfer writes, Anderson and his fellow disaffected small-town refugees had "attacked an abstraction with a counter-abstraction."[35] Even had they been able to go home again, to borrow

Thomas Wolfe's words, native-born Anglo refugees from small towns did not want to do so. When such places couldn't be forgotten entirely, the authors of this modern era hoped at least to be writing their elegies. The small town rarely presented itself as anything other than a trap from which most of its central characters seemed doomed never to escape. When George Willard manages to leave town at the end of *Winesburg*, it is nothing short of a miracle. Like Ishmael surviving the onslaught of Moby Dick on a piece of flotsam, George boards a train for the big city, the lone survivor of the slowly evolving cataclysm that was Winesburg, Ohio.

For their part, Jewish writers who sought to describe small-town existence before World War II presented a considerably less Manichean view of American geographical destiny. Because they had been drawn to their respective rural communities from a range of urban points of origin, Jews did not automatically equate cities with infectious corruption or rural locales with irretrievable innocence. These writers can be said to have "modified the myth to meet changing realities" as they experienced them.[36] Because they were often deliberately pursuing business opportunities in rural areas whose development, as they saw it, remained incomplete, small-town Jews reversed the typical American journey. The fact that many of them left for the country because they had exhausted possibilities for financial success in the cities did not necessarily mean that they believed city life itself to have exerted an evil influence upon them. Jews who moved to rural communities knew that they could, and often would, return from whence they had come, in part because they were the inheritors of a cultural heritage that stressed the importance of spatial mobility. Because they were perpetual outsiders who generally retained their social and economic ties to the world beyond the small town, Jews who wrote about rural life were able to emphasize its ephemeral quality without lamenting the prospect of its obsolescence. They understood, as Janet Galligani Casey has recently written, that "rurality was enfolded into the modernist" sensibility as opposed to merely alienated from it.[37] Since they had never imagined small-town life to be ideal in the first place, they could write about it without mourning or celebrating its decline.

Since these writers did not expect to be thought of as native to small-town America, their most effective means of establishing such a claim was to show their readers a different version of small-town America than the one to which they were accustomed from prior literary exposure. By the early decades of the twentieth century, when significant, if relatively small, numbers of Jews began to settle in small towns across the United States, few rural locales could be said to resemble the utterly isolated, forlorn, and totally homogenous communities that writers like Sherwood Anderson had depicted (if they had ever been that way in the first place).[38] The absorption of small towns into a dynamic and globalizing market economy precluded their retention of the sorts of hard and fast regional distinctions that often made rural areas seem isolated in the first place.

In her recent writing on the legacy of Jewish peddlers, Hasia Diner points out
that, just by their presence in such places, Jewish immigrants reminded attentive people that regions that were "so long conceptualized by [their] own residents and outsiders as unique" had now "become like other parts of the United
States and the new world."[39] Across literally hundreds of small towns throughout the United States from the latter decades of the nineteenth century through
to the post–World War II period, a casual survey of the average downtown district yielded descriptions like this 1949 description of an unnamed village in
coastal Maine: "In addition to half of the stores on Main Street, the list of Jewish
enterprises includes two garages, the large wholesale meat business . . . three city
hotels, two junk yards, two chicken-shipping concerns, and sundry real estate."[40]

As Diner explains, the global Jewish peddling phenomenon, which extended
not only throughout the United States and Canada but across the entire western world and included the hinterlands of South Africa and Australia, has until
recently been overlooked.[41] On the other hand, Jewish peddlers who passed
through or, often enough, established retail stores and settled their families in the
American South were similar to Jewish peddlers and storeowners in Maine, California, and, for that matter, Scotland, South Africa, and Argentina. The ubiquity
of globally interconnected Jewish peddlers and merchants rendered common
assumptions about rural isolation problematic. The arrival of a Jewish family in
a small town, whether that family was to abide there only temporarily or remain
intact for several generations, was indicative of the larger economic and social
transformation that had been under way for decades. In the years preceding the
Civil War and throughout the developing rural communities of the South and
West, Adam Mendelsohn writes, "the arrival of a Jew often coincided with that
of canals, roads, and railways that hitched the town to the regional and national
economy."[42] For all of their apparent provinciality, the inhabitants of such places
were now linked, by virtue of the family and trade networks that connected Jews
to one another throughout the United States and across the ocean, to the wider
world. In fact, Diner argues, it was the very remoteness of these small-town environments that enabled the Jewish peddlers' success by presenting them with ideal
opportunities to make the most of their access to mass-produced goods and the
trade networks through which they were exchanged.[43]

Whether or not Jews could ever become thoroughly regionalized participants in the cultural life of places like the Deep South, northern New England,
or remote areas of the prairie or Rocky Mountain states in the early and middle
decades of the twentieth century, their long-term residence in such rural environments proved that regional differences had become themselves somewhat superficial or at least that the cultural barriers that appeared to distinguish American
regions from one another were permeable. The experiences of Jewish residents
of small-town America help substantiate just such an argument. In the face of
what Mark Bauman describes as a belief held by Southerners (presumably, of the

non-Jewish variety) "in a pastoral concept of 'place over time,' a sense of rooted-ness in which space of residence was imbued with an almost familial type of loy-alty," Jewish residents of small-town Southern communities generally had more in common with other American Jews than they did with other Southerners, culturally speaking.[44] As one 1952 writer put it, "In our highly mobile American society, even the most isolated group does not easily disappear from the body of American Jewry."[45] Unless they converted or intermarried en masse, small-town Jews rarely lost contact with their coreligionists in distant communities. The unity of Jews across American regions was at least slightly indicative of a broader unity that connected all rural areas to a rapidly developing national culture.

By the middle of the twentieth century, the reluctance to view geographical circumstance as equivalent to familial loyalty had long since become a function not only of Jewish cultural heritage but also of contemporary American social reality. Jews did not comprise the only segment of the nation's population who experienced or understood the contiguity of small towns with large cities. All the residents of small-town America had become participants, willingly or unwill-ingly, in a dynamically linked national economy. If small towns like Kalamazoo were culturally contiguous with larger cities, it was because their residents could not and did not absent themselves from that economy. An acute awareness of the space between the sentimental notions about and the lived experiences of small-town America was a central feature in Jewish American writing about rural life. Jewish Americans who described small-town life knew perfectly well that, among Americans, small-town life denoted cultural stability.[46] For various reasons, including the exposures to anti-Semitism to which they had been subject at least from time to time, they were under no delusions that life in the country could ever be as wholesome as they might have wished. At the same time, however, and unlike the often bitter, or at least disillusioned, refugees from rural life who had authored popular and critically acclaimed works in the *Winesburg, Ohio* vein, small-town Jewish writers were not interested in condemning, lampoon-ing, or even elegizing such environments. Instead, they wrote about small towns from the perspective of people who had never felt imprisoned by them in the first place. As self-conscious outsiders and newcomers, for better or worse, they were capable of avoiding the extremes of romanticization and embitterment.

In many rural communities, the activities of Jewish merchants and farmers were widely recognized as helping revive local economies. Moreover, many of the Jews who took up farming in such places were occupying fields and forests that had been neglected or abandoned by non-Jews. As the author of a book entitled *Massachusetts Beautiful* had written in 1923, old-time New Englanders "ought to be glad that anybody wants our country acres."[47] Across the United States, as the author of the *American Jewish Yearbook* wrote in 1900, native-born country-dwellers had all too been "willing to sell their ancestral homesteads at a great sac-rifice."[48] The "Alien Invasion of Connecticut Farms," about which a profoundly ambivalent reporter named Isabel Foster wrote in 1925, might have spelled the "obliteration" of Yankee farmers, but it could just as easily offer the possibility of "new life for all, a renaissance of strong pioneering spirit, of vigorous ambition and great accomplishment."[49]

For a small number of culturally adventurous Jewish immigrants, the soil that had nurtured the nation's vaunted agrarian heritage now represented the landscape of the Jewish American future, at least in the near term. Because their settlement of rural districts was commensurate with their eagerness to take advantage of newly available economic and social opportunities, Jews who tended to agriculture and rural life in general, as Earl Raab explained, often found themselves "settling on the farms of the country while the great population surge was headed in the opposite direction."[50] In the wider scheme of things, what made America different from Europe in the minds of its Jewish writers was its adaptability to rapid change and the restlessness with which its citizens not only faced but also embraced a mixed future. Jews in and of themselves neither accounted for nor orchestrated these tendencies, but Jewish American writers like Leiser and Ferber did not hesitate to emphasize that their headlong participation in the nation's modernization was indicative of a profound commensurability that linked American ideologies and Jewish predilections. "The United States," Edna Ferber proclaimed in *A Peculiar Treasure*, was "resourceful, adaptable, maligned, envied, feared, imposed upon." Every activity and quality that seemed to be shaping the twentieth-century American mentality, as far as Ferber was concerned, could easily be thought of as at least partly Jewish in origin. America's "people are travelers and wanderers by nature," she wrote, "moving, shifting, restless; swarming in Fords, in ocean liners; craving entertainment; volatile."[51] The existence of these parallel tendencies was what made small-town environments not only livable but sometimes ideally suited to the needs of their Jewish residents.

"THIS LAND IS MY COUNTRY, THESE FORESTS MY HOME!": JOSEPH LEISER'S *CANAWAY AND THE LUSTIGS*

With North American cities as their points of departure (even if their time in those cities, following upon their recent arrival from places like Germany and Eastern Europe, had been brief), the Jews who settled in small-town America from the latter decades of the nineteenth century to the middle decades of the twentieth reified the growing interconnections between the nation's small-town and urban economies. The literature that they produced spoke to their discrete experiences as rural-dwellers whose urban origins both inspired and shaped their small-town affiliations. While a number of first-generation (mostly German Jewish) writers had written privately published memoirs of their experiences first as traveling peddlers and eventually as settled merchandisers in rural

American during the nineteenth century, Joseph Leiser's *Canaway and the Lustigs* (1909) marked one of the first deliberate attempts on the part of any Jewish American writer to produce a sustained literary representation of small-town Jewish life.[52] Leiser inherited an American identity at birth and viewed the small-town experience as a waypoint along a continuum of possible American geographical identities. As he would write in 1925, his grandfather had first come to New York in 1843, whereupon, "with a pack on his back [he] gradually trekked till he reached Rochester."[53] *Canway and the Lustigs* was a fanciful and didactic work of juvenile fiction, and its central subject was the experience of a German Jewish merchant family in a rural district of the northeastern United States during the post–Civil War era. To a degree that no memoir could, Leiser's novel attempted to reconcile small-town American and Jewish values by hallowing the fortunate lives of clothing merchant Herman ("Dutch") Lustig's two young sons, Ludwig and Gottlieb. Leiser described Canaway as "simply a Western New York village, situated at the foot of Canaway Lake"; to all appearances, it was based on Leiser's actual birthplace, Canandaigua, New York. As the novelist put it, "To be born and live in Canaway is a rare good fortune to anyone."[54]

Leiser employed a somewhat biblical metaphor in describing the town's rural location, pointing out that the lake stood as "bridegroom" to the town's "bride." Echoing one of the central defining features of the Promised Land itself, Canaway featured "the most deliciously flavored grapes raised in North America." Comparisons to the Land of Israel aside, the town provided the ideal setting for boys to run around barefoot, play with firecrackers, fly kites, and assist their mostly benign gentile neighbors in driving stray cattle. The convergence of such an idealized American setting and his protagonists' Jewish heritage constituted Leiser's main fare. "We are tempted to say that Herman Lustig and his sons are of special interest because they lived in Canaway," Leiser wrote, but within a few decades of Mark Twain's publication of *The Adventures of Tom Sawyer* and *The Adventures of Huckleberry Finn*, books featuring barefooted boys learning life lessons in the American countryside were hardly in demand. Accordingly, the "chief interest" that the author stated for his writing about the Lustigs was "due to the fact that they and their mother were the only Jewish people in Canaway."[55]

Leiser knew that what made his book of potential interest to readers was its combination of two seemingly incommensurate cultural milieus—that of immigrant Jews and that of small-town Americans. Because he was a fiction writer, however, he was not bound by social facts. Being forthrightly Jewish and being a longtime inhabitant of a small rural village in upstate New York were not mutually exclusive, in other words, as long as the writer enacted his ingenuity to shape the circumstances he was describing to his ideological preferences. He could boldly assert, for instance, that though the Lustigs "were the only Jewish people in Canaway," "nobody paid any attention to that matter"[56] and, instead, thought of them as "Germans." Moreover, Leiser's protagonist, Mr. Lustig, could only find kind words to say about the townspeople and their treatment of him when he had first arrived in the town as a traveling peddler. No one had "ever said an unpleasant word" to him, and even when his customers had already spent large sums of money on purchasing his goods, "they would not accept pay for a night's lodging, and very few would accept pay for meals."[57]

Leiser also assigned special symbolic weight to the starting point for his Jewish characters' American odyssey. The fact that "Dutch" Herman first arrived in Canaway on "the day after the battle of Gettysburg" (which also happened to be July 4, although the writer himself did not point that out) couldn't have appeared to be coincidental to anyone other than the fictional character himself.[58] After all, since the battle's outcome was widely perceived to have been predictive of the war's result, no single moment could have been more pivotal, symbolically speaking: the North's victory signaled the ascendancy of industrial capitalism over rural agrarianism. Herman Lustig's urban and Jewish incursion into the small-town milieu was fitting. Even if it was historically fantastic, Leiser's description of an unequivocally welcoming gentile community opening its doors to a recently arrived German Jew on one of the most auspicious days in American history was dramatically appropriate. The writer's ideological interest in reconciling Jewishness to a rural American setting constituted the foremost shaping factor for his narrative, and it certainly outran any sense of obligation he might have felt to relay sociological facts.

That abstract concerns so dominated Leiser's one attempt at fiction-writing should not be surprising, given the tenor and subject matter of his one other published book. The more mature and programmatic Leiser would go on, in 1925, to author a work with the ambitious title of *American Judaism: The Religion and Religious Institutions of the Jewish People (A Historical Survey)*. Among the work's several polemical purposes, Leiser's eagerness to establish his case for a properly understood Jewish birthright to America was central. In the face of the age's "spurious anthropology" that insinuated "racial differences where none exist," Leiser argued that it was "essential to trace the settlement of the Jews" in America and "show that their tenure is long established." Jews, Leiser asserted, had been "living on this continent as long as any other racial group and longer than the 'nordics.'" More important, Jewish and American ideals were entirely commensurate with one another. The arrival of Jews in America was not an accidental "shift of fortune, but a historical sequence" that amounted to the "fulfillment of prophecy." Jews were "inherently democratic," Leiser asserted, and America had merely comprised "the verification of [their] own vision." In the "large and liberal sense" to which this American-born Reform rabbi subscribed, "the religion of Judaism [was] expressed in service to . . . American democracy" itself. In his extended repudiation of the nativist sentiment that rose to its twentieth-century peak during the period that *American Judaism* was published, Leiser unequivocally stated that "the American Jew [was] part and portion of no other country save America." Accordingly, Jews could and did belong in the countryside as well as in the nation's cities.[59]

Leiser's fixation on reconciling two disparate worlds strained credibility, but it allowed him to address abstract and hypothetical possibilities that few of his contemporaries or successors would even have considered. He made his strongest case for the commensurability of Jewish and rural American life through his depiction of his Jewish characters in their capacity as roundly appreciated, and even welcome, agents of modernization who had chosen to live in communities whose residents longed for such exposures. He depicted Lustig's clothing store as an outpost of civilized, though entirely practical, elegance—a place that supplied local farmers and mechanics with the "coats, trousers, vests, overcoats, overalls, shirts, underwear, neckties, paper collars, and linen dusters" that their work and respectability required of them.[60] In the bigger picture, as Hasia Diner points out, establishments like Lustig's Rochester Clothing Store had helped not only redeem Jewish merchants in the eyes of their gentile neighbors but also elevate them to the status of cosmopolitans.[61] As Leiser described it, the fact of his protagonist's foreign birth, rather than alienating him from his Canaway neighbors, had only made him more attractive to them. It didn't hurt matters that a significant number of the townspeople, though not Jewish, were also of German origin and viewed him as their countryman. When Lustig first arrived in Canaway, as he recounted to his sons, "all the Germans in town" had gone to meet him, shake his hand, and try to convince him to stay there.[62] They apparently viewed his European provenance as an asset. In later portions of the book, in which Leiser described the Lustigs' celebrations of Purim and Passover, gentile neighbors happily indulged their town's sole Jews' attempts to observe their ancient holiday traditions.

Toward the middle of the novel, Dutch Herman's high profile as Canaway's most eminent practitioner of cosmopolitanism in an American setting is briefly overshadowed by the arrival of the mysterious Trummer, a Polish (and presumably Jewish) cobbler who appears in Canaway after the Lustig family has already established itself there. Having identified their new neighbor as a gifted storyteller, Ludwig and Gottlieb manipulate him into relaying a poetic ballad whose contents capture the entire spirit of Leiser's lesson about the Jews' relationship to the landscape of the diaspora. Trummer's rendition of a poem called "The Troubadour Jew" recounts the appearance of a speaker called "the Good Suskind of Trimberg" at a poetry contest being held before the king in the "tiled palace court in old Trimberg." Echoing the tradition of courtly poetry, mimicking the patterns of folk memory, and invoking the pastoral spirit that had long shaped

European place-descriptions, Suskind's speech concentrates much of its attention on landscape. His lines come as close to articulating the abiding conflicts of
small-town Jewish life as those of any real-life memoirist.

Recounting the Jews' history as an eternally wandering "people of the book,"
the poet Suskind delivers a narrative of exile that doubles as an expression
of fondness for the natural features that define his eponymous hometown in
Bavaria. He argues a point that Jews have been making for their entire history as
a people: no matter how long they lived in a given place and no matter what they
had done to demonstrate their fondness for that place, they had been treated like
and made to think of themselves as outsiders.

> We have wandered with this [the Torah] through the seasons and the climes,
> Long ago by the Rhine we enkindled our fires.
> We were here when the eagles of Rome were elate;
> We encamped amid desolate ruins and mounds.
> So of Trimberg I sing, and the woods of the state
> Of Bavaria, and what in it abounds.
>
> Before German was, then my fathers were here,
> And they sang of a peace that was sweeter than wine.
> With the harp that was David's, and not with the spear,
> They greeted the vales of the Saale and the Rhine
> Oh, this land is my country, these forests my home!
> Here, my altars of praise and of household were set.
> Overflowing with love of my townsmen, I come,
> And I offer a friendship that none shall regret.[63]

Not surprisingly, Suskind of Trimberg's high regard for the forested landscape
of Bavaria and his eagerness to find common cause with its proprietors go unrequited in Trummer's story. Leiser would go on to strike a similar chord in *American Judaism*, pointing out that "it is not a new sensation for the Jew to be told that
he is not one of the people among whom he lives."[64] Though silently "touched
to the core," Suskind's courtly audience responds with indifference to his
plea. "This minstrel of Judah," as Trummer himself sings, has been "elected by
fate / To sing a new song to the children of men," but his would-be "neighbors
and kinfolk" are unable to hear it, and the bard himself sadly "strode forth from
the gate / Of the town that he loved," presumably never to return to it. His descendants would have to wait several centuries until the founding of the United States
before they would ever see an opportunity to claim a land they inhabited as their
native home. Upon the conclusion of this strange episode, Trummer himself
vanishes from the novel as mysteriously as he has first appeared in it. When he
leaves town, no one, including the Lustigs themselves, has any inkling of where
he has gone or, for that matter, why he came there in the first place.

Enthusiastically embracing the conditions of modern life, the Lustigs themselves eventually depart from Canaway, though their doing so occurs after a more predictable and in a more triumphant fashion than Trummer's. After beginning their rudimentary education in the "aleph bet" with "Hyman Goldstein, D.D., professor of music and languages," yet another emissary from the outside Jewish world, Ludwig and Gottlieb return home one day to hear their father's news: he has sold his clothing store and arranged "to go into a bigger business in Rochester." Following in the footsteps of other "successful" small-town Jews, Dutch Herman had never viewed his sojourn in Canaway as anything other than a phase in his Americanization. For him, as for other small-town Jewish householders, "business strategy and planning for the future of the family were inexorably intertwined."[65] He desired a better future for his sons and "did not wish his boys to feel satisfied with an easy life, such as Canaway afforded them." Life in Rochester was sure to allow them wider social exposures—"they would go to dancing school, to parties on Chanukkah, attend the Sunday school picnics and go to the theaters on Saturday afternoons with their mother." Given the passion with which Leiser first introduced his readers to the virtues of country life and proximity that it could afford young Jewish children to wild nature, the Lustigs' relatively untroubled departure from Canaway comes as a bit of surprise to readers. Though Mrs. Lustig cries as she bids her neighbors farewell and Mr. Lustig maintains a "very sober" demeanor on the day of their departure, Leiser describes the boys themselves as having "waited with impatience the dawning of the morrow." At the novel's close, it is only the natural world itself that expresses deep disappointment, as "the lake dimpled" and "the hills frowned disapproval of the family's departure."[66]

"The Jew among Nations": Edna Ferber's *Fanny Herself* and *A Peculiar Treasure*

Joseph Leiser and Edna Ferber both recounted their small-town experiences at the prime of their careers, reflecting a retrospective mood and both acutely aware of how surprising their stories would be to a readership comprised of people who assumed that all Jews had grown up in and lived in big cities. These writers' status as *former* residents of small-town America who published books *about* small-town America, in and of itself, did not set them apart from many of their non-Jewish contemporaries. Even as they had faced some level of social ostracism in rural communities, however, small-town Jews were less harshly condemnatory of their places of origin than the "revolt from the village" authors tended to be. The gentile who left small-town America for the more tolerant atmosphere of the big city had declared self-exile from a place that had once defined and even encompassed him or her. A writer like Edna Ferber, on the other hand, knowing that none of the three upper Midwest communities in which she had grown up had ever truly been her family's home in the first place, could write about small-town life in a less strained and more generous fashion. To her way of thinking and as the child of parents who had never abandoned their connections to city-dwelling friends and family members through the period of their extended rural sojourn, the small town in which she had grown up and the big city where she now lived had never been so far apart in the first place. In her novel *Fanny Herself* (1917), as well as in *A Peculiar Treasure* (1939), Ferber described the places where she had lived as points along a dynamic American continuum, each part of which she was eager to embrace. Her books did not shy away from recounting traumatic episodes, but their central purpose with regard to her small-town origins was a celebratory one, and one of its primary vehicles for achieving such a result was the attention it lavished on describing the lively atmosphere of the towns in which she had grown up and by which she had been introduced to the idea of American diversity in the first place.

While the looming prospect of an ultimate leave-taking comprised the central dramatic motif both within the canonical and in Leiser's and Ferber's Jewish American depictions of small-town America, the Jewish story began, at least, in a manner far less bleak than its gentile counterpart did. Both Leiser's and Ferber's representations of small-town life opened with a journey backward to a time in which the small-town beckoned as an exciting place promising economic, and possibly social, prosperity. Its initiatory episodes were stories of arrival and restoration. In the story's prelude, the immigrant progenitors (either the parents or grandparents of the speaker) left a desperate situation in Europe and after a difficult passage across the ocean arrived safely in an American port. After experiencing some form of disillusionment there, they made their way, usually against their own better judgment and in defiance of the advice of their fellow Jews, through the countryside to the small town in question. Following from its author's account of familial success and neighborly feeling across religious and cultural divides, the narrative moved on to recount its subject's charmed childhood, relatively untroubled adolescence, and first steps toward promising adulthood. By necessity, at this exact point, the account then formally announced the wider backdrop that had been forming all along—a proposed move to the big city, which the writer then reified through the depiction of a somewhat sad but by no means heartbreaking departure.

The undercurrent of tragedy and doom that dominated canonical representations of small-town life was largely absent from Edna Ferber's writing. Despite the challenges that Jewish families like hers faced in the small towns in which they lived, such places did not necessarily stipulate bleak portrayals. In fact, two of their most significant attributes in the imagination of the writer consisted of their resemblance to the big city where the writer now resided and the access they afforded to other places. The Ferbers had left Kalamazoo in the late 1880s, when Edna was "little more than a baby," gone on to live temporarily with Julia Neumann Ferber's family in Chicago, and settled in Ottumwa in 1890. As she recounted the trying period of time that her family spent in Ottumwa in *A Peculiar Treasure*, the writer recalled dazzling scenes, heightened emotions, and a colorful demography. Her father operated a store that did a brisk business with the town's population of miners and farmers. Even as she described the fatigued look of the Welsh miners as they headed into town to trade, Ferber managed to liven up the scene, referring as she did to the procession they formed in "their trade caps, with the little miner's lamp on their heads, [and] their tin lunch pails in their tired hands."[67] The town itself "swirled down Main Street on Saturday night," Ferber wrote, and she took special pleasure in "sit[ting] in a tiny chair in a corner" from which she could "survey the crowds shuffling by." Ferber was not sure why she enjoyed crowd watching, but she owned that even as an adult, her "notion of bliss would be to sit in an armchair at the corner of Broadway and 42nd or State and Madison, or any other busy intersection in America, and watch the town go by."[68] It had all begun during her family's seven-year ordeal in Ottumwa, Iowa.

A Peculiar Treasure did not hold back from recounting some of the most painful episodes of its author's life, most of which had taken place in Ottumwa. It described the daily harassment that Edna experienced at the hands of other girls and boys, which frequently took a violent turn. It narrated the bitter history of "The Lawsuit," in which Ferber's father took a thieving employee to court but was himself found to have been libelous for having done so and was "made to pay some thousands of dollars to the employee alleged slandered."[69] The book also told the story of Jacob Ferber's degenerating health and journey into blindness, and it chronicled Julia Neumann Ferber's heroic and stalwart attempts to keep the family afloat in the midst of its greatest distress. Nonetheless, the book was sustained throughout by Ferber's tenacious optimism, which had been fueled no doubt by the substantial success she had met as an author and public figure. Seen through the lens of her later achievements and financial triumphs, her descriptions of life in Ottumwa—and to a still greater extent, her descriptions of life in Appleton, Wisconsin—were ebullient, forgiving, and even hopeful at times. She recalled visiting a friend of her mother's at home and watching her kind father grind flour in his mill. She "attended Chautauquas, revival meetings, political rallies, political parades, ten-twenty and thirties, [and] the circus."[70] If nothing else, she seems rarely to have experienced a dull moment, claiming that, one year during her family's time in Ottumwa, "there were seven murders . . . and no convictions." To her horror, she even witnessed a lynching on the town's main street.[71]

Life in Ottumwa was rarely pleasant and frequently traumatic, but despite its dark atmosphere of terror, Ferber the autobiographer made it her business to draw attention to its dynamism and eventfulness. Bitter as her experiences there had been, they may have been the point of origin for her lifelong fascination with

America and, for that matter, her career-defining interest in representing inter-ethnic encounters against a multiregional background. As the child of small-town Jewish retailers, Ferber was uniquely poised to witness such interactions daily. By selling their goods to and cultivating business relationships with all comers, small-town Jewish shopkeepers like Ferber's parents engaged in "transgressive behavior" as a matter of course.[72] As more than one historian has pointed out, Jewish storeowners throughout small-town America routinely "extended credit to other immigrants, to Indians, and to blacks when others would not."[73] Not-withstanding the apparent provinciality of its inhabitants, which often proved to be the source of her own and her family's suffering, the population of Ottumwa was not homogeneous.

Besides the Welsh miners and Anglo farmers, there were the "hired girls" (Fer-ber's mother always employed one to take care of Edna and her sister). Ferber named these women as alternatively "Irish, German, Swedish, Bohemian, Hun-garian, [or] Polish," and as a fiction writer whose subject was always America itself, she was well aware of and eager to acknowledge the importance of the historical and cultural forces that had "catapulted [them] across the ocean and into the melting pot" of small-town America. The hired girl "brought into the Eastern and Midwestern middle-class American household a wealth of European ways, manners, customs in speech, religion, festivals, morals, [and] clothing," as well as "old-world folk tales, dances, myths, [and] songs."[74] The town was also the site of an active political life, and Ferber recalled being "in the dense crowd that heard Bryan's Cross of Gold speech," as well as the sight of members of Coxey's Army passing by "hungry, penniless, [and] desperate" in a flotilla of rafts on the Des Moines River. All in all, her time in Ottumwa made for an "interesting child-hood." In her novel-writing days, when she followed the habit of conducting research on regions as disparate as Texas, Alaska, and Connecticut, she had been able to prepare a description of a Mississippi flood without having to set foot in a library. As a girl in Ottumwa, she had seen "bridges as they swayed. . . . houses tossing like toys in midstream, while sheep, cows, pianos, rocking chairs, [and] bedsteads floated and bobbed by."[75]

At its worst, Ottumwa, Iowa, represented the darker side of small-town life and bore "all the sordidness of a frontier town with none of its picturesqueness."[76] As Ferber described it, the Iowa town was "like some foreign provincial town in its narrowness and bigotry."[77] The writer's choice of the word "foreign" was deliber-ate. Since bigotry was un-American, Ottumwa was in fact an American anomaly. By contrast, Appleton, Wisconsin, to which the Ferbers moved in 1897 when Edna was twelve years old, "represented the American small-town at its best."[78] In its welcoming environment, Ferber spent "a superlatively happy adolescence."[79] Life in Appleton was not only lively but graceful as well, and Ferber's experiences there inspired her to write about them twice—not only in *A Peculiar Treasure* but also in *Fanny Herself*, the semiautobiographical novel that she published in

1917. Either the bitterness of the Ottumwa experience or the distance of age exercised a powerful influence over Ferber when she wrote about Appleton in her autobiography. Describing her family's first arrival in the Wisconsin town in *A Peculiar Treasure*, she imagined that they were reliving the experiences of the "pioneer families" of the 1840s who, as they were "coming upon a cool green oasis after heart-breaking days through parched desert and wind-swept plains," had breathed a sigh of relief. Appleton was "a lovely little town of sixteen thousand people; tree-shaded, prosperous, civilized."[80] Her parents had come upon it in flush times, relatively speaking, and their store did a brisk business there among the town's large population of factory workers and farmers.

Every one of the town's positive attributes (and it seemed only to have positive attributes) derived from its encompassment of what Ferber wrote about elsewhere as quintessentially American traits. Appleton embodied a version of the "complex pastoral."[81] Ferber's description of the place in *A Peculiar Treasure* made it sound positively utopian, and she called consistent attention to a correspondence between the loveliness of the landscape with the civility and ingenuity of the people who inhabited it. "All about it lay small prosperous towns like itself," she wrote, invoking the same "music and mystique" that had so endeared Kalamazoo to her writer's imagination—"Kaukauna, Neenah, Menasha, Little Chute." These were places where "giant elms and oaks, arching overhead, made cool green naves of the summer streets." Nature's bounty played host to "substantial, intelligent, [and] progressive" people who "owned their houses, tended their lawns and gardens, . . . read . . . traveled, went to the theater, heard music, [and] educated their children" at colleges far and wide.[82] Not surprisingly, in "the sun of Appleton's warm-generous friendliness," the "fog" that Ferber had associated with her family's years in Ottumwa dissipated. Jews, who comprised "about forty" families, as Ferber recalled, were comfortably established in small business, most of the men trading in horses and agricultural acreage, the women "placid and home-loving," and the "sons and daughters well educated and intelligent."[83] Despite, or maybe owing directly to, the Jews' relative numeric minority in the town, Appleton's mayor was a Jew. So too was its most famous native son—Erik Weisz, otherwise known as Harry Houdini.

Ferber's warm depiction of Appleton resulted in part from her grateful memory of how welcoming that town had been to her family when they came there after their purgatorial experience in Ottumwa. Its wider significance derived from its resonance with her lifelong conviction that America's and the Jews' destinies were intertwined, that "the founding myth of Judaism and the myth of America [were] one."[84] In Ferber's imagination, Appleton's ideal qualities were the selfsame qualities that distinguished America itself, which Ferber referred to as a "work hive since the fifteenth century."[85] Moreover, because "she perceived Jewishness and Americanness as positive and not contradictory influences" and "Jewishness as not . . . vastly different from Americaness," she could argue that Appleton's embodiment of American values made it an appropriate environment for Jews.[86] Its economic expansiveness and social inclusivity represented the promise of perpetual renewal that Ferber viewed as intrinsic to both Jewish and American worldviews. Ferber readily acknowledged her lack of any grounding in Jewish religious thought, and she made no claims that rabbinical Judaism might offer a precedent for claiming the American way of life as the embodiment of a Jewish ideal. Since she drew her associations between the Jews and the Americans from her secular experience within the modern world, however, she felt at liberty to pronounce the similarities as she saw them.

If opportunities for self-expression, productivity, and the expansion of one's worldview represented the ideal conditions for human existence, then a place like Appleton seemed to offer its residents a pleasing opportunity to live out the good life. The town's inhabitants were universally engaged in business and work activities. The Fox River valley, as Ferber wrote, "hummed with commerce." She described a region that "abounded both in manufacturing and agriculture," where paper mills employed large numbers of men and women and people earned livable wages. The town's many institutions—its schools, libraries, and music and theater venues, as well as its countless venues for healthy outdoor activity—were powerful bulwarks against the sort of torpor that dominated in places like Ottumwa. In short, Appleton offered most of the amenities of urban life while at the same time conferring upon them daily exposure to the soul-renewing pleasures of the natural world. Within sight and sound of the busy mills and downtown, the town was "lovely with its ravines and woods and jew-ellike lakes."[87] Ferber was particularly enchanted by the natural environment because, surrounded by its echoing silences, she could easily conjure the distant past in which Indians had once peacefully camped. It was, as she acknowledged, a precarious world, liable to disruption and extinction as the forces of the very same economic progress that had made the town so attractive and welcoming to families like hers threatened to eliminate the surrounding forests that ensured its atmosphere of charm. In this respect, Ferber's celebration of Appleton resembled Joseph Leiser's paean to Canaway. She appreciated its joys while calmly accepting their ephemerality.

Ferber's ebullience concerning life in Appleton seemed for the most part to have been an extension of fond memories she treasured of the lively educational and social experiences she and her family had enjoyed there. Nonetheless, the attention she paid to the town's unique landscape features spoke still more volubly to the very same "improbable" aspects that distinguished America from Europe and had made it a preferable environment, from her Jewishly informed perspective. In *Fanny Herself*, Ferber's only book in which Jewish characters and themes figured prominently, the protagonist devotes considerable attention to her childhood and adolescence in "Winnebago, Wisconsin," a town she would readily identify later as having been entirely based on Appleton. Fanny Brandeis is the energetic and ambitious daughter of a recently widowed storeowner, the practical-minded proprietor of Brandeis' Bazaar. In her youth, Fanny had once had a realization that she was different from the other children of her town and that the difference "was temperamental, or emotional, or dramatic, or historic, or all four."[88] What set her apart was her imagination, and what had touched off her imagination was the sense experience of the natural world that had been the direct result of her small-town upbringing. Far off in the woods, Ferber's protagonist had her first and evidently life-changing encounter with the multiracial, multiethnic myth of America.

Fanny and her friends were playing tag "in one of the cool, green ravines that were the beauty spots of the little Wisconsin town." These spots, as she recalled in the novel, "nestled like exquisite emeralds in the embrace of the hills." The town's "civic surge had not yet swept them away in a deluge of old tin cans, ashes, dirt and refuse." The presence of an order of "plump Capuchin monks," some of whom enjoyed sunning themselves in the vicinity, added a mysterious human dimension to the scene. The surrounding silence caused Fanny to "stop quite still in the midst of her tag game, struck with the beauty of the picture it called from the past." In her imagination, the "wild, free, sovereign" Indians of the conquest-era past formed a "thrilling mental picture" as they encountered the "silent, powerful" Jesuits who had first explored the Wisconsin woods in the seventeenth century. Joseph Leiser had ventured a similar image as he described his two boy heroes' frequent visits to an island in Canaway Lake where Indians had "at one time held a war council."[89] "Little Oriental that she was," Ferber wrote, Fanny had brought together the "dry text of her history book with the green of the trees, the gray of the church, and the brown of the monks' robes."[90]

Inspired by her protagonist's first woodland "encounter" with Native Americans and French explorers, Ferber would devote the rest of her writing career to authoring numerous regionally specific novels whose purpose it was to "examine American ideals."[91] Each episode would be set in a specifically American geography. As Lori Harrison-Kahan writes, "From the Oklahoma frontier of *Cimmaron* to New England in *American Beauty,* from the Wisconsin lumberyard of *Come and Get It* to the Texas ranches and oil fields of *Giant,* from the prairies of the American heartland in *So Big* to the new territory of Alaska in *Ice Palace,*" Ferber produced a series of grand American narratives in which geography equaled history and conflicts over place were the launching point for drama.[92] In their own way, each of those books would argue the case for American pluralism, celebrating, as Steven Horowitz and Miriam Landsman put it, "the variety of American communities; the beauty and diversity of the landscape; the heterogeneity of the American populace . . . and its democratic ideology."[93] Granted, most of Ferber's romantic fictions trafficked quite heavily in cultural stereotypes, some of which were injurious to various parties of racial Others, especially blacks and Indians. In *Fanny Herself,* Ferber had gone out of her way, for instance, to point out that the Sioux, Pottawatomies, Winnebagos, Menomonees, and Outagamis whom she had conjured in her imagination were "taciturn, and beady-eyed, and lithe, and fleet," and bore no resemblance to the "rather smelly Oneidas who came to the back door on summer mornings" in order to sell "baskets of huckleberries" to her mother.[94] Her novels, plays, and screenplays, as Harrison-Kahan argues, were racist in the way that Harriet Beecher Stowe's *Uncle Tom's Cabin* had been racist.[95] In pursuit of a middle-class white readership and in hopes of urging progressive and inclusive values upon that readership, she freely dabbled in Western and minstrel-show motifs, seeming all the while to lack any awareness that her character portraits of various minorities, even when they were intended to dignify those minorities in the face of mainstream oppression, were demeaning at best and exploitative at worst.

For all of its clumsy oversimplicity, Ferber's "romance with America," notwithstanding its idealization of small-town life and apparent reluctance to engage directly with the deeper questions of Jewish identity, was forthright in its insistence that Jews (and other minorities) were not strangers in the land but, in fact, instrumental players in assuring its American distinctiveness.[96] In direct opposition to the myth of a homogeneously Anglo past, Edna Ferber invented and recounted an alternative version of the American landscape in which members of many outlying cultural groups occupied center-stage in the national drama. Her Jewishness was primarily a reactive force within her career as a writer by which she tried to account for her sense of pride in difference. Ferber embraced the tie between Jewishness and a sense of exile and exteriority. Rather than allowing such a view to diminish her claim to American belonging, however, Ferber repeatedly posited America's own exteriority as indicative of its Jewishness.

The small-town environment had been an ideal starting point for a career like Edna Ferber's. Whether she was recounting its torturous aspects, as she had in her descriptions of Ottumwa, or reliving its blissful legacies, as she did when she wrote about Appleton, Ferber conjured the small town as a quintessentially American, and therefore dynamic, landscape. Her descriptions of these places bore little resemblance to the desiccated portrayals that writers like Sherwood Anderson had supplied. The central factor in bringing about such a result was Ferber's tendency to view small towns as contiguous with other American environments. The lives enacted in them took shape on the same grand scale that formed the backdrop for every other drama that was taking place in the modern world. Rather than portraying small-town life as a diminished sphere uniformly populated by weak and ineffectual actors whose glories lay in the distant and inaccessible past, she wrote about it as an environment that was similar in many respects to every other American locale. What had made both Ottumwa and Appleton worth writing about in the first place had been the social encounters that took place there daily. Like the cities that were playing host to an ever-larger proportion of the American populace, small towns presented opportunities for the expansion, expression, and perpetuation of pluralistic, democratic values.

"SHIFTING FOOTHOLD WITH FRANTIC ROOT-TOES": THE LANDSCAPES OF THE JEWISH AMERICAN FUTURE

Fanny Herself was Ferber's one and only novel in which the question of Jewish identity was paramount, and its author's expansive treatment of the small-town landscape seems to have been more than incidental to it. Even once the protagonist has long since left home in Winnebago, she continues to be transfixed by the idea of place. As Joyce Antler suggests, the young novelist who wrote it now "traveled so frequently [that] the notion of home became important to her."[97] An early episode in the novel features Fanny coming to the rescue of one of her fellow Jewish students who has been set upon by a gang of anti-Semitic boys like the ones Ferber would later write about as the scourge of her existence in her autobiography. Clarence (later, in an effort to further Americanize himself, he renames himself "Clancy") Heyl is harassed for both his Jewishness and his physical frailty—a "bum lung." By the middle of the novel, Clancy has become a healthy, proud, and willful actor, no longer in need of rescue at the hands of his female classmate and coreligionist. That he has also become a professional chronicler of American geography whose work takes him to every wild corner of the nation can hardly be the result of a mere coincidence in Ferber's characterization.

On an extended sojourn with Fanny in Chicago, Heyl tells his story in detail. In doing so, he explains how the remotest mountain peaks, the skyscrapers of New York City and the tree-lined streets of Winnebago all comprise different facets of the same dynamic American landscape. While holed up in the mountains, he happens to have been visited by a writer from the New York *Star* newspaper named Carl Lasker. After accompanying Heyl on a month-long horseback-riding trip in the backcountry, the newspaperman offers him a job in the big city. "You see, I'd never seen a chorus girl," Heyl explains to Fanny, "or the Woolworth building, or a cabaret, or a broiled lobster, or a subway, but I was interested and curious about all of them."[98] Clancy Heyl's rendition of his employer's speech collapses all of America into one singular pluralistic geography, arguing that "the fresh viewpoint" available to a perpetual outsider like Heyl (or his future wife, Fanny Brandeis) constitutes a magic ingredient that can bring every place to life and maintain its vital connection to modernity. As Jews, these two young people can see and appreciate the complex beauty that other Americans have long taken for granted. Having been raised in a place like Winnebago, but also having embraced the dynamism of American urbanism, Fanny and Clarence embody what Ewa Morawska characterizes as a Jewishly informed "pragmatic rationality, individual responsibility . . . and a future-oriented optimistic approach to life."⁹⁹

It is fitting, then, that in the immediate aftermath of this conversation, Fanny and Clancy head south of Chicago for a picnic among the dunes along Lake Michigan. "A stretch of cinders," recalls Fanny, "then dust, a rather stiff little hill, a great length of yellow sand and—the lake!" Within streetcar distance and in the presumed shadow of America's Second City, the young couple in the making enjoy one another's company. They are free to enjoy "mountains of sand, as far as the eye can see, and on top of them, incredibly, great pine trees that clutch at their perilous, shifting foothold with frantic root-toes."¹⁰⁰ From here, the novel angles toward an impossibly neat and happy outcome. Fanny rejects a promising career opportunity that would necessitate her turning her back on her Jewish past and instead travels to remotest Colorado herself in order to join her fellow small-town Jew in matrimony. As implausible and predictably sentimental as this outcome is, its geographical implications help set its main characters apart from their gentile counterparts as featured in the Sherwood Anderson school of small-town fiction. To Fanny and Clancy, America's greatest promise is made manifest through the combination of dazzling natural landscapes and imaginative and self-actuated personalities.

When Ferber published *Fanny Herself* in 1917, her belief in such a promise was entirely plausible, at least in the nation's more economically prosperous rural communities. Jews continued to flow in relatively large numbers into rural communities across the nation and a wartime business boom was under way. While events like the 1915 Leo Frank lynching could not but have had a chilling effect on would-be Jewish migrants to small towns, Jewish life in places like Appleton thrived. The anti-Semitism that was to peak in the 1920s and 1930s would be the result of a resurgent nativism that worsening economic conditions and rising class animosities had not yet brought to the fore. While Ferber herself had long since left Appleton to embark on her writing career, the adolescence she had spent there had instilled in her an understandably optimistic and untethered perspective on Jewish American geographic destiny. The shape of things to come, however, was quite different from the future that Ferber projected in *Fanny Herself*. While Jewish retailers, agriculturalists, and professionals would continue to maintain a visible presence in small towns throughout the United States through the coming decades, the combined effects of advancement into the middle class and rising educational achievement, along with the growing appeal of suburban environments would soon begin to siphon off large numbers of erstwhile rural Jews. The "classic era" of small-town Jewish life had been just that—a heyday that had been born of the adventurism instilled by economic necessity.

In the years following World War II, as more and more small-town Jews departed for the attractions of increasingly livable cities and burgeoning suburbs, those who remained looked around and sought the right words with which to frame a vanishing world. In a retrospective mood not entirely unlike the one that the earlier gentile refugees and exiles from rural America had evinced in their variations on Thomas Wolfe's "you can't go home again" dictum, a growing number of formerly small-town Jews would write and publish memoirs that recounted their rural experiences.[101] The overall tenor of these works tended toward wistfulness and wonder. Maine resident Toby Shafter captured their spirit with lyrical precision in her 1949 contribution to *Commentary* magazine. "The scenery is still superb," she noted with reference to the one unchanging fact of small-town life. "Yet beneath the even tenor of life there embellished by the incomparable jagged rocks, towering pines, and the jewel-blue bay dotted with islands," she continued, "one can observe a certain nostalgia over the gradual weakening in the real ties that once bound together the Jewish community."[102] Absent the ideological fervor that had infused Joseph Leiser's production of a novel that argued so forthrightly for Jews as natural-born inheritors of the rural tradition and the energy and optimism that had fueled Edna Ferber's insistence that America was itself a profoundly Jewish environment, latter-day small-town Jewish authors could do little besides pinch themselves and marvel at what had once been.

4

"THE LONGED-FOR PASTORAL"

IMAGES OF EXURBAN EXILE IN PHILIP ROTH'S *AMERICAN PASTORAL* AND ALLEGRA GOODMAN'S *KAATERSKILL FALLS*

The Impoverishment of Plenitude

In 1998, literary critic Michael Galchinsky suggested that all Jewish narratives could be encompassed by the following sequence: "Prosperity-Transgression-Diaspora-Repentance-Redemption."[1] Galchinsky may have intended his cyclical configuration of Jewish stories as a tool for historical insight, but at the turn of the twenty-first century it bore an even greater poignancy by hinting toward a contemporary Jewish impasse. Postwar Jewish Americans were not only beneficiaries of white skin privilege but had become by far "the most middle class and affluent of America's ethnic groups."[2] How could they ever reclaim the redemptory mantle of exceptionality? Softened through extended exposure to postwar plenitude and increasingly aware of their exalted racial status, Jewish Americans confronted an anomie borne of their collective inability to bring Galchinsky's cycle to completion.[3] In assigning particular symbolic importance to the escapist fantasies and exurban landscapes invoked by their titles, Philip Roth's and Allegra Goodman's novels *American Pastoral* (1997) and *Kaaterskill Falls* (1998) emphasized this feeling of stasis. Both books associated the geography of removal with the moral compromises of American individualism and the elusiveness of Jewish redemption. The contrast between their protagonists' bucolic aspirations and the postindustrial degeneration that surrounded them was disconcerting.

Thirty years earlier, during the period that Roth's and Goodman's turn-of-the-millennium novels would depict retrospectively, the sociologist Marshall Sklare seems to have anticipated just such a result. At the outset of his 1967 study of suburban Jewish life in the Illinois community of "Lakeville," Sklare acknowledged that "it is easier to treat the Jews of the 'ghetto' sympathetically than it is to do the same for those of the 'gilded ghetto.'"⁴ Mainstream literary representations of the nation's rising white middle class were critical of suburbia because in its inhabitants' purported uniformity of style it posed a threat to the primacy of the empowered self. Jewish writers articulated profound ambivalence in the face of their improved social and residential status, but fear of individual erasure was the least of their concerns. Rather, what made the flight to the elitist preserves of suburbia (and, eventually, exurbia) problematic from a Jewish American literary perspective was its elevation of the self over the community. In the context of the "inexplicable anxiety" that accompanied their compromised existence as a privileged minority within a nation that was now beginning to consider itself to be "multicultural," such acts of hubristic seclusion could have fatal consequences for people who were historically unaccustomed to cultural empowerment.⁵ As critic Ranen Omer-Sherman writes, "Complete liberation paralyzes, rather than frees, Jewish energy."⁶ Jewish writers who examined life in the gilded ghetto of shaded residential streets, high-powered educational institutions, and disproportionately remunerative professions were not worried about being like everyone else; they were worried by their increasing isolation from the main body of human experience.

The freedoms and privileges that resulted from such a hermetic existence did not comport well with the idea of what a Jew is and how Jews ought to live. Previous phases of their history had not entirely freed Jewish Americans from similar dilemmas. As long as Jews continued to think of themselves as outsiders seeking entry, however, progress toward collective Jewish redemption seemed possible. Jewish American geography offered a range of uplifting options, both for belonging to America and for remaining Jewish. By contrast, the men and women bred to material comfort and social success in the nation's postwar gilded ghettoes lived in a world apart and could not help but doubt their relevance and relatability, both to the wider Jewish world and to the American milieu in which they lived. As historian Deborah Dash Moore points out, Jewish Americans' relatively sudden achievement of "an unprecedented level of security, affluence, integration, and freedom" coincided with the rise of identity politics in public discourse.⁷ Increasingly isolated from all but the most affluent and privileged of their gentile neighbors by virtue of their economic and social achievements, and frequently cut off from a meaningfully Jewish life by virtue of their pursuit of individual success, premillennial Jews inhabited a rarified geography. While the rest of American society was coping with the ravages of racial disparity, economic disenfranchisement, and environmental degradation, a handful of Jews was seeking personal and spiritual fulfillment in a paradise of gated woodlands and fairways. While Israeli Jews were cultivating a Jewish homeland, settling the land of the Bible, and defending themselves from terrorists, Jewish Americans were indulging the awkward banalities of a superficially Jewish life in the land of plenty, from staging bar mitzvah ceremonies in football stadiums to installing Hanukkah bushes in their living rooms. Even the most religiously devoted among Jewish Americans, the various sects along the Orthodox continuum, appeared to be locked in petty quarrels among one another and bent on making their presence known to the rest of the nation in their capacity as chronic litigators and manipulators of exurban zoning ordinances.[8]

The existential woes and moral shortcomings of postwar suburban Jewish American life were part and parcel of a wider societal descent into the destructive atomization that accompanied such events and phenomena as the Vietnam War, Watergate, Reagan-era "greed is good" mentality, and even the cessation of the Cold War. One of the primary instigators of this result had been the postwar economic boom, which attempted to wipe away the legacy of the Depression by removing huge numbers of newly prosperous white Americans of every ethnic background from central cities and installing them in tidy suburbs. As a growing middle class spread itself out across the subdivided and largely segregated outskirts of dozens of once vibrant cities thanks to the federal government's "possessive investment in whiteness," those cities' central districts were all but abandoned to an increasingly impoverished and isolated racial underclass.[9] The suburbanization of America, as Kenneth Jackson described it in his classic study, *Crabgrass Frontier* (1985), was the "most unadulterated embodiment of contemporary culture" to be found anywhere in the United States. It was an important marker of nearly every social ill that could be seen eating away the nation's moral fabric—"conspicuous consumption, a reliance upon the private automobile, upward mobility, the separation of the family into nuclear units, the widening division between work and life, and a tendency towards racial and economic exclusiveness."[10] The superficial benefits that had accompanied their remarkable and rapid acceptance as "sovereign selves"[11] and white folks in suburban and exurban America were demonstrably *not* "good for the Jews" as a people.

Seymour "the Swede" Levov, the protagonist of Philip Roth's *American Pastoral*, epitomizes this state of delusional isolation as he asserts his obsessive and oddly ahistorical geographical proclivities. The Pulitzer Prize–winning story of the hero humbled and heartbroken by his daughter Merry's acts of politically motivated violence is by far Roth's most landscape-centered novel. Having freed himself from the "traditionally Jewish habits and attitudes" and madly in love with the freedom he associates with the North American continent, the Swede announces his intention of purchasing "a hundred acres of America" in order to clear a path to an untainted future for both himself and his progeny.[12] Destructive as it proves to be, his eagerness to leapfrog out of the urban enclave in which he was born, past the all-too-circumscribed and "cozy" mediocrities of suburban Maplewood and South Orange and into the "decidedly blue-blooded exurb of Old Rimrock,"[13] New Jersey, is an extension of his longing for Emersonian transcendence. Like the romantic idealists of mid-nineteenth-century New England, the Swede doesn't want "to live next door to anybody."[14] As a Jew living in the postwar United States, the Swede has achieved his personal freedom by extracting and abstracting himself from the maelstrom of the surrounding world. His exceptionality is a species of what Arnold Eisen refers to as a "chosenness hollowed out from within."[15] The Swede has not obtained an American identity at the cost of his Jewish identity. In pursuit of the unattainable pastoral, he has forsworn all communal identities in favor of what Ranen Omer-Sherman refers to as a "precarious selfhood."[16]

American Pastoral explores the postwar exurban environment in order to tally the purported costs of assimilation. In a much gentler but no less disconcerting fashion Allegra Goodman's *Kaaterskill Falls* situates its characters in a similarly bucolic atmosphere (which, like Roth's Rimrock, also happens to be about a two-hour drive from Manhattan) in order to draw attention to the high price that men and women must pay in order to maintain their separateness as Jews in a pluralistic and increasingly atomized American society. While *Kaaterskill Falls* has been described as a meditative and Austenesque "novel of manners" and a paean to committed individuals who understand and appreciate "the joys of limits,"[17] each of its characters suffers from and is largely defined by the unrequited longings borne of the postwar fracturing both of the Jewish world and of American society. Goodman's portrayal of an extended community of modern Orthodox "Kirshners" who divide their time between an urban enclave in upper Manhattan's Washington Heights and a group of summer cottages in the fictional town of Kaaterskill between 1976 and 1978 does not shield its readers from a constant awareness of the discomfiting and frequently vertiginous forces of outside influence. On the contrary, Goodman's characters fall short of realizing their most Jewish and also their most American aspirations. The characters' seasonal recourse to the sheltering mountains only reproduces and magnifies both their alienation from and their susceptibility to the machinations of a morally and spiritually bankrupt mainstream culture. In the town of Kaaterskill, an exploitative real-estate developer (who happens to be a Jew, albeit of the secular and intermarried variety) vies for power with a tight-fisted and bigoted judge. For all of their eagerness to maintain their spiritual autonomy, the Kirshners cannot help but entrust the future of their community to these figures and others like them.

The reason that both *American Pastoral* and *Kaaterskill Falls* explore the lives of postwar Jewish protagonists against the fraught backdrop of historically sanctified Anglo-American landscapes is that Roth and Goodman are troubled by the specter of Jewish American obsolescence. As long as Jewish Americans inhabited and possessed an "ironic awareness"[18] of their precarious status as residents of dynamic American landscapes, from mid-nineteenth-century frontiers to late nineteenth-century cities to prewar small towns, they could maintain both

sides of their identity. Their existence in those places as a people apart who happened at the same time to be fully engaged, at least commercially, with their gentile neighbors allowed for the prevalence in their lives of a dynamic and uniquely
bicameral communitarian ethic. But as aspiring members of the American elite
or would-be religious separatists, the characters who populate Roth's and Goodman's novels appear to be in full retreat from modernity. They are people who
have forgotten that escapist and individualistic thinking has never served American, let alone Jewish, interests. In renouncing either a vibrant Jewish geography
or a pluralistic American geography in favor of the hallowed but sterile terrain of
the exurbs, these figures represent the social stagnancy and imaginative impov-
erishment of the postwar condition.

"You Can Do Whatever You Damn Please": The Geography of Individual Freedom

For generations, the ordinariness of suburbia has been recurrent fodder for
American commentators. Fiction writers, playwrights, journalists, filmmakers,
and documentarians of every stripe—not to mention a host of academic spe-
cialists trained in several fields—habitually depict suburbia as an atmosphere
defined by conformity while placing considerably less stress on the powerful
strain of pastoral individualism that also informs it. This strain has been no
less important in shaping its cultural geography. Political liberals rail against
its inhabitants' collective acts of environmental destruction and wastefulness,
perhaps failing to see that the very existence of suburbia is the result of many
individuals' longing for access to open space. Conservatives place a similar
emphasis on suburbia's vaunted patterns of cultural normality, whether by lion-
izing SUV-driving "soccer moms" or by counting on suburbanites as a critical
component within their base of supporters. In order to champion suburbia's
supposed virtues as a font of "family values," however, conservative pundits elide
the decidedly atomistic tendencies that gave rise to its development and fuel its
growth.[19] Regardless of its informing ideologies, the thematic focus on suburbia
as a monotonous place populated by norm-seeking people has been a common
motif in postwar American literature and popular culture. From John Cheever's
"The Five-Forty-Eight" to The Simpsons to American Beauty, the American jury,
constituted in large part by people who themselves have been the very progeny of
suburban life, has singled suburbia out at best as a "contrived [and] dispiriting"
landscape. In the worst case scenarios, it is depicted "as a landscape of imprisonment and control" or "an amoral refuge of luxury and waste" worthy of being
labeled a "New Babylon."[20]

Postwar American literature abounds with characters who have either been
fooled into associating suburban normality with absolution from sin or are

disappointed to learn that the exasperatingly ordinary shelter it has conferred upon them is merely ephemeral. In such scenarios, suburbia's most salient characteristic is a culture of conformity whose imputed dullness provokes all manner of futile attempts at rebellion and repudiation. In John Cheever's "The Five-Forty-Eight" (1954), a commuter on his way back from his office in the city to his sheltered suburban paradise and sexually dormant marriage is confronted by a gun-wielding former female employee with whom he once had an illicit affair. Desperate for his life and evidently regretful of his having so long taken the tranquility of suburban life for granted, the protagonist cooperates with his captor's every command. Inwardly hoping that he might still escape the consequences of his previous flouting of middle class behavioral constraints, he envisions himself vanishing back into suburban mundanity upon alighting from the train. His ex-lover, Miss Dent, sees through his intentions, succinctly referring at once to his immediate hope of eluding her murderous intentions and his hypocritical exploitation of suburban anonymity as a platform for a career of philandering. "You're thinking you can get away from me in Shady Hill," she says to him, pronouncing the truth of what men like him have been doing to women like her since the invention of suburbs. Her decision to spare his life and allow him to return to the safety of his home only fortifies the accuracy of Miss Dent's assertion.[21]

If the deceptively static domestic environment of suburbia has inspired some fiction writers to describe pathetic and vulnerable characters trapped in it by their own habits of complacency and acquiescence, it has evoked still more disturbing treatments at the hands of authors whose fiction tends toward more deliberate social commentary. In the dystopian world of Don DeLillo, suburbia is so thoroughly normative as to function as a landscape of apocalypse. The narrator of DeLillo's 1985 novel *White Noise*, the "chairman of the department of Hitler studies at the College-on-the-Hill," resides in a town called "Blacksmith" with his wife and children. During the lengthy and tense prelude to the "airborne toxic event" around which the novel's action centers, Jack Gladney hears news of some missing neighbors from his wife. "The Treadwells had been found alive but shaken," she tells him, "in an abandoned cookie shack at the Mid-Village Mall, a vast shopping center out on the interstate." The landscape of the strip mall as DeLillo describes it is rendered all the more ominous by virtue of its myriad banalities, which make members of the lost couple family appear all the more hapless. After "wandering through the mall for two days, lost, confused, and frightened," they happened upon and took shelter in the cookie kiosk, "the weak and faltering sister venturing out to scavenge food scraps from the cartoon-character disposal baskets with the swinging doors."[22] Like Cheever, DeLillo associates suburban sprawl and normativity with the death of the human soul and the decay of civilization itself. What suburbia scholar Robert Beuka describes as the "totalitarian impulses that lurk beneath the fabric of centrist, middle-class culture" are rendered all the more menacing for the mockingly comic appearance that DeLillo confers upon them.

From its earliest projections in the popular imagination as a landscape that symbolizes stilted alienation and conformity, however, suburbia has also been a showcase for abundant, often rampant acts of individualism. Notwithstanding the stereotypical view of suburbia as a "grid of identical houses on identical streets,"[23] its landscape is also the real estate equivalent of those autonomous and quintessentially American selves who created the literary canon formed by *The Autobiography of Benjamin Franklin*, *Walden*, and even *The Art of the Deal*. It is an assemblage of separate and ostensibly imperial tracts, a landscape that resounds at every minute with a million simultaneous shouts of triumph. It is a dense array of oddly separate but disturbingly contiguous and uniform domiciles, perhaps most effectively conjured by Thomas Pynchon in his description of "San Narciso" in *The Crying of Lot 49* (1965) as an "ordered swirl of houses and streets" whose "patterns [form] a hieroglyphic sense of concealed meaning."[24] As a geographic entity, it is pregnant with significance but maddeningly opaque to interpretation. In the words of architectural historian Dolores Hayden, while "more Americans reside in suburban landscapes than in inner cities and rural areas combined," hardly any of them "can decode the shapes of the landscapes or define where they begin and end."[25]

From a Jewish perspective, the dangers posed by suburbia did not derive from its atmosphere of conformity so much as they did from its invitations to self-assertiveness and license to escapism. Abandoning the master narrative in which suburbia comprises the geographic backdrop for soulless acts of accommodation or doomed attempts to rebel against that soullessness, Roth instead devotes attention in *American Pastoral* to its other seemingly opposite but equally lethal facet: its "fatal detachment of the individual from the collective."[26] His novel addresses suburbia's appeal to misguided and delusional individualists seeking personal restoration and autonomy in a pastoral paradise. Seeking to transcend the ordinariness of suburban life, Swede Levov pursues an outward course that is at odds with the delicately ameliorative patterns that were themselves the result of countless individual acts of secession. This act on his part, however, is entirely commensurate with the same suburban mentality that impels so many of his coreligionists' flight to the subdivided paradises of South Orange, Great Neck, and New Rochelle. In eschewing a newly built split-level in Maplewood in favor of a Revolutionary War–era stone house in Old Rimrock, the Swede is only emphasizing the individualistic strain that has informed that mentality from its inception.

While such outbreaks of garden-variety American individualism are tightly repressed in Goodman's *Kaaterskill Falls*, it is worth noting that the members of the Kirshner kehillah are not done in by their acts of conformity with American

culture so much as they are by their common hope of achieving a separate collective autonomy within and especially beyond the physical bounds of the city.
Ironically, it is Andras Melish, a nonbelieving skeptic who is married to an observant woman, who asserts the basic principle that guides the community in its
actions. In hopes of encouraging his friend Elizabeth Shulman not to give up her
dream of maintaining a kosher store in Kaaterskill, Andras tells her, "This is the
United States of America. You can do whatever you damn please."[27] Andras Shulman's intention in uttering these words is to encourage Elizabeth's act of modest rebellion against the kehillah, but his pronouncement of such a libertarian
ethos also describes the actions of the Kirshners themselves. Their collective act
of secession from their surrounding communities in Kaaterskill and Washington
Heights, while appearing to be an assertion of Jewish agency, amounts instead
to an act of relinquishment. The Kirshners' retreat into the pastoral and their
cultivation of a tightly knit and severely ordered community sequesters Judaism
from the rest of American society. It enacts an American separatist and pietistic
tradition that dates back to the Pilgrims' settlement at Plymouth Rock, but in
doing so, it abandons any commitment to societal improvement and civic participation. It also promotes the invisibility of Jews within the American religious
panoply. For that matter, the group's strongly anti-Zionist stance also echoes this
antimodern impulse, ceding Judaism's place on the world stage.

Instead of expressing the typical anxieties about suburban conformity, the
authors of *American Pastoral* and *Kaaterskill Falls* explore the magnification of
the self that occurs against the backdrop of the exurban landscape, where people
in flight from the communal or societal pressures of life in a pluralistic society
go in hopes of asserting their autonomy and living out their romantic fantasies
of individual or in-group fulfillment. The actors in Roth's and Goodman's novels
are damaged by virtue of the excess of agency that their flight from mundanity
engenders. They might not fare any better as dull cogs in the workings of the
postwar American social and political economy, but their attempts to escape that
world entirely into the delusional realm of the pastoral doom them to a doubly
exilic fate. Their pastoral and individualistic fixations deprive them of their ability to function not only as Jews in the modern world but as engaged participants
in the life of the nation that has so forthrightly bestowed its gift of freedom and
plenitude upon them.

"LIKE SOME FRONTIERSMAN OF OLD": THE LANDSCAPE
OF INDIVIDUATION IN *AMERICAN PASTORAL*

Throughout *American Pastoral*, Philip Roth challenges readers to discern the
source of the all-consuming blight that has turned his protagonist from golden
boy to tragic figure. The novelist's attention to place is central to his vision. Roth's
depiction of the New Jersey landscape doesn't merely symbolize the Swede's

descent into chaos; the protagonist's obsession with that landscape is the very instigator of his downfall. The novel's tripartite structure, which moves from "Paradise Remembered," to "The Fall," to "Paradise Lost," announces Roth's equation of changing landscapes with changing human conditions. The allusions to the Bible and to Milton's seventeenth-century epic poem reinforce strong associations of place with notions of innocence, knowledge, and change. It is worth noting, however, that Roth's rendering of the journey from innocence to corruption inverts the pastoralism implied in both the biblical and Miltonic formulations. In *American Pastoral*, "Paradise Remembered" describes the entirely "past-situated"[28] communally rich joys of life in prewar, inner-city Newark, and "Paradise Lost" represents the spiritually bankrupt and atomistic cultural geography of semirural Morris County, New Jersey, in the postwar era. If such a thing as original sin exists within the heavily ironic and postmodern confines of *American Pastoral*, it would have to be the protagonist's movement away from the radically integrated and dynamic landscape of his birth toward the landscape of individuation where he and his family self-destruct. In this respect, the Swede's story is "the modern story par excellence."[29]

While Roth hardly limits himself to such topographical metaphors in his evocations of human frailty, the novel's titular emphasis on the deceptiveness of the pastoral mode proves to be its only consistent and reliable component. Like the author of Job, Roth's narrator Nathan Zuckerman is breathtakingly unreliable. He exhibits a habit of formulating incorrect theories about his characters' history and true motivations, readily owning that the story to follow is at best "a realistic chronicle" that he has "dreamed."[30] The changing landscape of New Jersey, like landscapes the world over, on the other hand, is a text that does not lie. Attention to the novel's representations of that landscape offers insight into both the Swede's and America's patterns of self-deception. In giving the lie to the dangerously false dichotomy upon which the pastoral mode rests, it presents readers with a viable basis upon which to interpret the entire story. Moreover, while Zuckerman admits to barely knowing the Swede, he does possess firsthand authority on the subject of pastoralism's uses as a "self-deluding desire for an idealized bucolic existence."[31] As he tells us near the novel's outset, Zuckerman himself is a self-described isolationist who lives, according to his distinctly Thoreauvian syntactical formulation, "alone, two and a half hours west of Boston, in the Berkshires."[32] Like his protagonist, he is a seeker of personal autonomy and an isolationist who has enacted his own seclusion in a bucolic paradise.

From our first introduction to his story, Zuckerman describes the Swede's love for America as an extension of his participation in a mythologically informed notion of the nation's settlement history. He tells us that as early as 1958, the Swede became the inhabitant of a fantasy world in which he was able to "commute every morning down to Central Avenue from his home some thirty-odd miles west of Newark, out past the suburbs." Referring to the Swede as a "short-range pioneer," Zuckerman hints that the "hundred-acre farm on a back road in rural Old Rimrock" is "a long way from the tannery floor where Grandfather Levov had begun in America." The Swede's tragic innocence, like that of the nation he loves so fervently, originates in his all too naive belief in this fantasy. What makes the Swede's fantasy problematic is its all too convenient abstraction of the pioneer myth from the exploitative forces that gave birth to it in the first place. The exploration and settlement of the hinterlands did not precede the development of tanneries; it formed the very basis for their development. Despite appearances to the contrary, the "thirty-odd miles" separating the two places from one another is no distance at all, and the Swede's pastoralism is an extension of his participation in a globalizing endeavor.[33]

Roth's Swede is the rare late twentieth-century embodiment of the American Adam, a holdover from the nineteenth-century works of James Fenimore Cooper, Ralph Waldo Emerson, and Henry David Thoreau and from popular press depictions of men like Daniel Boone and Davy Crockett. He is, as Brian McDonald writes, the "impoverished, atomistic, and deracinated" version of the American self who the sees the bounteousness of the land and decides on the basis of his proprietorship of it to establish a republic of his own in hopes of vanquishing history and negating the coercive power of family, community, and tradition.[34] Roth doesn't hesitate to associate the Swede's homestead with notions of utopian fantasy. It cannot be a coincidence that the place sits on a road called Arcady Hill. The Swede's purchase of a stone house "that had probably been standing there since the country began" confirms the notion that, as Derek Parker-Royal writes, the protagonist's entire life is an embodied "fiction."[35]

The main problem with the Swede's formulation of his own and his family's autonomy is that it attaches transcendent meaning to a place whose history is more complicated than he wishes or imagines it to be. Roth exposes the tragic folly of the Swede's pastoralism through his extended descriptions of the landscape of northern New Jersey. In contrast to the inventive approach that Zuckerman takes to conjuring the Swede's past, his surveys of local geography, as well as his brief expositions on the area's local history, take their cues from actualities. The plot device that allows Zuckerman to deliver this material within the narrative is his introduction of the man who will eventually become the Swede's rival for the love of his wife, Dawn. Bill Orcutt, a Princeton- and Harvard-trained law school graduate who eschews a career as an attorney in order to promote his own imperial self in the guise of an independently wealthy abstract painter, manifests all the characteristics of the landed gentry whose number one priority, as he tells the Swede, is "to keep the modern ills at bay." Shortly after introducing himself to the Levovs, this "country squire" offers to take them on a tour of the local sites. It is both a neighborly gesture and a transparent, if calculating, act of noblesse oblige on Orcutt's part. Orcutt himself is a pastoral dreamer, descended from a line of economically privileged "lawyers, judges, [and] state senators."[36] Though

Zuckerman's rendering of Orcutt presents the man as a dull, shallow, and self-serving foil, the insight that his tour and history lectures supply, to readers of the novel if not to the Swede himself, is crucial.

Orcutt's tour with the Swede supplies one of *American Pastoral*'s most extended descriptions of the local landscape, and its revelations get to the heart of why pastoralism poses such a threat to social equilibrium in the modern context. The day begins with the two men traveling "diagonally to the northwest corner of the county" and then "backtracking" along the "southward meandering spine of the old iron mines" that had once been the area's claim to fame. "Backtracking" is a key word in this context because the day-trip's retrospective aspect is exactly what proves to be the source of its revelatory importance. The green bucolic hills of north Jersey turn out not always to have been so green. From the earliest days of European settlement, they were never free of the taint of industrialism. Zuckerman's voice assumes the perspective of Orcutt, the Swede's tour guide:

> The towns and villages had been thick with rolling mills, nail and spike factories, foundries, and forging shops. Orcutt showed him the site of the old mill in Boonton where axles, wheels, and rails were manufactured for the original Morris and Essex Railroad. He showed him the powder company plant in Kenvil that made dynamite for the mines and then, for the First World War, made TNT and more or less paved the way for the government to build the arsenal up at Picatinny, where they'd manufactured the big shells for the Second World War. It was at the Kenvil plant that there'd been the munitions explosion in 1940—fifty-two killed, carelessness the culprit, though at first foreign agents, spies, were suspected.[37]

Neither Orcutt nor the Swede utters a word about the irony implicit in this description. For that matter, Zuckerman himself remains silent on the matter; he supplies the information but doesn't hint at its symbolic significance. But such a lesson cannot be lost on readers. The pastoral environs that surround the Swede's "impregnable" stone fortress of a house barely conceal the traces of a historical landscape whose very settlement coincided with and was identical to its industrialization. More striking still is that the area's industrial sites proved to be integral to the history of so many American military conflicts. Despite the region's pervasive appearance of bucolic calm, Orcutt's tour makes it clear that the bomb that the teenaged Merry Levov will eventually detonate in the Old Rimrock post office in an act of protest against the conflict in Vietnam will not have been the first explosion heard and felt in that part of the world.

In his imagination, the Swede believes himself to be "rather like some frontiersman of old," a man bent on "settling Revolutionary New Jersey as if for the first time." The story that Zuckerman tells about him, by contrast, seems largely intended to "deflate heroic pioneer narratives."[38] Orcutt's tour reveals a troubling truth about the place: it is an enormous graveyard that commemorates a past that was by and large death-strewn and violent. As for Washington's troops having been quartered nearby, one of the primary landscape markers of their presence is an old church cemetery containing the remains not only of those "killed in the war" but also of "twenty-seven soldiers, buried in a common grave, who were victims of the smallpox epidemic that swept the encampments in the countryside in the spring of 1777." What the Swede fails to see, his skeptical father, a determined antipastoralist and "undomesticated Jew,"[39] is eager to point out to him. The entire district, as Lou Levov puts it, is a predominantly Republican former stronghold of the Ku Klux Klan where anti-immigrant bigotry thrives even in the age of the tolerant Eisenhower. As for the stirring historical accoutrements that mark the house itself and its accompanying "hundred acres of America," the Swede's father refers to the place as a "mausoleum."[40] In the context of such a contentious American past and present, not to mention in the immediate aftermath of World War II and the Holocaust, the Swede's pastoralism amounts to a form of willful blindness.

Old Rimrock's nearness to so much historical death and destruction does not seem to faze the idealistic Swede. Like many other Americans, he views history as a bygone affair that can be harmlessly contained in a distant past. His zealous devotion to the myth of American innocence keeps him from feeling menaced by the traces of the past that surround him in the present. The Swede is no less susceptible to the fantasy that his spatial removal from the ugliness of the present era will protect him and his family from the worst effects of modern life. His failure to reckon with this latter aspect of the pastoral delusion is made clear at an earlier point in Zuckerman's description of the same excursion with Bill Orcutt. As the two men pause to overlook the Morris Canal, Orcutt explains how barges traveling its length once carried anthracite to a local foundry. His reference to the town in which the coal was mined in turn reminds the Swede's tour guide of the whorehouse in adjacent Easton, Pennsylvania, that young men from Old Rimrock used to frequent. Inadvertent or not, Orcutt's winking aside is a reminder that innocence always exists in precarious proximity to corruption, but the Swede pays no heed to it. Instead, Levov is startled by and then just as quickly becomes indifferent to a different realization: that the Morris Canal whose western end the two men are contemplating on their tour of the bucolic north Jersey countryside is the same Morris Canal that, at its eastern terminus, passed through the decidedly industrial and immigrant-heavy cities of Newark and Jersey City on its way to the waters of New York Harbor.

As Zuckerman notes, the Swede "knew of the Newark end of the canal when he was a boy and his father would remind him, if they were downtown or anywhere near Raymond Boulevard, that until as recently as the Swede was born a real canal ran up by High Street, near where the Jewish Y was." Whether or not its eastern end was still in use, the canal itself had been a connective tissue of sorts, an important precursor to where "there was now this wide city thorough-fare, Raymond Boulevard, leading traffic from Broad Street under Penn Station and out old Passaic Avenue onto the Skyway." The revelation, however brief it proves to be for the Swede, is that the "real" America of Old Rimrock and the immigrant America of urban New Jersey are contiguous geographical entities, literally connected to one another by their long-standing mutual participation in an encompassing industrial economy (or, in Eisenhower's terms, "military-industrial complex") that is as old as the nation itself. Instead of registering this revelation and noting its broader significance as the negation of his pastoral dreams, however, Zuckerman's version of the Swede proves vulnerable to yet another manifestation of Adamic thought. "In the Swede's young mind," Zucker-man speculates, "the 'Morris' in Morris Canal never connected with Morris County—a place that seemed as remote as Nebraska" to him when he was a child. Instead, in an act of imagination that erases all traces of historical complexity and eliminates the encumbering legacy of a collective American past, the Swede conflates the Morris Canal as his father introduced him to it with his deceased Uncle Morris, who died in the influenza epidemic of 1918. Even as an adult in Bill Orcutt's company, Seymour Levov "persist[s] in associating the name of the canal with the story of the struggles of [his] family rather than with the grander history of the state."[41] In an Emersonian vein, viewing all of America as an exten-sion of his own imperial self, the Swede dismisses the reality that it is he who exists as an extension of the nation.

After the tragedy of his daughter's bombing, as the Swede enters the hum-bling phase that comprises the rest of his life, he is disabused of his fanciful ideas concerning the quaintness of the American landscape and the prospect of his hermetic removal from the woes of modernity. In a series of pained visits that he pays to his fugitive daughter, who now lives poverty-stricken in a squalid dis-trict of riot-torn Newark, he discovers as if for the first time the urban blight he has spent much of his life trying to wall off. Merry has been living a mere "ten-minute car ride" from the site of the Newark Maid glove factory where the Levov family fortune was made during the first half of the twentieth century. The fact that it is "the one place in the world he would never have guessed had he been given a thousand guesses" that he would find her indicates the severity of the Swede's benightedness. Here, in the depths of the very city whose industrial infrastructure and immigrant history had made his own American story possible, is exactly where his daughter—the deliverer of what Roth calls the "indigenous American berserk"—must be. The fictive belief that had fooled him all along was the notion that history was just "the stuff you read about in books and study in school." Well before Merry's bomb had gone off, history had been no stranger to "tranquil, untrafficked Old Rimrock." From the 1777 smallpox epidemic onward, the town's "cloistered hills" had not only seen plenty of action but also maintained close communication with and economic dependence upon the looming urban expanse that lay to their east.[42] The existence of every bucolic paradise is and always has been contingent on and dependent upon its ironic proximity to the exact sort of place from which it tries to distinguish itself.

Roth's description of the landscape in which Merry (by 1973 she is renamed Mary Stultz) cowers in fear of detection by the FBI embodies the diametric opposite of the hopeful green hills of her birth. In an echo of the novel's overarching allusion to Milton and the English poetic tradition, the author's description of postriot inner-city Newark hints strongly toward William Blake's charged projection of his own industrial era's "dark satanic mills." Approaching Merry's hovel near the "dog and cat hospital," the Swede passes "the dark old factories—Civil War factories, foundries, brassworks, heavy-industrial plants blackened from the chimneys pumping smoke for a hundred years now." These ruined and decrepit buildings tell a story that few Americans wish to know, a story that many of them would just as soon leave behind in their quest for the bucolic shelter of postwar suburbia. As he walks the streets, it finally dawns on the Swede that "these were the factories where people had lost fingers and arms and got their feet crushed and their faces scalded, where children once labored in the heat and cold." Their more recent history, the result of the city's 1967 race riots, was even more blighted. The narrative of suffering European immigrants, the one that "her greenhorn great-grandparents" were rarely interested in recalling, had been succeeded by an even more desperate situation. By the 1970s, Newark's Puerto Rican and black inhabitants had been reduced to abject poverty from which few of them could never hope to escape, surrounded by a city that was now little more than an ash heap. As the Swede sees and experiences the place on his way to see Merry, all traces of civilization have now vanished, leaving in their wake a hellish scene of devastation where "walkways were strewn with broken pieces of furniture, with beer cans, bottles, lumps of things that were unidentifiable." In the far distance where the downtown skyscrapers are located, the mocking presence of a sign that reads "FIRST FIDELITY BANK" reminds the Swede of how wrong he had been to imagine himself or anyone else capable of keeping "the modern ills at bay" by maintaining a one-man republic in an old stone house. It has become, as Zuckerman puts it, "a sign in which only a madman could believe."

The tragedy of the Swede is that the naive hope for a permanent escape into an idealized America that impels him is entirely commensurate with the nation's highest ideals of individual freedom and prosperity. The Swede's guilt derives from nothing more than his haplessly innocent belief in the Adamic myth. This happens to be a condition that he shares with many a fellow American, Jewish and non-Jewish alike, but a scant few are ever made to reckon with its direct consequences. Only a few well-meaning upwardly mobile fathers will bring forth bomb-throwing children. Only a few such people will be forced as the Swede is to inherit the repercussions of their inadvertent acts of complicity. The culture whose rapaciousness has enabled their personal success resulted from circumstances larger than any one person could ever control, but just as individuals are its greatest beneficiaries, individuals can occasionally be made to feel its harshest consequences. The Swede does not deserve his fate any more than anyone else does. What distinguishes his story is its quintessential Americanness and, in particular, its powerful resonance with the atomistic yearnings that underlay the development of postwar suburbia. Few Jewish men of his generation fell prey to pioneering myths of an individual rebirth on the land. At worst, men of his generation demeaned themselves and diminished their Jewishness by acquiescing too readily to the conformist banalities and assimilative patterns of suburban existence. The Swede is and has frequently been written about as an avatar of the American Dream. The dream he sought to make manifest was a singularly dangerous one, however, because unlike the communitarian dream of consensual egalitarianism, his rejected assimilation and conformity in favor of outright secession.

"A Life of Greater Separation": Pastoralist Fantasy in *Kaaterskill Falls*

As Rav Kirshner, the elderly leader of the Orthodox community depicted in Allegra Goodman's *Kaaterskill Falls*, nears his death, he faces a sharp dilemma. His congregants expect him to pass his legacy of learning and wisdom on to one of his sons, but neither of the two men is a truly qualified recipient of so many centuries' worth of accumulated Jewish knowledge. Jeremy, the more intellectually accomplished of the two, has achieved much in the world of secular scholarship but is religiously unobservant and indifferent toward Judaic precedent. His brother Isaiah is a stalwart devotee of the faith but glaringly parochial in his every thought and action. Despite the evident contrast between the two sons, they are similar in one important respect: each in accordance with his own personal predilections is petty and self-absorbed. Reflecting on the uncertain future that his congregation faces, the elder Kirshner's meandering thoughts light upon the source not only of Jeremy's and Isaiah's individual shortcomings but also of his entire congregation's weakness: they are American-born. Having been constrained by the self-imposed and isolationist mentalities that define both the American ivory tower and the Kirshner community, the Rav's sons have cut themselves off from any true sense of community and living tradition.

For his part, German-born Rav Kirshner can't help but see America as a hopelessly inferior place. His congregants "seem to live in shadow," never having experienced the richness of prewar German Jewish culture, as he sees it. In Frankfurt, where the community originated and had hundreds of years to coalesce, their synagogue had "windows like jewels" and served as a "seat of learning and a soaring theater for prayer." Jews in the Old World, as Goodman allows the Rav to explain elsewhere in the novel, lead "expansive" lives.[43] In America, where the surviving remnant of Kirshners came in the late 1930s, the congregants have been tainted by individualism and deprived of the multilayered, complex cultural history that defined the lives of European Jews. "They keep one thing, the religious, alive," but "they have forgotten the poetry," as the Rav puts it.[44] Rav Kirshner was traumatized by the Holocaust and by his group's exile from Europe. When he arrived in New York, he knew he had to go out of his way to build "a community of vigilance, a careful, cautious American generation." Their piety, as he views it in retrospect, is in fact "a way of mourning," and its hermetic aspect only draws greater attention to Jewish Americans' "facile adoption" of a false distinction between sacred and secular ways of being Jewish.[45] In coming to America, Goodman writes, the Kirshners "chose a new way, a life of greater separation."[46]

Kaaterskill Falls explores the stagnancy and sterility of the American-born Kirshners by highlighting this "life of greater separation" against the backdrop of two contrasting places—an inner-city neighborhood and an exurban village. The novel's movement between these two places is determined by the calendrical patterns of Jewish worship, but it also resonates with Goodman's evident interest in exploring specifically geographical markers of separation. In both settings, the Kirshners and their extended body of friends and family members inhabit clearly delineated districts whose parameters accord with the stringent requirements of their religious tradition. Their physical separation from the rest of American society is by no means indicative of their oppression, however. Life in America has not restricted their travel but freed them to go anywhere, and the cloistered life that most of them lead is entirely volitional. Like many preceding generations of American-born religious separatists, they are secessionists at heart and have freely chosen a life apart in a highly "circumscribed world."[47] Among its most enduring legacies, separation leaves an impermeable barrier between the past and the present, severing connections between the generations and depriving people of the exact sort of historical awareness whose absence the German-born Rav laments.

In effect, by situating her story's action in both urban and exurban locales and in calling repeated attention to the contrast that distinguishes the two settings from one another, the novelist highlights the multiple acts of separation that underlie and shape the group's identity. From one scene to the next, the characters are always just arriving somewhere or poised to leave another place. Their sense of meaning in the world results from their multiple acts of coming and going, and their coming and going is symbolic of their apartness from the surrounding world. As Eileen Watts argues, Goodman's book demonstrates its "theme of separation" at many levels simultaneously. From the laws of kashrut that stipulate the separation of milk from meat to the *mechcitza* that delineates the women's portion of the synagogue from that of the men to the narrator's frequent recourse to descriptions of both the arrival of the Sabbath and the havdalah ceremony that marks its conclusion, the book is about boundaries. In their "self-created, self-imposed, self-restricted enclave,"[48] the characters who populate *Kaaterskill Falls,* for all of their adherence to an extremely strict form of Jewish orthodoxy, collectively assert their prerogative of religious freedom in accordance with a uniquely American formulation. "In America," the Rav thinks to himself, "everything is smaller and more private."[49] In fact, their most religiously Jewish moments and their achievement of maximal separation from their surrounding communities occur as the direct result of their wholehearted embrace of the same Adamic ethos that motivates the entirely secular Swede in his self-destructive acts of secession. The novel's attention to the theme of separation chronicles the movement "from corporate identity to individual identity" among postwar Jewish Americans.[50]

Like Roth's representation of the Swede's landscape fixation in *American Pastoral,* Allegra Goodman depicts the Kirshner community's winter and summer homes in order to highlight the effects exerted by the ideology of American individualism upon the fabric of Jewish communal life. In both instances, it is not the enticements of assimilation to American culture that pose the greatest danger to Jewish American continuity but the temptation of separation from it. While *Kaaterskill Falls* does present more than a handful of characters who wage some sort of rebellion against the immediate strictures of the Kirshner community, none of these figures seeks to leave the Jewish fold in order to become "more American" in the ordinary sense of deserting Jewish tradition in order to feel and partake of a sense of national belonging. The somewhat elegiac atmosphere that prevails in *Kaaterskill Falls* is a function of its characters' collective removal from the dynamism of the present, a removal that they have freely chosen as a direct result of their American autonomy. Severed as they are both from the larger Jewish world by virtue of their rejection of Israel and by their eschewal of secular American culture, their self-imposed exile leaves them to wallow in the empty shell of an unchanging, and possibly doomed, religious tradition. When they are at home in Washington Heights, they are intimidated by an alien and encroaching urban poverty. During their periods of summer residency in Kaaterskill, they fall into petty quarrels among themselves and acquiesce to the exploitative practices of local real estate developers in a desperate attempt to maintain their fraying communal order. The geographical descriptions that accompany Goodman's rendering of their story serve as a constant reminder of the isolation they have chosen to pursue in their acts of quintessentially American autonomy.

The atmosphere that defines the Kirshners' existence in upper Manhattan is decidedly constricting and hermetic—"small, shabby, and tight," as Goodman puts it. The novelist emphasizes this quality in part by highlighting the enclave's location on high ground at the northern tip of Manhattan Island. While she points out that the Kirshners never actually ascend to the actual Heights that define the neighborhood as a whole, her reference to the adjacent Fort Tryon Park, which happens to have been one of the sites where the Battle of Washington

Heights was fought during the American Revolution, hints strongly at the area's fortress-like attributes. So too does Goodman's reference to the Cloisters, the museum of medieval art whose displays of "icons and crucifixes" the Kirshners also ignore, for obvious reasons. Constructed out of the remnants of several monasteries that were moved, brick by brick, from France to the United States, the museum is as powerful an architectural symbol of a hermetic existence as can be conjured anywhere. The Orthodox Jews who live at the base of the hill upon which it sits may never approach the place, but its looming embodiment of monasticism resonates with the novel's wider theme of separation. At a later point in the novel, Elizabeth Shulman, the young mother who operates a kosher store in an act of soft rebellion against the community, imagines herself stranded by the tides at the monastery at Mont St. Michel.

Goodman's attention to separation as the central theme of *Kaaterskill Falls* receives its most salient treatment in connection with the novel's other, eponymous, setting in the Catskills. While the fortress-like aspect of the Washington Heights compound suits the Kirshners' needs to maintain their autonomy against the backdrop of New York City's multiple threats, the mountain village represents their most powerful redoubt of separateness. Its origin as a site for vacationing Orthodox Jews dates to 1948, when the Rav's wife Sarah first purchased a cottage there with reparation money she received from Germany. Given Goodman's interest in the notion of separateness and autonomy, the fact that Israel was founded in the same year is difficult to ignore. That nearly half of the novel occurs during the bicentennial year of 1976 further enhances this theme. Goodman's invocations of 1948 and 1776 bear roughly the same symbolic significance as Henry David Thoreau's announcement in *Walden* that he moved into his cabin "by accident, on Independence Day, or the fourth of July, 1845."[51]

By building his cabin in the Walden woods, Thoreau declared his personal independence from the nation whose founding was posited on the sovereignty of the individual. In applying her Holocaust reparation money toward the purchase of a cottage in Kaaterskill in the exact same year in which David Ben-Gurion declared the sovereignty of the first Jewish state since the age of Bar Kochba, the Kirshner rebbetzin, along with the congregants who quickly joined her and her husband there, was declaring the kehillah's independence both from the wider Jewish world and from the surrounding American scene. In both instances, the autonomous instinct is an extension of the individual's or the group's assertion of sovereignty. Despite Goodman's invocation of national sovereignty, the kehillah's movement to the Catskills is not meant as an assertion of the community's oneness with world Jewry any more than Thoreau's gesture was intended to be an act of solidarity with the American nation. On the contrary, both acts manifest the ideology of secession that underlies and often subverts acts of collective reinvention.

The story of the Jews who preceded the Kirshners in Kaaterskill presents a fascinating contrast to the Orthodox group's separatism. In keeping with the actual history of the Catskill region, Goodman's novel briefly but pointedly represents the experiences of Jews who came there at the close of the nineteenth century as part of the larger nationwide movement of Jewish retailers, farmers, and, eventually, resort-operators to small towns throughout the country.[52] The synagogue that houses the Kirshners' congregation dates to the 1880s, when it was built by "old man Rubin" on the top of Bear Mountain in order to serve the adjacent communities of Bear Mountain and Kaaterskill. The founders' command of Hebrew was so weak that they named the synagogue "Anshei Sharon," thinking that it meant "People of the Mountain" when it actually meant "People of the Plain."[53] The comic error is telling: either the first Kaaterskill Jews didn't know Hebrew because they had slipped too far into Americanism or they didn't know whether they were at the top or the bottom of a mountain because they had retained too much of their immigrant Jewish mentality to register the lay of the land. In symbolic terms, both scenarios suggest that the early Catskill Jews wanted to feel connected to a wider community of either Americans or Jews.

The novel's primary invocation of the lore of the Catskills occurs through its frequent allusions to the literature and art of the romantic era, which typically privileged images of solitude. In these scenes, it is always the members of the separatist Kirshner sect who are in thrall to the area's scenic charms. In this respect, they prove themselves to be no less susceptible than the year-round Catskill Jews are to the enticements of American ideology, but their embrace of romantic solitude shows that they favor its separatist over its assimilationist strain. The theme of romantic escape is never far from the surface of *Kaaterskill Falls*, and it reaches its peak in the portions of the book that address themselves to the sights and sounds of the storied Catskill Mountains. When the characters drive along the Washington Irving Highway on their way to their country cottages, they encounter scenery that closely resembles the dreamy tranquility and "magical hues" of the famed early nineteenth-century author's "fairy mountains."

Their approach, precisely timed for the arrival of the Sabbath, resembles Rip Van Winkle's entry into the "deep mountain glen" where he encounters Henry Hudson's ghost crew playing at ninepins and falls asleep for twenty years.[54] As their car nears the village of Kaaterskill, they enter a place where they "exchange the sunny afternoon for shade, and the light breeze for damper, stiller air" and where "old oaks overhang the road, roots flung up from the ground, while younger birches shoot up toward the light in thin stalks, like grass." The allusion to the enchanted landscape of "Rip Van Winkle" is repeated later in the novel, when Elizabeth Shulman introduces her youngest child to reading by showing her a picture-book version of Irving's story in which "elves are dancing up and down in the mountains in their peaked hats and pointed shoes."[55] The Catskills may be only a few hours' drive from Washington Heights, but their beauty represents the enticement of a world apart and the indulgent dream of escape into a fantasy world. Just as Rip seeks respite in the high peaks from the nagging presence of his sharp-tongued wife and misses out on the Revolutionary War, the Kirshners' summer respite in the Catskills (especially during the bicentennial celebration of 1976) is meant to relieve the stress of city life and mirrors their reluctance to play an active part in American and Jewish life.

One of the most readily recognizable earmarks of romantic-era literature and art is its invocation of the sublime. As Isaac Shulman and Andras Melish make the Friday afternoon drive from the city to the mountains, their approach to Kaaterskill Falls yields inspiring and fearful associations in equal measure. In a Jewishly inflected echo of Irving's description of the thundering game of nine-pins in "Rip Van Winkle," Goodman compares the sound of the rushing falls to the sound of "a thousand men praying, davening and turning pages." She describes the distant sight, through the trees, of an area of Victorian mansions that the Shulman children refer to as "Fairyland." But the approach to the falls also reminds the two men of death. As Goodman points out, "The low safety rail bolted to the road's edge isn't much to keep a car from tumbling down into the deep gorges, hundreds of feet below." Indeed, "there are car wrecks rusting down there under the leaves," one of which—as readers find out later—resulted in the death years earlier of a newlywed would-be father.[56] The interchangeability of fanciful views and chilling perspectives is indicative of Goodman's interest in exploring the hazards of solitude. The Catskill scenery is both enticing and deceptive. The romantic dream attracts idealists and abandons them in a world of isolationist fantasy. Any visual allusions to the charms of Currier and Ives prints or Norman Rockwell paintings that are contained in Goodman's description of the Catskills are accompanied, "more darkly," by the novelist's echoes of the sorts of images contained in Robert Frost's and Emily Dickinson's poetry.[57]

Romantic imagery echoes and accompanies the novel's most salient illustration of the separatist mentality. As if to underscore the collapsibility of real and imagined realms that characterized the literature and art of the era, the title of Goodman's novel refers not only to an actual place but also to one of the most famous canvasses of the romantic-era Hudson River School. Thomas Cole's 1826 painting "Falls of the Kaaterskill" captures its era's enthusiasm for the romantic sublime. Its autumnal palette indicates the artist's awareness both of natural splendor and of the passage of time. Its attention to the tranquility of the surrounding scenery and to the breathtaking sight of water rushing loudly through the cataract suggests the simultaneity of peacefulness and excitement. Accordingly, Thomas Cole's painting provides the inspiration for the novel's central plot device—Elizabeth Shulman's decision to open a kosher store in Kaaterskill.

Taking advantage of the opportunity to send her daughters off to day camp, Elizabeth accepts her friend Nina Melish's invitation to drive to Olana, the nearby home of another Hudson River School painter, Frederic Church. Glimpsing the Cole painting prominently displayed in one of the museum's galleries, Elizabeth "rushes over to examine it, leaning forward, hands clasped behind her." At first, she has mixed feelings about what she sees, perhaps realizing that its stunning depiction of a familiar waterfall and the beautiful solitude and imaginative liberation that it represents is illusory. She is prepared, in fact, to be skeptical toward its "overblown and clichéd" qualities, which she understands on an intellectual level to be "much more dramatic" than the actual place. The enormous painting proves to be as difficult to dismiss, however, as the beautiful fantasy of individual liberation that it symbolizes. As it turns out, she can't help but feel that "the unabashed romantic colors are right." Recognizing "Cole's integrity," she sees that "this particular landscape seems to mark the truth in all the others." The painting acts upon her like a drug. "Forgetting Nina at her side," she enters a world that is entirely of her own making, ready to follow a "pagan-poetic impulse" that may lead her into outright "idolatry."[58] She is as far from Washington Heights, from America, from the wider Jewish world, as can be imagined.

The Cole painting brings Elizabeth back to her firsthand experiences of the landscape that inspired it. Like Rip Van Winkle himself on the verge of his twenty-year slumber, Elizabeth experiences a profound reverie as she views the painting and recalls her own earlier trips to the Falls. Leaving the reader to decide whether the character has lost herself in the grandeur of the painting or in her recollection of the scenery it depicts, the passage follows Cole's lead and also obscures the distinction between fantasy and reality: "The sky, luminous above the trees, the crash of water. Piles and piles of yellow leaves pillowing the trail. Elizabeth slipped in them hiking once with Isaac and the children, and she fell right on her face, deep, deeper, falling gradually, losing her balance by degrees. She kept waiting to hit hard ground, expecting something sharp. But she never did hit. The leaves were so deep that she felt as though she were falling in a dream; falling farther and farther until she landed in her own bed." The vision that inspires Elizabeth equates the experience of natural beauty with a somnolent state of removal. It is an entirely private world whose allure derives from its indulgence of the self and its profoundest desires for individual fulfillment.

Elizabeth's view of the Cole painting and the memory that accompanies it confirms and stokes her desire to break free of her self-imposed constraints. Though she is quick to dismiss any hope of ever becoming a writer or a painter herself, Elizabeth's encounter at Olana with the idea of "a place and time that beautiful" inspires her in another way. She "wants to do something of her own" and decides at that moment that she "has to make something." Looking "intently at the painting, that brilliant piece of the world, and gazing at the color and the light of it she feels the desire, as intense as prayer" and decides that she must open a kosher store in Kaaterskill.[59] This moment of inspiration, which drives much of the novel's remaining action, mirrors her entire community's problematic susceptibility to separatist tendencies. Elizabeth's sudden decision is almost comical in the relative modesty of its aspirations, but Goodman's language makes it clear nonetheless that the reverie that leads to it is the product of a powerfully individualistic strain of thought that is doing irreparable damage to her characters' Jewish souls. Such self-indulgence cannot possibly be commensurate with either conventional Orthodox practice or, for that matter, the ameliorative patterns of small-town American life. As the assertion of individual will in the context of a tight-knit Orthodox community whose members frown upon actions whose primary purpose or outcome is personal fulfillment, it is doomed to alienate a beleaguered leadership that is already intent on exercising its own secessionist and patriarchal prerogatives. By the same token, as an attempt to insinuate Orthodox practice in the public square, it risks exposing halachic Judaism's incommensurability with American cultural life.

"Secret Forests": The Geography of Jewish Obsolescence

While *American Pastoral* and *Kaaterskill Falls* appear to comprise a study in contrasts, the parallels between them are arresting. Notwithstanding their seeming opposite interests in depicting flagrantly secular and deeply religious Jews, these novels' mutual focus on geographical escapism as a trope for the separatist postwar Jewish American mind-set constitutes their most salient theme. Against the backdrop of the suburbanization of American Jewry, with all of its disappointing and embarrassing bourgeois banalities, the Swede and the Kirshners appear at first blush to be heroic exceptions, quixotically bent on avoiding the worst consequences of assimilation—the loss of self and of group autonomy, respectively. Their acts of withdrawal into the storied hinterlands of American mythology bring unintended consequences, however. Rather than achieving a oneness either with an authentic America or with a purified Judaism, these men and women are carried off into flights of fancy that result in their willful separation from all forms of lasting, dynamic community. They have become believers in fairy tales, subject to the dangerous delusion that the most reliable route to self-determination and renewal is a life apart from others. To borrow from Goodman's introductory description of Elizabeth in *Kaaterskill Falls*, these late twentieth-century Jewish Americans devote themselves to "the idea that there are secret forests where you can become someone else."[60] That such forests can only provide temporary and provisional shelter from the chaos of the surrounding world and in the face of the diaspora's "failure of communal identity"[61] is made absolutely plain to the readers of both Roth's and Goodman's novels.

These two novels' common focus on the pastoral mode is striking given both the tumultuous period that their central action depicts and the unsettled atmosphere in which they were written. When Roth and Goodman wrote their respective novels, the gift of hindsight rendered both the Swede's and the Kirshners' attempts to escape an untoward engagement in the American and Jewish crises of their day all the more transparent. With the idealism of the 1960s long since shattered by riots, assassinations, political intrigue, and ascendant corporate greed, an era of American innocence had metamorphosed into what one psychologist referred to as an age of "radical individualism." As the title of his 2000 book strongly hinted, David Myers' *American Paradox* was a fitting companion to Roth's *American Pastoral*. Rampant individualism, Myers argued, had yielded a "social recession" which "imperil[ed] children, corrode[d] civility, and diminishe[d] happiness."[62] In the face of such developments, novels depicting the dream of pastoral withdrawal, whether they were jaggedly cynical on the order of *American Pastoral* or gently elegiac on the order of *Kaaterskill Falls*, comprised a logical medium for an "ever-widening examination of the complacency that is at the heart of Jewish American culture."[63]

That the pastoral comes into play for both authors as a Jewish motif is surprising on a certain level given its profoundly antimodern implications. According to Grace Paley's diasporic formulation, after all, Jews "are not supposed to take up space but to continue in time."[64] It may be tempting to dismiss Roth's and Goodman's novels as straightforward repudiations of the pastoral, but neither book warrants such an interpretation. While no argument for Jewish American exceptionalism is likely to withstand nuanced scrutiny, particularly in the context of the transnational turn of recent years, the lives of Jews in the New World have been appreciably different from the lives of Jews elsewhere by virtue of the mythology of spatial expansion that occurred concomitantly with their passage of the Atlantic Ocean. Whether America was Zion, Babylon, or merely another iteration of the European diaspora, for Jews, America was America by virtue of its inhabitants' belief in, or skepticism toward, a prevailing notion of geographical separateness. In the land where, as Charles Olson once put it, "SPACE" is "the central fact," pastoralism has been a recurrent motif.[65] Jews have tended for the most part to constitute a less than reliably compliant constituency for the perpetuation of the pastoral myth. Yet just as they have come closest to achieving acceptance in American society through their "embrace of whiteness,"[66] Jewish Americans have become especially susceptible to the promise of individual sovereignty and the belief in what Sidra DeKoven Ezrahi refers to as "a remythification of the Jewish fantasy of return to a pre-lapsarian, pre- (or post-) exilic state."[67] They have shed their former inhibitions around the notion of geographical redemption in favor of what Sarah Phillips Casteel refers to as "gesture[s] of emplacement."[68] The result, at least as Philip Roth and Allegra Goodman make manifest in their millennial novels, is a mixed one. Neither the Swede nor the Kirshners are contemptible in our eyes. We can easily empathize with their respective attempts to find inspiration in the surrounding natural world even as we perceive the tragic folly that follows from these attempts. As readers, we can't help but note, however, that in their particular "appropriations" of the myth of pastoral escape, Roth and Goodman have "put pressure on the myths themselves" that few other American writers have imposed.[69]

~~~

RETURN TO THE SHTETL

FOLLOWING THE "TOPOLOGICAL TURN" IN REBECCA GOLDSTEIN'S *MAZEL* AND JONATHAN SAFRAN FOER'S *EVERYTHING IS ILLUMINATED*

TURNING TIME INTO SPACE: THE SHTETL IN THE POSTASSIMILATION, POSTMODERN IMAGINATION

Rabbi Max Wall wasn't sure where his images of the Polish shtetl of Hatna originated. "You get transmitted not only your personal memories," he explained, "but the memories of people who were living there . . . and you begin to think that you actually remember those places." In an oral history interview I conducted with him when he was 91 years old, the Vermont rabbi strained to recall the place of his birth. He remembered that when he was three years old, he accidentally rolled a hoop through the open door of a church. "Somebody came out, took a look at me, slapped me violently across the face, and called me a Jew Christ-killer in Polish," he said. Wall grew up to attend rabbinical school in Manhattan. As a chaplain at the end of World War II, he participated in the liberation of Dachau. He became Burlington's most beloved rabbi. So many years spent in so many places left him with only a threadbare recollection of the shtetl in which he had begun his life. He knew that his mother's uncle kept a store "that had a long porch like you see in some of the Western towns where they raise the sidewalk."[1] As they lived on in Rabbi Wall's imagination, the church doorway and the store porch bore the hallmarks of "multidirectional" *postmemories*—examples of "the past made present" as the result of a lifetime of superimposed impressions, experiences, and formulations.[2]

That these two fragmentary memories constituted his only images of Poland said as much about Rabbi Wall's life in America as it did about what life had been like for his family in that shtetl. What he could call to mind in a Burlington restaurant in 2004 constituted a poignant and ambivalent commentary on the Jewish American geography of the entire twentieth century. Among Jewish Americans at the turn of the millennium, the Eastern European shtetl had long since acquired the status of what one critic terms a "poetic construct" and another refers to as a "literary topos."[3] Its legacy lived on for all kinds of reasons and in all sorts of ways because Jewish Americans were both relieved to have left it behind and mournful at its passing.[4] The shtetl comprised a geographical metonym for everything that was beautiful and praiseworthy about traditional Jewish life in a modernizing world—its strong communal ethic, its rich religious culture, its legacy of humor in the face of tragedy. Among twentieth-century Jewish Americans, most of whom had roots in Eastern Europe, the shtetl also represented the worst things about their Old World experiences, as Rabbi Wall's recollection attested. The facility with which authors could depict it in both wistful and unstintingly harsh ways made the shtetl an ideal foil for Jewish American writers who were either discomfited or delighted by their lives in the United States. Some may have felt that their "claim to difference as Jews" within a highly racialized American society was in question.[5] An imaginative return to the shtetl could serve to remind both Jews and non-Jews not only of how different they had once been but also of the miracle of their collective survival into the new millennium. It offered new "possibilities for Jewish American fiction in a post-historicist, post-assimilationist era."[6]

For Jews who lived in the latter half of the twentieth century, the shtetl had also evolved into even more of a fraught and painful construct by virtue of its cataclysmic disappearance in the 1940s. The Eastern European Jews who had come to America around the turn of the twentieth century chose to leave it behind. Fleeing the oppressive regime of an anti-Semitic czar, with its policy of near lifelong conscription for Jewish males, periodic pogroms, and stifling poverty made sense from a certain standpoint, but it had also been entirely volitional. Within a few decades of this mass migration, the majority of Jews who chose to remain in Eastern Europe were dead. The shtetl as a cultural landscape literally vanished in the onslaught of Nazi violence that all but destroyed European Jewry. For many Jewish Americans who sought to conjure its memory after World War II, the shtetl could not but have been "emptied, drained of color, texture and complexity" in the aftermath of the Shoah.[7] Max Wall's desiccated description of Hatna was a case in point. Memories like his conveyed profoundly mixed emotions and meanings. From a material standpoint, to have left Eastern Europe for the land of plenty had been a blessing. In spiritual terms, perhaps, the shtetl might have been the richer of the two environments, but the point was moot. Whichever of the two environments one preferred in the abstract, there could be no going back. As a locale to be written about, on the other hand, the shtetl would become a unique touchstone to the Jewish American literary imagination.

Despite, or perhaps because of, the piecemeal and fraught nature of shtetl images, third- and fourth-generation Jewish American fiction writers who lived at the turn of the millennium could not resist the temptation to reclaim and recolor it as a territorial basis for their projections onto the collective Jewish past and future. On the one hand, they had "little to say about Jewish existence" in their own country of birth, which they could not view as anything other than the land of the eternal present.[8] At the same time, these Jewish American authors could not help but take note as other minority writers of their time found opportunities to counteract their invisibility within American culture by inscribing their collective presence onto a reimagined historical landscape.

With a firm belief in the abiding immanence of the past, accompanied by a tragic post-Holocaust awareness that the Eastern European Jewish legacy could only be felt as "the presence of an absence,"[9] these writers reinhabited a fanciful shtetl that was at once joyfully, hermetically, and permanently Jewish. At the same time, the millennial-era literary shtetl was doomed for every minute of its existence to inevitable extinction. It was impossible to imagine such a place without knowing all along that it derived its very meaning and significance from the fact and knowledge of its destruction. As Michael Chabon wrote about it in a controversial 1997 essay that was a point of inspiration for his 2007 novel *The Yiddish Policemen's Union*, the imagined shtetl of the millennial era had, on some level, to be a world where "millions of Jews who were never killed produced grandchildren, and great-grandchildren" and whose "countryside contained large Yiddish-speaking pockets."[10] It was entirely fantastic and yet entirely recognizable. Its salient attribute as a device for memory was its haunting physicality. To revisit such places in their present state was to undergo an unstinting confrontation with the cruel facts of history. One could only engage in such a pastime if one were willing to exhume the dead, reinhabit their souls, and attempt to return to ordinary life afterward. Such acts, as William Boelhower writes, had the effect of spatializing time, which is to say that they superimposed the fixations of a historical consciousness onto a haunted landscape.[11]

Although Rebecca Goldstein's *Mazel* (1995) and Jonathan Safran Foer's *Everything Is Illuminated* (2002) were by no means the only works of their time period that explored the shtetl trope, the centrality in both of these novels of what one critic refers to as an insistence on "spatial and temporal multidimensionality" marked their contributions as distinct.[12] While its middle portions recount its protagonist's long journey from an Eastern European shtetl to Warsaw's experimental theater in the prewar years, Holocaust-era Israel, and later New York, Goldstein's novel begins and ends in the American present. Foer's book shuttles back and forth between the early history of a shtetl, its elimination in the Holocaust, and its protagonist's search, in the 1990s, for traces of the lost community. With their frequent resort to an experimental aesthetic, both novels cope with the absence of memory by freely supplying invented detail and mixing it in with what appears to be documentary evidence. Though unbridgeable gaps in both time and space exists between them and their subjects, Goldstein and Foer negate the ordinary parameters of both dimensions. Goldstein's writing emphasizes the continuities between the present and the past so that even as her book appears to be following a fairly conventional chronological arc, the lineage that connects its characters to one another can be read backward or forward. Foer's novel also treats time as a fluid entity, but its primary innovation derives from its flagrant superimposition of American pastimes and fixations over the pre-Holocaust Eastern European landscape.

When they revisited the vanished landscapes of Jewish Eastern Europe, the shtetl reinventors of millennial America were also participating in what one critic refers to as "the topological turn in ethnic narration."[13] The fact that the Jewish Old Country was an intrinsically inaccessible and unrecoverable land of enchantment and horror was both heartening and disquieting from an artistic point of view. It was also of a piece with an existing trend that had developed across the spectrum of ethnically situated writing of the era. From Native American authors who reconsecrated the stolen landscapes of their tribal pasts to African American writers who reinhabited the blood-soaked geography of the rural South, a growing interest in place as a locus for renegotiated American identities and postmodern consciousness affected writers of an increasingly past-obsessed and present-disoriented era. This trend, as Anna Ronell describes it, reflected the eagerness of late twentieth-century ethnic fiction writers to "nourish identity" and "draw on the resources of collective memory."[14]

In Native American oral and literary traditions, the landscape of North America was an agent of restoration—the beginning and ending of all communal and spiritual endeavors. Defiled as it was by the rapacious practices of its European colonizers, it continued nonetheless to speak to its original inhabitants and recall them to their most edifying memories and traditions. Amid the tragedies and injustices of reservation life, with its rampant alcoholism, brutal violence, and abject poverty, the land had the power to bring people back to themselves. It had, after all, witnessed their entire history as a people. For members of Native American tribes who had their land and very often their cultural pastimes taken away from them, the land underfoot, regardless of who held its title, also offered geographical confirmation of time's cyclical nature. In Leslie Marmon Silko's 1977 novel *Ceremony*, for instance, the protagonist's adventure in the New Mexico highlands brings him into a healing proximity with an entity called "time immemorial." For African American writers of the late twentieth century, the landscape of North America, having been forced at the hands of brutal white racists to absorb the blood, sweat, and tears of millions of black bodies, continued to waft its sweetness toward the victims of oppression as an act of ironic defiance. Cotton fields, swamps, and urban ghettoes alike bestowed the most unlikely gifts upon the most unlikely recipients, perhaps most notably including the characters who populated Toni Morrison's *Song of Solomon* (1977) and Gloria Naylor's *Mama Day* (1988). Continually surrounded by the land where their fathers and mothers had died, Native American and black authors of the postmodern period, as William Boelhower puts it, developed the habit of "mining memories as if they were sites."[15] Their fiction explored the legacy of recent and present-day oppression through the experience of landscapes whose features continued to bear the mark of their communal histories.

What distinguished the Jewish American shtetl fictions from the topological creations of other minority writers of the postwar and millennial period was not merely the fact of their reversion to the "foreign" landscapes of Eastern Europe as a means of access to a fraught ethnic past, although that factor was not insignificant to their uniqueness. Their central point of departure from other topological fictions of the era period resulted from the much more significant temporal and spatial distance that existed between the Jewish past and present. Writers of color could not help but be confronted daily with physical reminders of an oppression that continued to link them to the legacy of the past. Historical American landscapes could help sustain Native American and black spirits, offering authors from those two traditions a comforting corrective and corroborating witness to the sad and age-old story of their dispossession. Jewish writers, conversely, often experienced and depicted the American landscape as a neutral receptor for their lives in the present that had little, if anything, to say about their past. On the bright side, America was a singularly *un*haunted place from a Jewish perspective. With a few notable exceptions, Jewish bones that lay in its soil could rest easily. From a Jewish perspective, America could only be the continent of the eternal present. Any attempt to recuperate an ancient Jewish lineage and attach it to a particular place on the North American continent was doomed to fail.[16] America had been too kind, or at least indifferent, to Jewish narratives to confer such numinous meanings upon them.

Young Jewish American writers of the late twentieth and early twenty-first centuries had to strain their imaginations in order to reclaim a Jewish past. Their "recollections" of the shtetl could only be filtered through the disconcertingly comforting (if spiritually alienating) experience of social and economic stability. From their homes in American suburbs and largely through the instrument of their educations in elite American institutions, millennial-era Jews sought to recover a sense of the past and of Jewish distinctiveness by revisiting the Eastern European landscapes from which their grandparents had escaped to the land of plenty. To reverse Boelhower's formulation, instead of mining memories for sites, these writers felt compelled instead to mine sites for memories. In order to claim their rightful place within a literary milieu that viewed place-inspired narratives of oppression as a means for reasserting group identity, Jewish writers had to recross the Atlantic both figuratively and literally. Owing to the profoundly racialized conditions of American life, the framework according to which they operated demanded such alignments. In the postwar era, "the more distant they became from their minority social status," writes Eric Goldstein, "the more Jews felt the need to highlight their difference from white society."[17] Such a task could not be achieved against the backdrop of America itself, whose recent

history and social, economic, and even cultural facts all seemed to point to Jews
as a singularly, if only newly, privileged group. The spatial dimension of Jewish
oppression simply did not exist in America. Unlike minorities of color, Jews had
not experienced the adverse effects of colonialism. Jewish collective trauma
had been largely inflicted on the opposite shore of the Atlantic. For Jews, the millennial moment was less a function of postcolonial existence than it was a result
of the "post-assimilation" experience.[18] In order to conjure the very idea of a
tight-knit Jewish community, the millennial-era shtetl inventors of the latter-day
imaginary realms of "Yiddishland" and "Ashkenaz" could only draw upon what
they knew from firsthand experience in the bland suburban districts of the land
of their birth.[19]

TRAVELING TO THE RUINED SHRINE: MULTICULTURAL
WRITERS REPOPULATING THE LANDSCAPES OF THE PAST

Like their non-Jewish counterparts who created topologically inspired fiction,
the Jewish American inventors of latter-day shtetls were the products of a postmodern consciousness whose agents sought and found opportunities to explore
what critic Merle Bachman refers to as the "thresholds" of identity and history.
Among the millennial writers, exploration of the spatial realm was transformational because it sought to reshape the past entirely. The fluidity of postmodern
motifs could allow for the radical decentering of inherited social and racial hierarchies and their replacement with more syncretic and dynamic models of the
sorts of histories that had been lived out on the American land among communities of color. Within the overall pattern that defined the topological turn, ethnic writers sought to "employ a local mind as they set about haunting American
democracy."[20] They might challenge the master narratives and mythologies of
frontier dominion, military conquest, urban expansion, and even immigrant
success by proffering images of subversive autonomy and indigeneity. Within
this framework, blacks would become the uninhibitedly inventive and resourceful inhabitants of a dynamically reconfigured South whose land and culture bore
the imprint of their African origins even as it continued to be haunted by the
ghosts of slavery. Native peoples could maintain an even more long-standing
continuity with the American land. They did so by virtue not so much of the
ancient treaty rights that the dominant culture frequently ignored but as a
result of their adherence, through oral tradition and ceremony, to a spiritual
legacy and storytelling tradition whose entire meaning was linked to a sense of
place and rootedness in the landscape. For writers of color, legacies of perseverance as well as of suffering, of liberation as well as of captivity, could all be
reflected and superimposed upon the geography of North America, which had
been the scene of great drama for them. As fiction writers of diverse origins
and orientations grew ever more interested in literary representations of the

threshold in the postwar era and millennial eras, place presented itself as an ideal stage for inverting or at least complicating preexisting stories of the American past. It allowed its practitioners to reclaim stolen lands and stolen lives.

What held such fictions together across ethnic and racial divides was the notion of transcendent otherworldliness that adhered to the landscapes they featured—often despite those very same landscapes' superficial and circumstantial removal from their immediate purview. Tayo, the Laguna Pueblo protagonist of Leslie Marmon Silko's 1977 novel *Ceremony*, has spent nearly his entire life in northern New Mexico, but only his traumatic return from combat and imprisonment in the jungles of the Pacific during World War II enable him to see and appreciate the landscape of his origin as a forgiving, transformational force in his life. In the ceremonial journey that he undertakes in order to recover a herd of stolen cattle and thereby complete his healing, he continually discovers that the landscape features he once took for granted or, worse, had written off as no longer his in the first place, have never been indifferent to him or his people. "The Texans who bought the land fenced it and posted signs in English and Spanish warning trespassers to keep out" proceed as if it is theirs to manage and demarcate, but Tayo knows better. "The liars had fooled everyone," he thinks to himself, and "as long as people believed the lies, they would never be able to see what had been done to them or what they were doing to each other."[21] The salient development that makes such a realization possible for him in the first place is his growing awareness that his people's removal from the land is a temporary condition and that the cyclical view of time that prevails among them is the only form of lasting historical truth.

Otherworldliness is an attribute of late twentieth-century African American fiction writers' depictions of place as well. Notwithstanding divisions of the land that typically rewarded whites and dismissed blacks as unworthy of holding title to anything but the least desirable parcels, in the work of a writer like Gloria Naylor, black-owned land takes on a powerful, even supernatural, significance. In her book *Mama Day* (1988), Naylor describes a place called Willow Springs that appears to be modeled, at least in part, on the Georgia Sea Islands. Having survived in unrelenting succession "malaria," "Union soldiers," "sandy soil," "two big depressions," "hurricanes," and "real estate developers who think we gonna sell our shore land just because we ain't fool enough to live there," the people of Willow Springs maintain a connection to the land by virtue of both their sheer tenacity and the enchanting power of the stories they tell about the place nearly two hundred years after their initial settlement there. "It ain't about right or wrong, truth or lies," the narrator says—"it's about a slave woman who brought a whole new meaning to both them words." Sapphira Wade, the woman in question, is the originator of the unique atmosphere that asserts itself to anyone who dares to "cross over here from beyond the bridge." Having succeeded in marrying her white owner, bearing seven sons by him, and finally murdering him 1823, she achieved an even greater accomplishment: perpetual ownership of "every inch of Willow Springs" for the island's black inhabitants. Sapphira's power derives not only from her historical legacy but also from her mystical wake, which "don't live in the part of our memory we use to form words."[22] Gloria Naylor's formulation, like Leslie Marmon Silko's, relies heavily on the testimony of the land itself as a recuperative antidote to the historical and present-day oppression of its most devoted and deserving caretakers.

The starting point for such formulations is an act of injustice committed by a ruthless oppressor. Because racialized victims of European colonialism were hardly in short supply in North America, stories like Tayo's and Sapphira Wade's were both widespread and easily linked to the American landscape. For Jews, however, whose entire history in America seemed to be one of gradual economic advancement, civic enfranchisement, and social ascension, such acts could only be played out in a foreign territory that had all but ceased to exist in the lived experiences of actual people. Within the wider framework formed by the post-war and millennial reclamation of ethnic space, Jewish topological fiction had no recourse but to revert to a reimagined Eastern European shtetl if it wished to replicate the "archaemythological"[23] interests and proclivities of the era. That Jewish writers would even bother to engage in such exercises was the result of their long-standing and somewhat anomalous (for people of "white" stature, at least) interest and investment in multiculturalism. As the nation's quintessential "insiders who are outsiders and outsiders who are insiders," Jews were both reluc-tant to relinquish their mantle of persecution and eager to embrace the nation that seemed willing to confer its bounteous blessings upon them.

The millennial reinventors of the shtetl fiction enacted a "reacquisition of the spatial dimension" that fairly closely resembled the recuperative projects of their nonwhite American counterparts.[24] Millennial-era shtetl fiction offered Jewish writers an opportunity to address the skeptical inquiries of critics who, as Jen-nifer Glaser puts it, were "hard-pressed to identify any particular Jewish differ-ence from the American body politic."[25] In the multicultural American context, in which the recovery of roots and of originating landscapes served as a central component in the search for identity, the reimagined shtetl was, in many ways, a profoundly American, as well as Jewish, *topos*. Rebecca Goldstein Americanized her shtetl by drastically reducing the gaps in space-time that existed between it and its postwar New Jersey suburban counterpart. Jonathan Safran Foer described a shtetl that sounded like a cross between a small American town, a circus encampment, and a Jewish version of the Land of Oz. For both authors, to return to the shtetl through fiction was to reinhabit a land that, while it had never been anything other than a site of exile, represented a version of Jewish wholeness that was absent in contemporary America. At a moment in American literary history when place was being newly accorded with an ability to redeem oppressed and objectified peoples, the reconstituted shtetl offered Jewish writers an opportunity to revisit their past and reshape their present. In order to address what Amy Hungerford refers to as "the ... problem of American insignificance,"[26] these authors attempted to escape America entirely. Ironically, their apparently insignificant experiences in America had constituted the most important and evident launching points for these flights of fancy.

The shtetl was a problematic site around which to build such endeavors. The fact that it had been located several thousand miles beyond the borders of the United States constituted an admission that America itself was not and might not ever become a genuinely Jewish place. While it appeared to make no claim to Jewish legitimacy on American soil, in establishing, or seeking to establish, the Jews' collective legitimacy as a historically grounded and tradition-bound people with a direct stake in the living out and articulation of American multicultur-alism, shtetl fiction mimicked the topological fictions of Native American and black authors. Shtetl fiction allowed "younger self-identified Jewish writers ... to function as part of [the] new multicultural world" that was taking shape all around them.[27] In its direct engagement with the facts of the Nazi genocide, the shtetl fiction of the millennial era also depicted the grandparents of American-born Jews as racialized Others who had been made to suffer for their Jewishness. It emphasized the legacy of that historical trauma in the lives of present-day Jewish Americans. By spatializing identity and projecting their own people's his-tory upon a recognizable and particularistic geography, writers like Goldstein and Foer participated in a wider attempt to challenge, if not dislodge, the myth of Americanization. No matter how materially comfortable they might have become in the United States, these novelists' eagerness to reanimate the shtetl was indicative of their continuing misgivings about such a prospect.

At the same time, the efforts of the shtetl reinventors to create a uniquely Jew-ish imaginary space only emphasized the wide chasm that had begun to form between themselves and other minority groups in the United States. The Jews' acceptance in America had in large part been a function of their willingness to acquiesce to the rules of a society whose openness and prosperity were posited on a historical and systematic exclusion of people of color. Ironically, while the work of the shtetl reinventors may have been intended at least in part to be a gesture of solidarity with the members of other minority groups, it only suc-ceeded in setting Jews farther apart from their fellow Americans. It may well have been intended to serve as a reminder of the trauma of Eastern European anti-Semitism and of the Holocaust, but the drastic acts of invention that it required of its participants had by necessity to confer upon their work an odd, storybook quality. From a distance, after all, these books could not help but conjure famil-iarly American "happy endings" of latter-day survival and prosperity. The authors of works like *Mazel* and *Everything Is Illuminated* drew attention to the wide, essentially unbridgeable gap that existed between their grandparents' legacy of Jewish Otherness in Eastern Europe and their own inheritance of Jewish success

in America. That these writers could only represent Jewish difference in their fiction by conjuring a vanished and extra-American landscape was a discomfiting
reminder of the radical displacement and exilic mind-set that characterized the
Jewish American experience. Their shtetl fictions, as Andrew Furman remarks,
betrayed a "nagging fear on the part of contemporary Jewish American writers that their culturally specific experiences" would strike readers "both as less
'American' and less 'strange' than the experiences of [other] minority writers."[28]

IMAGINING "THE FOREST'S DARK SCENT": TIME
TRAVEL IN REBECCA GOLDSTEIN'S *MAZEL*

That Rebecca Goldstein's novel begins and ends in the suburban town of Lipton, New Jersey, speaks both to its profoundly American implications and to
its attention to the theme of radical displacement. The town's fictional name
meant to suggest Lipton's equivalency to the town of Teaneck, which is just
across the George Washington Bridge from upper Manhattan, but perhaps its
play on the familiar brand name is also meant to imply an equivalency between
America itself and corporate blandness. The book's protagonist Sasha (in the
portions of the book that take place during her childhood in the shtetl, her name
is Sorel) is extremely vocal in her disapproval of Lipton and everything it stands
for.[29] Because the author's telling of her story is occasioned by the wedding and
childbirth of Sasha's American granddaughter, however, Lipton exerts an unes-
capable, binding influence on everything else in Goldstein's book, including its
account of the protagonist's experiences of shtetl deprivation and escape from
the Holocaust. While Goldstein seems at pains, mostly through her depiction
of Sasha's well-adjusted granddaughter Phoebe, to redeem Lipton or at least its
devoted Orthodox Jewish residents as latter-day stalwarts of an ancient tradition,
her main character despises the place. The tension between these two perspectives on the meaning and importance of her characters' "North American acculturation"[30] in the New Jersey suburb can only be left unresolved, owing in large
part to the dual tragedies that shape the book's interior portions: the childhood
suicide of Sasha's sister and the *Shoah* itself. Are the survival and propagation
of the Jews in postwar America indications of triumph, or are they legacies of
loss? The juxtaposition of Sasha's and Phoebe's opposing attitudes toward life in
Lipton convey the magnitude of Goldstein's and her readers' dilemma.

   Both women's perspectives on the New Jersey suburb are shaped by its apparent resemblance to the shtetl of Schluftchev, where Sasha was born. Outwardly,
Lipton bears all the earmarks of a distinctly contemporary American place. As
Goldstein puts it on her opening page, each home in Lipton "comes equipped
with all the clichés of suburbia—including a redwood deck with a gas barbe-
cue."[31] From Sasha's perspective, at least, Lipton's sterility is a function of its
residents' lazy conformity, and she finds the groom's family, and his mother in

particular, to be insufferable, typically Jewish American bores. On the angry walk she takes with her daughter Chloe through Phoebe's neighborhood in order to blow off steam prior to the wedding ceremony, the proudly eccentric and bohemian grandmother takes note of the town's "regulation split-levels." While she marks the presence of blooming magnolias that have been evenly and deliberately planted to run "the length of the avenue," she can't help but notice that the blooms are "just beginning to turn brown and drop to the ground."[32] When she returns from her walk, hundreds of pages later and after the author has delivered her lengthy recounting of a life story that began in an actual shtetl, Sasha passes her final judgment on Lipton: it is, she says exasperatedly, "Schluftchev . . . with a designer label."[33] The book's very structure supports such an idea, since Sasha's promenade through the streets of Lipton occurs in exact simultaneity with readers hearing about her shtetl beginnings. "While she is in Lipton," as Murray Baumgarten puts it, "Sasha is also in Schluftchev."[34]

Sasha's pronouncement fits Goldstein's representation of Schluftchev as more of a trope for coming to grips with the Jewish present than an attempt to render an accurate description of a historical phenomenon. It is, as one critic explains, entirely "unmoored from the 'reality' of historical fact."[35] When the narrative moves backward in time in order to recount Sasha's childhood in the shtetl, readers' sense of the town is, by necessity, filtered through their prior introduction to Lipton. We can only see the Jewish past through the American present, just as Sasha herself can only view the American present through the filter of her Eastern European past. To her way of seeing things, the close-knit suburban community, which she views as closed-minded, represents a failure on the part of Jewish Americans to progress past their circumscribed past. For Sasha, as for other contemporary American shtetl-viewers, such places' function in the present is "inherently retrospective." As Jeffrey Shandler writes, the shtetl in the modern literary and popular cultural imagination is exactly equivalent, by definition, to "a place, a language, habit, or ethos understood as having been left behind." For Jewish American writers, the shtetl cannot be viewed on its own terms but only as a device for time travel. It either prefigures the Jewish American topos of late twentieth-century suburbia or it hearkens backward, as a "metonym for a bygone way of life."[36] A metonym is a trope, not an actuality, however, and the shtetl that Goldstein has created is "an imaginary place" and a "fantasy."[37] Even if readers are meant to consider the possibility that Sasha is wrong to pass such negative judgment upon Lipton, the shtetl still functions as her device for understanding and grappling with the lived facts of Jewish American social geography.[38]

On its own terms, the shtetl of Schluftchev is a symbolically rich, if somewhat visually obscure, place. Its most pervasive quality is a surrounding and creeping darkness. As its protagonist experiences her childhood there, she perceives the nighttime as "inky black," compares it to a "black ocean," and even goes so far as to imagine it liturgically as "opaque as the night that had once fallen on Egypt."[39]

In the prelude to the crisis that precipitates her older sister Fraydel's suicide, Sasha considers running away from home with Fraydel and joining the gypsy encampment that has been occupying space on the immediate outskirts of Schluftchev. What she imagines doing feels all the more daring to her because of the exposure it would afford her to the surrounding darkness. Whether the darkness of the shtetl is meant to represent terror, benightedness, isolation, or—in keeping with the Egyptian parallel—divinely ordained punishment, its repeated deployment as a metaphor signals Goldstein's tacit recognition that she is employing it as a symbolic device whose meaning is meant to be carried forward into her characters' lives in the American present. She is certainly not attempting to render a topologically accurate description of an actual place. After all, the effect that the darkness has upon readers is only to impede its depiction as an illuminated, visible geographical entity.

Goldstein's depiction of a handful of the shtetl's geographical features allows her to represent her characters' Jewish legacy as a singularly unfixed and fluid inheritance—one that is commensurate with the inventions of her contemporaries in the multicultural American scene. The "ancient" and "little crowded cemetery on the hill" stands as an outward sign of the ponderous and constricting weight of tradition to be escaped, but it is also a changeable, even temporary, feature. As Goldstein explains twice in nearly the same exact words, the stones of the cemetery cluster "lean together like old friends," but no one in the Jewish community of Schluftchev has any illusions about remaining there forever.[40] While it is nowhere near as haunting a site as the cemetery on first glance, the puddle at the center of town presents itself as an off-putting and intimidating physical obstacle to be avoided. According to Fraydel, whose imagination and spiritual depth serve as the greatest inspiration to her younger sister, the puddle is the reification of what she calls "the stink of Evil, pure and simple."[41] After their younger brother, Bezalel wanders into the puddle against the wishes of his third sister and caretaker, however, Chana, Sasha, and Fraydel entertain one another endlessly, reminiscing over the comical sight of their overweight sister having chased him to the very brink of this "Evil." Eager to emphasize the puddle's prominent, if ambiguous, place within the novel's symbolic landscape, Goldstein affords her readers a whiff of it in Lipton. Sasha wonders aloud what the source of the "putrid smell" is on her walk through Phoebe's suburban town. "It's that little brook that wanders so prettily through the neighborhood," her daughter Chloe tells her, as if to say the smell and the meaning reside in the beholder alone.

Owing in large part to their drabness, neither the cemetery nor the puddle bear down as palpably on Sasha's forming consciousness as the forest outside town does. For their part, the cemetery and puddle comprise evidence of the shtetl's oppressive atmosphere, its impermanence, and ultimately, its utility as fodder for the imagination. Perhaps because they are so familiar to her, however, neither of these features intrudes too deeply into the girl's psyche.

The forest, on the other hand, which she only visits on one occasion, exerts a more transformative influence over her view of the world and her future existence. The forest proffers the tantalizing prospect of physical escape into a new and mysterious world of dangerous possibility. In part because it is located on the outskirts of the Jewish settlement, it embodies the outside world for the Jews who live in its proximity. It is a pagan preserve and a distinctly un-Jewish environment whose natural elements both magnetize and repel Sasha. The shtetl's rabbis are aware of the danger the forest and places like it pose and, as Goldstein explains, "had instructed the Jews to avert their gaze from pagan thoughts" and to avoid the "pull of [its] alien enchantments." The forest, which Goldstein's descriptions associate several times with the enlivening scent of pine trees, may represent the end of Jewish continuity, but it also hints at the culturally—and even religiously—restorative richness of life lived in the diaspora and in proximity to alien peoples. The episode in which Sasha and Fraydel spend time in that forest comprises one of *Mazel*'s most memorable moments, and it is certainly the novel's liveliest depiction of Sasha's life in Schluftchev. The episode is indicative of Goldstein's use of place as an instrument for exploring the dilemmas of Jewish identity in a modernizing, pluralistic society.

Goldstein ventures her most detailed and sensually indulgent descriptions of the shtetl's surrounding landscape in connection with the one moment in time when the arrival of strangers entirely transforms its physical appearance and especially that of the nearby and otherwise forbidding forest. When a band of Gypsies camps at the side of the very same river where Schluftchev's Jews have only recently held their tashlich ceremony for Rosh Hashanah, both girls are fascinated by sudden splashes of color that intrude upon the otherwise gray environs of the town. Wearing "brightly colored kerchiefs" over their skin that is already the color of "strong tea," the Gypsy men stride about in the town, trading horses and noisily drinking toasts in the tavern. The Gypsy women, too, are "strange and shameless," their heads topped with "inky black hair," their bodies decorated with "brass-colored jewelry" and clothed in low-cut and loose-hanging bodices. It takes the arrival of Gypsies to lend color and memorability to an otherwise drab atmosphere and, for that matter, to remind the Jews that they are Jews in the first place. For a writer like Goldstein, herself a product of a pluralistic American environment, to hearken back to the dynamic geography of the Eastern European Jewish past is to cast her readers forward into the lively geography of the American present.

Like the culturally diverse suburbs and cities of contemporary America, the shtetl was an environment within which Jewish difference was not necessarily easy to maintain. As more than one scholar has pointed out, actual shtetls were far from hermetic environments. The superimposition by some latter-day writers of "an ethno-geographic segregation" over the landscape, which placed "Jews in the center of the town [and] the goyim in the suburbs and surrounding villages," was, as Israel Bartal points out, a fictional device.[42] For her part, Fraydel associates the Gypsies with magical powers and speculates that they are the descendants of the ancient Egyptians. Goldstein's depiction of the Gypsies' sojourn in Schluftchev focuses primary attention on how the visitors' temporary occupation and transformation of the local landscape draw her central characters to the outdoors, away from their self-imposed benightedness and beyond the sheltering walls of their homes. Before the arrival of the Gypsies, Sasha and her sister experience the forest outside of town as a concept—a place to be thought of but never ventured into. Before long, however, as Fraydel becomes increasingly eager to act on her impulses and decides to visit the Gypsies on their own turf, her younger sister too begins to smell and be enticed by "the forest's dark scent."[43] To be enticed by this scent of exposure to the outside world without succumbing entirely to its charms is the trick. To be able to venture among strange peoples, appreciate the physical beauty of the land, and dwell in it without relinquishing one's sense of self as a Jew proves to be the most difficult achievement of all, both in shtetl-era Eastern Europe and in contemporary America.

One night, after the "evening soup" that they consume in the sheltering darkness of their mother's safe kitchen, the girls venture off in the direction of "the dark mass of the forest" where the Gypsies have set up their camp. Surrounded by the "moist woods," the encampment spreads out with its bright colors and varied noises—snorting horses, thudding axes, and crying babies. By now, the girls have traveled further into the forest than they have ever been, past the river crossing where the tashlich ceremonies have been held for generations and into its darkened, but now lively and suddenly illuminated, interior. As Goldstein explains, it is if "the two sisters had crossed foreign seas and faraway lands." When they encounter a pack of the Gypsies' dogs with their "yellowish white . . . stiff short fur [and] terrifyingly sharp teeth," the girls barely resist the temptation to run away and are rescued by a small boy who manages to disperse the dogs by throwing a rock at them.[44] Sasha and Fraydel spend the next several hours in the company of the Gypsies, who are both entertained by the sight of the frightened Jewish girls and warmly welcoming toward them. They watch as a Gypsy boy entertains his friends by prancing around in Fraydel's oversized shoes. They pass the cooking fires of the Gypsy women, smell their spicy meat being roasted in the night air, and observe another young boy dressing a dead hedgehog to be added to the evening meal. No longer defined by the darkness that their religious tradition and families and have imposed upon it, the shtetl has revealed itself to them as one element within a diverse cultural geography. This new way of seeing the place dooms Fraydel, but it liberates her younger sibling.

The adolescent Fraydel experiences the aftereffects of her time among the Gypsies at a critical period in her life. She knowingly faces the immediate prospect of an entire life spent within sight but beyond the physical reach of an outside world. Close on the heels of her evening in the forest, she nearly runs off with the Gypsies when they leave town, leaving her sister in despair at the prospect of living in a "black night-world" without her. Fraydel changes her mind and returns home mysteriously on the very night of the planned departure (having confided her initial intentions to Sasha ahead of time), but she is now lost to her loved ones, having become "something indecipherable" to them in her insanity.[45] "In danger of disappearing down the well of her own thoughts," "Fraydel, Fraydel, *da meshuggena maydel*" comes under ever closer scrutiny by her mother and younger siblings. After bringing ridicule and shame upon herself by flaunting Jewish custom and picking flowers on the Sabbath, she is betrothed to a man whom she has no interest in marrying. Feigning acquiescence to her parents' wishes and to tradition, she staves off discovery long enough to plan her suicide, which, like Ophelia in Hamlet, she completes by drowning herself in the river around which the Gypsy camp had once spread itself out. It is Fraydel's experience that embitters her younger sister against shtetl life and causes her to feel and express suspicion toward traditional Judaism. All the same, the night in the forest among the Gypsies, which offered both girls a glimpse of the inconceivably alien world outside the Jewish fold, is not only the event that precipitates Fraydel's final act but also the one that leads to Sasha's self-liberation.

For Sasha, who is still too young and attached to her parents to act on her childhood whims, the evening spent with the Gypsies serves as a future point of reference and especially as a touchstone to the imagination. Whether as a young adult in prewar Warsaw, where she will make her way as a member of an experimental Yiddish theater group, or as the lone middle-aged protester dancing a Balkan-inspired snake-dance during the 1968 anti–Vietnam War Columbia student strike in New York City, Sasha internalizes the spirit of the Gypsy encampment wherever she goes. "Sasha had hated shtetl life," Goldstein points out near the end of *Mazel*, because it was "close and narrow" and "shut off from the great wide world." Even recalling it gave her a feeling of "claustrophobia."[46] While the resentment that she later evinces through her critique of Lipton, New Jersey, suggests a lingering bitterness on her part toward shtetl life, however, nowhere in her life story does there appear any evidence that she will contemplate leaving the fold of her family or of the Jewish community. Rather than poisoning her attitude toward Jewish life, her shtetl experience, and her one evening spent in the company of the Gypsies in the forest in particular, has taught her how to inhabit an exilic landscape without relinquishing her Jewish autonomy within it. At her granddaughter's wedding, while outwardly put off by the orthodoxy that surrounds her, she suddenly asks that Phoebe identify herself as Fraydel on the ketuba. During the party at the Sheraton Meadowlands that follows the ceremony, even in the midst of her muttering complaints regarding the "reshtetlization of America," she allows herself to be "dragged" toward and then shoved onto the dance floor by an unidentified friend of the groom's. Unhesitatingly, she joins her daughter and granddaughter in a motion whose wild circularity is both

Jewish to the core and, in its own way, oddly reminiscent of the Gypsies' "exuber-ant" dance by the campfire in Schluftchev's forest.[47]

While Sasha is consistently harsh in her condemnation of shtetl life, Gold-stein weaves such a forgiving irony around both the character and the situa-tion in which she finds herself as a great-grandmother-to-be in 1990s America that readers cannot so easily dismiss Schluftchev's important, even affirming, contributions to her story. The protagonist's bitter and tragic experiences as a child in Schluftchev have prepared her to lead a daring and dynamic life on the edge of great change. As Goldstein describes the early influences upon her pro-tagonist, including the shtetl's physical environs, she does so in such a way as to emphasize their numinous, liminal, and transformational qualities. She rep-resents the "black-night" that surrounds the shtetl as both a dangerous threat and an inviting world of possibility. She describes the cemetery as both stark and warmly familiar—a dark place that is full of "the bones of ancestors" and, at the same time, an outdoor space where the stones lean crowdedly together like "old friends." Even Schluftchev's puddle proves to be both a toxic receptacle and a site where comic relief plays itself out. The "dark mass of the forest," too, represents both unspeakable tragedy and the shtetl's most obvious access point for freedom. While it is Sasha's adult life and high achievement as a stage-actor and writer that serves as the source of her pride and sense of self as an adult, Goldstein makes it clear through her sustained and detailed narration of the character's upbringing in Schluftchev that such humble-seeming beginnings provide more than mere background to her story but the actual ground upon which a self-affirming, uninhibited Jewish identity can originate. While it is the time in Warsaw that "crystallizes" characters like Sasha, as Murray Baumgarten writes, "the deep structure of their personalities has been shaped by the experience of the shtetl."[48]

Like the dancing that occurs at its lively conclusion, the pattern of *Mazel* is circular, but the completed circle is not indicative of retrogression. The novel's principal character suffers through and survives the loss of her sister and the dissolution of her family. She is a bystander and near-victim to the destruction of European Jewry. Notwithstanding Sasha's misgivings about it, the New Jersey shtetl to which her granddaughter "returns" does not replicate the circumscribed atmosphere of Schluftchev. While Schluftchev's "study-house" accommodated men and boys only, the end of this novel presents us with female characters who occupy tenured positions at Ivy League universities. At the wedding that closes the novel, even the cynical Sasha cannot help but note that the world has changed. When Phoebe approaches the chuppa, she is accompanied by her two best friends and fellow Princeton mathematicians Cindy Chan and Shanti Chevru. Goldstein's deliberate inclusion of their singularly non-Jewish (and nonwhite Anglo) names is a clear signal that the New Jersey version of Schluftchev is far from culturally homogenous, let alone patriarchal. Goldstein's symbolic vocabu-lary hints strongly at the notion that the seeds of this new world were sown in the life of her imaginary Eastern European shtetl. As fixed and impervious to change as that realm seems to have been, it was not a stable milieu in the first place but a world that was itself poised at the edge of an abyss of unmeaning and *mazel*, or fortune, whose inhabitants had only clung to habit and tradition out of necessity.

Mazel settles on a fairly tenuous note with regard to the geography of the Jewish American future. No particular place among the novel's several successive settings is meant to represent lasting comfort or security for the members of Sasha's family. Schluftchev has long ceased to exist. Warsaw as the novel's characters knew it was completely and brutally destroyed in the aftermath of the ghetto uprising of 1943. Israel, where Sasha fled in the face of the Nazi invasion, provided her with temporary shelter, but its citizens' reinvention of themselves as Hebrew-speaking Middle Easterners made it a barren cultural environment from the perspective of an actor whose greatness derived from her achievements on the Yiddish stage. Even New York, which is where Sasha has made her home since the 1950s, falls short of ensuring an autonomous Jewish future because it fails to contain enough of a Jewish past to offer the comfort that would be needed for such assurance. What Goldstein offers instead of any notion of Jewish topological permanence is an entirely alternative and provisional "home-making" space which "disentangles homes from predetermined landmasses and [Jewish identity] from notions of authenticity."[49] Her ability to conjure such an entity in the first place is a function of her having projected a world of reconstituted memories backward and forward onto the landscape of the Eastern European shtetl, which her novel casts as at once densely symbolic and tragically ephemeral.

"How Could Anything Have Ever Existed Here?": Negotiating an Empty Present and an Invisible Past in Jonathan Safran Foer's *Everything Is Illuminated*

One of the features that makes Jonathan Safran Foer's fanciful shtetl of Trachimbrod unique in comparison to Goldstein's Schluftchev is the fact that the novel's narrator actually goes there and sees it. *Everything Is Illuminated* is the product of the period when the demise of Soviet communism inspired significant numbers of Jews from the United States and elsewhere to travel to Eastern Europe in search of their roots. Though the novel's ostensible "hero" is a latter-day Jewish American traveler in Ukraine, what he experiences and sees in the land of his ancestors exercises little influence over his descriptions of the place. Foer's text is deeply ironic in several ways, but its most salient irony is its studied failure to "report back" with the slightest degree of verisimilitude on life in the contemporary Ukrainian countryside. The book avoids any such attempt because its author is preoccupied with other matters. Like Rebecca Goldstein, his purpose is to bring the past forward into the present, but in visiting the shtetl that birthed his grandparents, he discovers that there is no past to be encountered in the landscape of the present. All that he has to work with are two bodies of factual knowledge, both of which entirely negate the significance (to him) of latter-day Eastern European geography. The first body of knowledge upon which Foer draws is his experience of America. The second is the legacy of the Holocaust, whose impact and scale were large enough to render the landscape of present-day Eastern Europe irrelevant and therefore invisible to him. It is the dynamic interplay between these two informing presences that shape *Everything Is Illuminated*. Foer's invention of Trachimbrod attempts to account for and describe the unfathomable space that separates two impossibilities: American bounty and European genocide.

In this sense, the novel enacts what Walter Benjamin once described as "the storm from Paradise." To borrow from Jonathan Boyarin's formulation, we might say that *Everything Is Illuminated* is a book that, like the idea of a "'storm from Paradise,' emphasizes both the howling gap between us and the past *and* the past's proximity to us"[50] (my emphasis). This howling gap is nowhere more evident than in the cities and suburbs of the millennial-era United States, where Jews may either practice their religion freely or ignore it entirely while constituting the nation's single-most economically privileged ethnic subculture. Within the wider framework of the American political economy and social hierarchy, Jews are fortunate sons and daughters whose present-day existence separates them, as a people, from the suffering of other peoples, especially people of color. More important, that existence insinuates an enormous distance between themselves and their own historical suffering, all of which took place in an earlier era, on a distant continent. American plenitude is the "howling gap" that separates Jewish Americans from Jewish history. In its daily experiences, which Foer's novel renders all the more banal for his comically ironic purposes, it is impossible for Jewish writers to feel connected to their past in the same way that writers of color can be connected to theirs. All they can do in pursuit of their heritage and in order to shore up their claims to historical suffering is to travel, either imaginatively or literally (or both), to the mythic land of their origins.

That this sort of travel is easier to conceptualize than to execute is a function of the second body of knowledge upon which Foer must rely as a novelist: the legacy of the Holocaust. To borrow from the second half of Boyarin's formulation, if the howling gap is America, the proximate past is the destruction of European Jewry. It is proximate because it is unforgettable and because, despite the comfort and banality of present-day American existence, its repercussions are always felt, even by Jews who were untouched by it in any concrete sense. For all of its psychic and spiritual proximity, this legacy is painfully intangible, not to mention so full of unfathomable cruelty that it is unrepresentable. The search for it inspires the likes of Jonathan Safran Foer to travel overseas to Ukraine in hopes of achieving some reckoning and reconciliation to both eliminate the howling gap and simultaneously alleviate the strain of history's threatening proximity. When he arrives in Ukraine, however, the novelist quickly learns that he will not succeed at either objective. No matter what lengths he may be willing to go to in order to recapture his family's Eastern European Jewish past, he is not capable of shedding his American identity. When the landscape can be made to reflect people back to themselves, as it has been in the work of Native American and black authors, the topological turn is a viable strategy for the recovery of communal identities and the revaluation of historical experiences. Foer's passing glimpse of the Ukrainian countryside and reimagining of the shtetl of Trachimbrod will not allow for such transformations.

In writing his shtetl novel, therefore, Foer takes multiple liberties with his descriptions of Trachimbrod. From start to finish, he shapes the descriptions of the land he views there, whether he passes by it in a car, encounters it on foot, or imaginatively conjures its earlier phases of history in the portions of the novel that purport to supply the town's history, by drawing upon his two informing elements: American lightness and Holocaust weight. As several critics, including Foer himself, have pointed out, the novelist was not literally forced to invent Trachimbrod out of thin air but instead made a deliberate choice to do so. Trochenbrod, the actual place upon which Foer based his fictional account, was a shtetl with a long history, and the handful of its former inhabitants who survived the war went to extraordinary lengths to tell the story of its people and its destruction. Like the former inhabitants of several other shtetls, these men and women prepared a *yitzkor*, or memorial book, in which they recounted Trochenbrod's founding in the 1790s, its history throughout the nineteenth century, and the names of many of its most illustrious people.[51] While he was perfectly familiar with that volume's contents, and even referred to them as "more fantastical"[52] than his novel, Foer elected all the same to ignore or bypass the town's actual story in order to create his own memories of "a place to which he had never been and events he had never witnessed."[53]

The somewhat eclectic structure of *Everything Is Illuminated* supports Foer's untethered approach to describing the shtetl in several ways, each of which sheds a slightly different light on its author's specifically American mode for conceiving of places and people. Those sections of the book that tell the "outer" story of Jonathan Safran Foer's journey to Ukraine are narrated by an invented interlocutor, Alexander Perchov, whose obsession with all things American results in a portrait of the story's ostensible "hero" that doubles as a quasi-anthropological description of the millennial-era Jewish American mentality. In the portions of the novel that encompass the historical account that the "Jonathan Safran Foer" narrator purports to be writing about it, Trachimbrod is a totally blank slate. It is a community whose founding on one particular day in 1791 resembles the establishment of a town on the American prairie. Even the sections of the story that are composed as letters from Alexander to Jonathan, written after the "very rigid journey" has come to an end and Foer is back in the United States, betray an unmistakably American-centered perspective on the author's part. While the letters purport to be Alexander's metafictional commentary on the "Foer" character's metafictional invention of Trachimbrod's history, their consistent subtext is Alexander's narration of his own family woes and, by extension, an expiation of Eastern European guilt for the Holocaust.

Everything Is Illuminated reflects Foer's profound ambivalence toward Jewish American existence and his eagerness to part ways with the preexisting canon of Jewish American literature that has so consistently depicted and viewed America as "home."[54] At the beginning of the novel, as Jonathan makes his first contact with Alexander, his attempt to explain his quest to return to Trachimbrod offers insight into just how difficult it is both to articulate and to understand such a hankering for a connection to the ethnic past. Why, Alexander wonders, would a Jewish American ever want to "return" to Ukraine? Jonathan's answer to Alexander's question supplies the necessary insight. It isn't enough for "the hero" to know his grandfather's story, or even to have in his possession a photograph of the person from that community who saved his family from destruction. Born in a country where historical memory is woefully short and where Jewish inhabitants in particular have never quite felt encompassed by that memory, he longs to make a physical connection to the place whose history accounts for his very existence.

His attempt to explain this to Alexander is halting and awkward, however, in part because a person in Alexander's shoes can't help but find the quest to be an odd one and in part because it is an obscure and doomed quest in the first place. The ironic distance that Alexander's Ukrainian perspective supplies is integral to our own apprehension of Jonathan's nearly incomprehensible hankering: "'I want to see Trachimbrod,' the hero said. 'To see what it's like, how my grandfather grew up, where I would be now if it weren't for the war.' 'You would be Ukrainian.' 'That's right.' 'Like me.' 'I guess.' 'Only not like me because you would be a farmer in an unimpressive town, and I live in Odessa, which is very much like Miami.'"[55] Alexander's cluelessness has myriad points of origin. For one thing, he cannot appreciate Jonathan's inability, as a Jew, to turn back the clock and imagine himself simply as a "Ukrainian." Neither can he fathom that, sixty years earlier, a person of Jonathan's background would *not* have been like him, even if he *had* lived in Ukraine. Alexander is still more confused regarding Jonathan's apparent interest in reestablishing his connection to a rural community like Trachimbrod. From Alexander's perspective, if an American were to make the mistake of visiting Ukraine in the first place, he would be much better off seeing Odessa, whether or not it is "very much like Miami." The Ukrainian

has a difficult time understanding why people who live blessed lives in techno-
logically advanced countries cultivate such strange preoccupations as Jonathan's.

At an earlier stage in the novel, before Alexander has even set eyes on Jonathan,
he evinces a similar befuddlement regarding the Jewish American obsession with
a past that he would imagine they would just as soon forget. He explains that
his father "toils" for a travel agency called "Heritage Touring" that specializes in
escorting Jewish American tourists like "the hero" who "have cravings to leave
that ennobled country America and visit humble towns in Poland and Ukraine."
Having grown up in a place where Jews either were not physically present in the
first place or, if they were around, were invisible to non-Jews, Alexander freely
admits first to his ignorance about them and also to having once cultivated a
contemptuous view of them. Not only had he "never met a Jewish person until
the voyage" (i.e., his trip to Trachimbrod with Jonathan), but he "had the opinion that Jewish people were having shit between their brains." His reason for
the latter view had less to do with his having inherited his countrymen's anti-
Semitic stereotypes and more with his having observed their strikingly counterintuitive behavior. "All I knew of Jewish people," Alexander explains, "was that
they paid Father very much currency in order to make vacations *from* America
to Ukraine."[56]

When Jonathan himself speaks, both through Alexander's representations of
him but more especially as the omniscient narrator of the shtetl history that
occupies nearly half of the novel, what he says offers even more direct evidence of the novel's consistently American preoccupations. Following in the
footsteps of the Yiddish masters of a hundred years earlier, Foer's approach to
describing Trachimbrod's history necessitates mythologizing the place. Where
writers like Sholem Aleichem had done so in order to "satirize, critique, and wax
nostalgic over the dilemmas and absurdities of Eastern European Jewish existence," however, Foer's apparent lack of knowledge about that subject allows him
to pursue an alternative mythology.[57] While they bear some superficial resemblance to the Chelm tales and other works of the Yiddish masters, the wild inventions that comprise his rendition of Trachimbrod's story are inspired by Jewish
American exposures and rooted in Jewish American obsessions. Foer establishes
the facts of the shtetl's founding, which dates back to the occasion "when Trachim
B's double-axle wagon either did or did not pin him against the bottom of the
Brod River" as if it were a film spectacle of small-town American life.[58] Between
the colorfully named characters, the hints both of lighthearted comedy and of
cosmologically minded mysticism, and the immediate dissent that arises over
the question of what actually happened when the wagon either did or didn't get
pinned and Trachim B's daughter Brod was rescued from the wreckage, the story
of Trachimbrod's founding is above all a commentary on how space is mythologized. Foer also emphasizes this point by highlighting the yearly commemoration

of the "Trachimday" festival that has forever enshrined the founding event in history. He describes the proceedings of this holiday in such a way as to draw a strong resemblance between them and a Fourth of July parade.

Perhaps because their initial settlement of the land has been so pivotal to Americans' sense of themselves and their history, stories like the one about the wagon running aground, an accident that sparked events that led to the birth of a town, are widespread in the canon of American folklore. Their ubiquity speaks to an eagerness on the part of their original tellers, who were generally newcomers from other places, to establish a sense of their rootedness in a local geography by generating narratives from their first encounters with it. Lacking other points of cultural commonality, Americans have gone out of their way to mythologize the land itself and to establish a mystical connection between it and themselves. At least as far back as the works of early nineteenth-century writers like Washington Irving and James Fenimore Cooper, American literature has sought to historicize the North American continent. But this habit is not common in Jewish literature. The combination of mythology and history that Foer presents in the shtetl history sections of *Everything Is Illuminated* suggests an interest on his part in inventing a landscape of Jewish origin and American provenance. It speaks to his own and his generation's quest to find or fashion a physical space, or at least an imaginary physical space, that might alleviate its sense of dislocation in both history and geography.

Foer's shtetl inhabitants also appear to be modeled on the Jews one would have encountered in a late twentieth-century American suburb. Before the town's "official" founding in 1791, in fact, the Jews of the locale that eventually became Trachimbrod were divided into two factions, the Uprighters and the Slouchers. While Eastern European shtetls most certainly knew their share of dissenters of various stripes, Trachimbrod's division along such clearly delineated lines is more indicative of its resonance with a postwar Jewish American mentality than of any similarity to the actualities of shtetl life. Jews in prewar Eastern Europe argued about more than what level of Jewish observance was important to maintain. When they weren't preoccupied by esoteric matters, their debates followed political and social developments throughout Europe. They argued about whether secular knowledge was commensurate with Judaism. They either resisted or yielded to the multiple influences of Jewish emancipation, socialism, and Zionism. The characters in *Everything Is Illuminated*, by contrast, appear to be too self-absorbed to be bothered by such matters. Their disagreements, both petty and momentous, stem in large from their mutual suspicion regarding each other's levels of Jewish observance. In their superficial sectarianism, the Jews of Trachimbrod seem to be humorously conceived caricatures of Jewish Americans of the postwar era. In their relative obliviousness to the world that is changing around them, they hint at a still more immediate and topical concern on the novelist's part. Like the

Jewish beneficiaries of American plenitude, they fail to appreciate both their own vulnerability and the fact that they inhabit a wider world.

Every step of the way, Foer shapes *Everything Is Illuminated* by juxtaposing his dual preoccupations with the Jewish American experience and the Holocaust. Perhaps it should not come as a surprise, then, that when destruction comes to the shtetl's inhabitants, it occurs on Trachimday, the very occasion that they have devoted for more than a century to a pageantry that betrays a pagan, or at least postmodern American, mentality rather than a traditionally Jewish one. Destruction rains upon the town while the Trachimbroders are marking their uniqueness in a celebratory fashion. A float decorated with blue and black butterflies passes by. A girl wearing an electrified tiara is surrounded by a group of seeming-cheerleaders. Fiddlers play patriotic songs while old men seated on the banks of the Brod River reminiscing about the old days. In this scene that precedes the German bombing of Trachimbrod, Foer has set his lighthearted replication of an American Fourth of July pageant on a collision course with his depiction of the Holocaust. The episode's closing lines remind us that the inevitability of the shtetl's destruction has been hovering at the margins of its history all along. Poised to describe the commemorative dive, the historian suddenly breaks rank with his own narrative stream and supplies a parenthetical sentence that speaks directly to the tension that has existed at the heart of his story from its beginning. His words admit to the unbridgeable distance that has always interceded between himself and the characters that populate his shtetl history. "Here it is impossible to go on," he says, "because we know what happens, and wonder why they don't. Or it's impossible because we fear that they do."[59]

Foer meant to confront that impossibility by coming to Ukraine. By representing his protagonist's travels, he suggests that a physical reckoning with the landscape of Eastern Europe offers the most effective means of highlighting the tension between his modern-day American sensibility and his fascination with the Holocaust. This is why most of the novel's direct attention to the Holocaust is mediated by Alexander Perchov's narration of Jonathan's travels. In the course of Jonathan's invented history of Trachimbrod we hear relatively little about the Holocaust. The story of what actually happened to the shtetl's inhabitants can only be told as Jonathan interacts with witnesses to its destruction on the sites where that destruction occurred. Since the novelist is fully aware that any resolution between his dual preoccupations is impossible, it hardly matters that these interactions and these witnesses are fabrications. Like so many other novels that depict the Holocaust, *Everything Is Illuminated* describes a latter-day encounter with the event as opposed to the event itself. The encounter engenders the opposite of resolution and closure. Instead, it calls attention to the "storm from Paradise," the simultaneity of separation and nearness that defines the Jewish relationship to history.

"The Jewish past . . . overwhelms encounters with present-day life in Eastern European towns," as Jeffrey Shandler writes, and physical proximity only magnifies the effect by which "distance shapes engagements with *shtetlekh*."[60] Though Jonathan is surrounded by the very forests and fields where his grandparents' shtetl once stood, the gulf that separates him from the actualities of the Holocaust has only grown wider. As Alexander asks for the directions to the site where Trachimbrod once stood, the local inhabitants' responses to his inquiries call attention to this notion. "I have lived here my whole life," an elderly man tells them, "and I can inform you that there is no place called Trachimbrod." As Alexander puts it, "It was seeming as if we were in the wrong country, or the wrong century, or as if Trachimbrod had disappeared, and so had the memory of it." For Jonathan, the emptiness of the encounter results in a return to his original impasse. *Everything Is Illuminated* does not alleviate Jonathan's inability to reconcile his present-day existence as a Jewish American with the facts of his family's past in Eastern Europe. As Foer wrote in 2010, "Trachimbrod will never be redeemed, and we will never, next year, be there."[61]

"A Utopian Impulse Turned Cruel and Ironic"[62]: The Tragedy of No-Place

If Rebecca Goldstein's and Jonathan Safran Foer's shtetl inventions achieve any sort of breakthrough, it is by virtue of their negation of narrative linearity. They remind us that time and space are malleable and plastic dimensions that often reflect back upon one another. Foer's encounter with the geography of Eastern Europe itself does not reconcile the horrors of the past with the numbness of the present, but his attempts to revisit and Americanize it succeed at collapsing the distinction between the two realms. Likewise, Goldstein's explorations of events from her protagonist's remote past allow us to see that physical distance is of small importance where human inheritance is concerned. Neither novel grants predominance to time or space as shaping influences over its characters. Neither novel "prefers" America or Eastern Europe, and neither privileges the present over the past. These refusals are essential to their enterprise. The fictional repopulation of the shtetl gestures toward the goal that motivates the topological turn in general, the reclamation of cultural agency within the framework of a multicultural America. Only by asserting such control are writers enabled to challenge the myth of their erasure.

That geographical space is important at all to these writers' formulations is the result not only of literary and cultural influence from other minority traditions within the American canon. While attention to the "spatial dimension of time," as William Boelhower refers to it,[63] has been a stable component of ethnic American literature for some time, it has always been a factor in Jewish literature. The eagerness of writers like Goldstein and Foer to conjure notions of Jewish geography is entirely commensurate with "the tension between homeland and diaspora" that informs their fiction.[64] The uniqueness of the Eastern European shtetl as a site for such acts of invention derives from its status as an exclusively imaginative entity. Shtetl fiction of the millennial era did not, as Jeffrey Shandler puts it, "rejoice in the amassing of turf" but in the exploration of exile as a condition of the soul.[65] It was a stay against assimilation. The genre allowed its creators and readers alike to read their present existence through the lens of the past before the enticements of the American present caused them to lose contact with it. At the same time, the very existence of shtetl fiction constituted evidence of a discomfiting truth. In order to reacquaint themselves with their origins, its inventors had to abandon the United States, the only place where they had ever felt at home, and reimagine a time in a place whose natives had sought their complete destruction. Their recourse to such a "heartbreakingly implausible"[66] tactic marked their persistent inability to attach a meaningful Jewish past to the American geography whose disconcertingly familiar contours defined their existence in the present.

6

~~

TURNING DREAMSCAPES INTO LANDSCAPES ON THE "WILD WEST BANK" FRONTIER

JON PAPERNICK'S *THE ASCENT OF ELI ISRAEL* AND RISA MILLER'S *WELCOME TO HEAVENLY HEIGHTS*

EXILES AND IMMIGRANTS IN THE PROMISED LAND

Jon Papernick's short story collection *The Ascent of Eli Israel* (2002) and Risa Miller's novel *Welcome to Heavenly Heights* (2003) depict Jewish American would-be pioneers failing to redeem themselves as immigrants in the Land of Israel. After Eli Haller puts a cataclysmic end to his marriage by raping his wife in the presence of his young son, he hears the voice of God commanding him to "go to the house of Israel."[1] When he arrives at his new home on a Judean hilltop surrounded by Arab villages and olive groves, his old drinking and drugging buddy Zev whoops, "Welcome to the wild, wild West Bank!" Though Risa Miller's characters are not as deeply troubled as Papernick's no-goodniks, their eagerness to move to Israel is motivated by similarly American preoccupations. Fed up with an unsatisfying life in a Baltimore suburb, Tova wishes "for sidewalks and a ten-minute walk to the library," and Mike has "set his mind on open air and a mountain view."[2] Papernick's and Miller's fiction portrays dismayed Jews who project the recuperative power of open space upon the ancient landscape of Israel. Papernick's use of the word "ascent" and Miller's reference to "heavenly heights" hint strongly at the notion that these characters believe themselves to be acting for the good of the Jewish people by making aliyah, especially at the height of the Second Intifada. Their move to Israel, however, proves to be of far greater personal rather than communal import. Both writers depict Israel's

130

frontier regions as a troubling and alien backdrop for their characters' ineffectual attempts to redress misgivings that result from their peculiarly American condition of social isolation and spiritual anomie.

Within the wider framework of Jewish American literary history, the regression to such a disturbingly atomistic pattern has been doubly ironic. After all, the handful of Jewish writers who represented life on the frontier of the United States during the mid-nineteenth century associated migration to the west with the cause of communal rebirth and civilizational reprise. Their narratives of frontier travel depicted the wilderness as a potential outpost not only of emancipatory American democracy but of redemptory Jewish spirituality. By contrast, stories about American-born Jews fleeing their unfulfilling lives in the developed portions of the United States in order to settle the borderlands of Israel at the turn of the millennium convey a less heartening set of implications. By emphasizing the spatial dimension of Jewish American identity as it operates in a barren, even dystopian, landscape far outside the borders of the United States, these works postulate an end to the dream of Jewish American homecoming. The irony of the situation is compounded by the fact that literary representations of Jewish American immigration to Israel can also not help but bear at least a faint resemblance to the hundred-year-old narrative of redemptive immigration from Eastern Europe to America. At the heart of both Papernick's and Miller's fiction lies a sense of dislocation and longing for renewal that, three and four generations ago, defined and impelled the work of such immigrant writers as Abraham Cahan, Anzia Yezierska, and Henry Roth. The experience of Israeli life instigates a renegotiation of self and community that is analogous to the adjustments that late nineteenth- and early twentieth-century Jews (and immigrants of other ethnic origins) had to make upon their arrival in America from the Old World.

Circumstantial and qualitative differences abound, however. By and large, turn-of-the-century Jewish immigrants to America left stagnant and predominantly Jewish environments in the hopes of acquiring the rights of access and fluid modes of existence that they associated with life in a modernizing, pluralistic, and urban milieu. Many of them subscribed to "'grand narratives' of emancipation and enlightenment" that stipulated "the rejection of religion."[3] Adjustment to America was a deliberate act that both improved and complicated the lives not only of Eastern European Jews but of newcomers from all over the world who attempted to bring their religious and ethnic traditions with them. No single strain of Jewish American literature could compare, in terms of its influence upon and congruence with the wider developing patterns of American literature, to the work of the first- and second-generation immigrants who wrote about their arrival experiences. Their very alienation, as Sidra DeKoven Ezrahi writes, laid the groundwork for the "democratization of individualism" and "the negotiation between self and society" that shaped American literature for decades to follow.[4]

Invented, proliferated, and perfected as the nation's trend toward urbanization and industrialization reached its peak, the immigrant story has played an instrumental role in the development of the modern American character, up to and including the work of contemporary writers such as Edwidge Danticat, Chang-Rae Lee, and Junot Diaz. As they echo this long established and still vibrant interest in cultural adjustment and assimilation, even while fashioning characters who are leaving the United States behind, Papernick and Miller mark their convergence with the wider patterns of American letters. On the other hand, as they depart from it in order to highlight those same characters' troubling social isolation in Israel, they introduce a darker element that goes against the grain not only of an American but also of a canonically established Jewish American precedent. As the Canadian-Israeli author Matti Friedman has recently written, readers of contemporary Jewish American fictional works about Israel can't "miss their distance from the brash and rooted tone" of Saul Bellow's "first to knock, first admitted" *Augie March*, among other works of literature.[5]

In Papernick's and Miller's depictions, in sharp contrast with the tendencies we find in the American immigrant tradition, Jews who leave the United States for Israel at the turn of the twenty-first century do so in order to leave American pluralism behind and in a futile attempt to recover a sense of integral Jewishness that they believe will only be available to them in Israel. The millennial-era characters who choose to repatriate to Israel employ immigration somewhat naively as an attempt to simplify their condition by re-Judaizing their environment. The "return to the land," however, "has the potential to undermine the power of its own metaphors."[6] Regardless of the historically Jewish setting in which this literature is situated, and regardless of the deliberate acts by which its characters seek to differentiate themselves, both from their stay-at-home American family members and from the populations of non-Ashkenazi Jews, Arabs, and otherwise "alien" peoples who share space with them in the Middle East, the characters we encounter in Papernick's and Miller's books generally fall far short of the Jewish fulfillment that they are seeking. Their most profound moments of recognition occur in the fleeting moments when they relinquish the dream of inhabiting a transcendently Jewish territory and give up on their attempts "to shore up American lives that feel short on meaning."[7]

That these two writers even bother to write about Israel as an actual place is the result of a profound change that occurred in the relationship between Jewish American writers and Israel at the end of the millennium. Bernard Malamud spoke for many Jewish American authors in 1973 when he told a reporter for *The Harvard Crimson*, "Many people tell me I should write about Israel, but that's absurd; I don't know the country, I haven't been there enough."[8] Without the "landscapes and languages and people and day-to-day commotion of Israeli life in their eyes and ears all the time," as Alvin Rosenfeld and Moshe Davis put it, how could Jewish American writers, who were the "products of this country," be expected to write meaningfully about it?[9] Even as late as 1997, as one critic points out, Jewish American writers were still devoting more attention to the historical memory of the Holocaust than they were to the present-day reality of Israel.[10] From a late twentieth-century American standpoint, Israel was a sideshow whose existence deepened and complicated Jewish Americans' sense of their place in the world as Jews but whose quotidian realities lay beyond their typical or even occasional scope of interest. Alternatively, as Michael Kramer has recently written, for Jews whose perpetually insecure and unstable assimilation to American society has been a mode of self-actualizing empowerment, the collectively and diversely Jewish environment of Israel also represented a disconcerting "loss of power, a loss of imagination, [and] a loss of self" that was too potent for comfort.[11]

Several factors contributed to the Jewish American reluctance to engage Israeli life. One may very well have been the fact that the founding of and earliest decades of Israel's existence had coincided with the period during which Jewish Americans were reaching their pinnacle of domestic economic, social, and cultural success. Israel provided an inspiring example of renewal, courage, and gusto, but Jews were making it big in America and had no need of such things in the 1950s, 1960s, and 1970s. Taking into account "the freedom of invention" that America allowed them, even while denying them the privilege of "territorial sovereignty," Jewish American writers could only view Israel as a curious but only marginally important source of distraction.[12] The handful of Jewish American writers who had been sufficiently piqued by its existence to venture there often found it difficult to come to terms with it as a real place populated by ordinary people. Instead, Jewish American writers writing about Israel developed the habit of mythologizing it in their wonderment at its very existence.[13] Near the conclusion of his 1969 novel *Portnoy's Complaint,* as he narrates his protagonist's brief sojourn in Israel, Philip Roth describes the amazement he experiences upon his arrival at Lod Airport in Tel Aviv, where not only "*the passengers, stewardesses, ticket sellers, porters, pilots, taxi drivers are Jewish*" but even "the writing on the walls is Jewish—Jewish graffiti!"[14] While most of the action in *Operation Shylock* (1993) also takes place in Israel, Roth's experimental combination of postmodern self-reflexivity and spy novel antics voids the novel of any verisimilitude on the subject of Israeli life. As Tresa Grauer writes, in Jewish American literature, Israel "almost never appears as a real place . . . as an actual physical landscape or as an identifiable location."[15] Its remarkability, from a Jewish American standpoint at least, has warranted bemusement, symbolic play, and treatment in a minor key—but Israel as anything other than a pure (or tainted) signifier of Jewish identity has only recently entered the Jewish American literary imagination on its own terms.

Owing to the dual pattern by which Israel has been either mythologized by its sympathizers or demonized by its detractors, contemporary Jewish American writers like Jon Papernick and Risa Miller have faced an increasingly difficult task when they have chosen to address its existence in their works.[16] One of their primary tasks has been to humanize the place and its inhabitants—to depict its topography and its architecture, its slang and its foodways. By necessity, they have, to borrow Sidra DeKoven Ezrahi's phrase, sought to turn "dreamscapes into landscapes."[17] In a sense, such work implicates them in trying to undo the work not merely of decades of Jewish American representations of Israel but of centuries of Jewish (and non-Jewish) mythologizing of "the Holy Land."[18] In order to write meaningfully about Israel, they have had at once to desacralize and rehistoricize its hallowed topography. They have had to people its ancient spaces with disconcertingly modern, migratory, and shockingly diverse populations not only of European Jews on kibbutzim and Middle Eastern Arabs in olive-growing villages but also of dark-skinned Yemenites speaking on cellphones, African American Hebrews inhabiting desert compounds, and Filipino nurses patrolling hospital wards. These more grounded, even realistic, renderings of Israeli places and people fall far short of transcending the "drastically bifurcated" view of Israel that inheres in the Jewish American perspective.[19] Nonetheless, their frank attention to the "diverse, conflicted, character of Israeli culture and society" achieves a breakthrough that has been thus far absent from Jewish American literature on the subject of Israel.[20] These writers have succeeded in writing about Israel because, in large part through their attention to its cultural landscapes and the difficulties they have faced in adjusting to them, they have challenged the mythological views that have so consistently shaped its reputation among Jewish Americans. In doing so, they have also highlighted the exact sorts of complexities that it shares in common with their country of origin.

LEAVE-TAKING AND HOMECOMING: THE INFLUENCE OF THE IMMIGRANT TRADITION

First- and second-generation Jewish American immigrant fiction achieved a similar breakthrough. In anticipation of their arrival in the New World, many Eastern European Jews had at first mythologized it beyond recognition. Enthralled and occasionally misled by a "goldene medina" mentality that promised not only freedom from religious and ethnic persecution but the attainment of great material wealth and opportunity, Jewish immigrants to New York's Lower East Side and other American locations generally experienced disappointment before they found success. Only a gradual or sudden reckoning with the complexities of American life could disabuse them of their illusions about their collective future and, in turn, infuse the works of these early twentieth-century writers with the energetic force that it would take to overcome the power of mythology. Inspired by their exposures to literature by non-Jews and acting upon their burgeoning interest in formal experimentalism, writers like Cahan, Yezierska, and Henry Roth managed to describe a Jewish encounter with America that defied expectations and stereotypes. As writers, they labored to dismantle mutually reinforcing mythologies of American glitter and Jewish stagnancy and instead depict the New World as a complex environment whose most well-adjusted citizens prospered by upholding tradition in the midst of change. Their work cast a long shadow. In the latter decades of the same century, immigrant writers whose families originated in such disparate places as the Caribbean, the Indian subcontinent, and China began to produce fiction that also challenged mythologies of origin and negated expectations of complete assimilation. Their work described an expansive, if frequently hostile or indifferent, urban America whose streets and neighborhoods were no single group's rightful property.

Anzia Yezierska's *Breadgivers* (1925) told the story of a young woman whose journey from Eastern Europe to America and early life in the Lower East Side ghetto nearly convinced her of the incommensurability of traditional Judaism and modern America. After a period spent in grudging servitude to her maniacal father, Sara Smolensky manages to gain a foothold in the New World through entry to a teachers' college outside New York City. Her description of the day of her departure cribs the language of American mythology: "I felt like Columbus starting out for the other end of the earth . . . like the Pilgrim fathers who had left their homeland and all of their kin behind them and trailed out in search of the New World."[21] Tempted as she is to abandon the repressive religiosity, patriarchal regimentation, and clannishness of her father's traditionally Jewish outlook, however, Yezierska's narrator learns that she cannot honestly face her American future without acknowledging and straining to maintain a vital connection to her past. Several decades subsequent to the early twentieth-century heyday of Jewish American immigrant fiction, writers from an ever-widening array of cultural backgrounds have continued to build on its achievements. Refusing their final allegiance either to tradition-bound places of origin or to an American multiplicity that vanquishes all traces of those allegiances, the authors of works such as Edwidge Danticat's *Breath, Eyes, Memory* (1994) have balanced the pull of the past with the enticements of the present. In Danticat's coming-of-age novel, a young Haitian-born immigrant arrives in New York and reflects, literally, on how far she has come in twenty-four hours. She describes what she sees as she looks in the mirror: "New eyes seemed to be looking back at me. A new face altogether. Someone who had aged in one day, as though she had been through a time machine, rather than an airplane. Welcome to New York, this face seemed to be saying. Accept your new life. I greeted the challenge, like one greets a new day. As my mother's daughter and Tante Atie's child."[22] For many modern immigrants, an airplane is, in fact, a time machine. That being said, the new life that Danticat's narrator begins in an American city does not stipulate the abandonment of her roots. If anything, she is better equipped to face the challenge of the future with the help and inspiration of her foremothers. For that matter, access to airplane travel also allows for a proximity that helps negate the distance between Haiti and the United States. Danticat's protagonist maintains her intergenerational family connections in spite of the geographical space that separates her from her place of origin. She reduces the determinative power of mythology to shape her readers' understanding of both locales.

Millennial-era fiction on Jewish American immigrants to Israel challenges the mythological constructs that have shaped its characters' repudiations of America, but it also concentrates on their disappointing encounters with the Land of Israel. The problem with these would-be Israelis of American origin, at least as writers like Papernick and Miller have so incisively depicted them, is that they no longer have the capacity to be at home anywhere because, to them, the entire world has become an alienating extension of America. Their problems are not external but specific to their individual condition of anomie. By virtue of their characters' self-imposed exile, mythologies of place vacate all possibility of their achieving contentment anywhere. Despite the fact that they "feel at home in America," however, they have also come to believe that America is no longer "[their] homeland" because it isn't sufficiently Jewish for them.[23] Their flight to Israel, as Naomi Sokoloff writes, "signifies [their] impatience with self-centered values, exaggerated individualism, assimilation, sexual indulgence, and the failures of political liberalism."[24] Their arrival in Israel, though they expected it to alleviate their susceptibility to these sorts of corruptions, only renews their despair. Ironically, given the fact that these characters originate in America, Israel proves to be "too heterogeneous to be home" for them.[25]

Instead of adhering to the convention of Promised Land projection, both writers seek to invest the Land of Israel with a full range of possible meanings, ranging from the numbingly mundane to the eerily transcendent. Their ability to do so has been a function of two primary tendencies in their work, both of which operate according to a dynamics of comparison and both of which result at least indirectly from their North American affiliations and perspectives. The first of these patterns is perhaps the more obvious one: while both Papernick and Miller attempt to render realistic descriptions of Israeli cultural geography, they are both deliberate in their consistent representations of its points of convergence with and divergence from American cultural geography. Both Papernick's title story and Miller's novel deploy and emphasize the "wild West Bank" theme from beginning to end. Their doing so highlights more than mere wordplay. It calls necessary attention to the larger frame of reference according to which Israel, for all its Jewish eccentricity and Middle Eastern alien-ness, has imbibed what Jerold Auerbach refers to as "the corrosive moral relativism that has infused American culture."[26] In addition, as both authors feature American-born protagonists settling or sojourning in Israel, they refer consistently back to the places from which these characters originate, often through flashbacks whose denouement complicates (and clarifies) action in the present. Debby, a Kentucky-bred convert who lives in Miller's Heavenly Heights, sees, experiences, and reflects upon her life in her East Jerusalem compound through the lens of the formative years during which she spent "nine months a year" sitting on a porch glider, "thigh to thigh" with her granny under the shadow of Pinnacle Mountain.[27] Kravetz, the main character in Papernick's story "Lucky Eighteen," infuses his life in Israel with the searching and intoxicated spirit of the years he spent haunting punk rock clubs in Lower Manhattan.

The second motif by which Papernick and Miller approach the task of demythologizing Israel takes shape as they apply an insight that has perhaps been most effectively articulated by the anthropologist Jonathan Boyarin. In a 1996 essay, Boyarin points to the contrast that exists in the popular imagination between the monumental and "most famous Jewish ruins" of the Western Wall and Masada and the naturalized ruins of more recently destroyed Arab communities "which easily blend into the landscape."[28] American writers, whose geography bears a hundred thousand hidden and not-so-hidden remnants of a dispossessed native population, cannot help but be familiar with such a concept, at least unconsciously. To monumentalize a landscape is to impose abstractions over it that, ironically, consign the people who identify with its ancient history to the status of modern interlopers. To naturalize a landscape, on the other hand, is to erase or demean the historical significance of its most accessible features and to doom its indigenous population to a form of psychic extinction. Both Papernick and Miller avoid such a result by virtue of their attention to the built environments and cultural landscapes that mark Israel and Palestine as modern entities populated by modern peoples. Their settings eliminate symbolic distinctions between Jewish and Arab experiences by monumentalizing action in the present and naturalizing action in the past. When Papernick's Eli Israel murders a young Palestinian boy and carries his body to the trunk of his car, he looks up to see "black smoke" rising skyward from the place "where the local Arabs burned garbage."[29] For all of Eli's efforts to conceal his deed from others, the sky itself reminds readers that his violent act replicates and perverts the legacy of Abraham's near-sacrifice of Isaac. Near the conclusion of *Welcome to Heavenly Heights*, as several of the novel's main characters are visiting the Jewish sites of Hebron, the passage of "a fat Arab woman balancing a covered basket on her head and a barefoot toddler mouthing an open can of Coca-Cola"[30] hints powerfully that the holiest of shrines cannot be abstracted from the modern contexts in which we encounter them.

"This Is Your Home?": Americanizing the Land of Israel

When Jon Papernick's short story collection and Risa Miller's novel were published in 2002 and 2003, both the United States and Israel had just entered a particularly embattled phase in their collective modern history. Though some sort of strategic alliance between the two nations extended several decades into the past, it was the events of the early 2000s that suggested a deeper, even existential, affinity between them. In the immediate aftermath of the Al Qaeda attacks on New York City and Washington, DC, American intelligence cooperation with Israel became more frequent. American police departments eager to protect against further terrorist attacks hired Israeli security experts and consulted with Israeli firms.[31] Despite many attempts on the part of Bush administration officials and other representatives of the United States government and State Department to argue that Muslims or Arabs were not America's foe in the global war on terror, the "common enemy," such as it was, was comprised entirely of Arab Muslims. For the first time in their mutual history, in other words, Israel and the United States were united by the perception that they faced a common foe whose goal it was to destroy both of them. Whatever grounding that perception may have had in the facts of the case, and whatever political persuasion one adhered to, the points of convergence could not be ignored. Whether Israel and the United States stood firm as the world's most solid bastions of civilized resistance to "Islamofacism" or whether Israel was a malicious pawn of predatory Euro-American colonialism, the ties that bound them to one another within the American imagination solidified in the aftermath of the 9/11 attacks.

Papernick's short story collection may or may not have been directly inspired by these political circumstances, but its contents reflect its author's interest in exploring the two cultures' mutual habit of mythologizing their landscapes. As American security experts began to speak about protecting "the homeland" and the Sharon administration announced its policy of asserting Israel's "facts on the ground," the land itself took on a new set of determinative meanings. When Papernick's Eli Haller first arrives in Israel, a refugee from a ruined marriage and a tanking career in television production, the narrator tells us that his friend Zev refers to their new home as "the wild, wild West Bank." Immediately afterward, readers learn that the two men first met while attending "a John Lennon memorial at Strawberry Fields in Central Park."[32] Both of these American reference points are quintessentially mythical in their makeup but in contradictory ways. If the open space of the Wild West is strongly suggestive of violence, lawlessness, and robust individualism, Strawberry Fields would have to be its antithesis. Named after the 1980 assassination of John Lennon, the two-and-a-half-acre section of Central Park has come to represent the communally minded and nonviolence-aspiring legacy of the counterculture. Insofar as they represent diametrically opposing facets of American spatial history, Papernick's use of these two place references is indicative of his broader interest in highlighting his Jewish American characters' inability to adjust properly to their adoptive geography. Should Jewish American life in Israel postulate a showdown or a love-in? The disturbing outcome of "The Ascent of Eli Israel," in which Eli shoots and kills a young Palestinian boy who has been throwing rocks at his car, would suggest that the OK Corral prevails over the Human Be-In, but the dilemma itself originates in Eli's tendency to impose meaning over places without coming to terms with the complex experiences that shape human geography in the first place.

Zev, whose aliyah precedes Eli's and whose purported acclimation to Israeli life is already complete when Eli arrives there, plays the part of the would-be mentor. In that capacity, he does not hesitate to emphasize the possibilities for mayhem and gun-fighting. After introducing his old friend to a rabbi who justifies his own militant Jewish fervor by saying, "I don't want to be a fascist, but I have no choice," Zev tells Eli that he must adopt a new mind-set if he is to survive in "the Holy Land." "If you want to be secular, go to America," he tells the newcomer, even as his admonitions to proper action in Israel borrow almost exclusively from American precedent in order to explain life in the Middle East.[33] When the two men go off into the Hebron hills so that Zev can instruct Eli on how to fire an automatic weapon, Zev is firm in his counsel. "You really need something with a cartridge out here," he says. "This is the OK Corral, man. Injun country."[34] Only the Israeli soldiers whose charge it is to guard the safety of these aspiring Jewish American frontiersmen speak out against their brash behavior. "Tell me," demands one tall IDF (Israel Defense Forces) soldier, "why is it that all of the scum of the world comes to Israel?" Suggesting that Zev and Eli return to their homes in "Brooklyn or Miami," he announces the facts of the case: "You come to Israel because you are a Jew and you act like a maniac."[35]

Eli's newfound freedom combines biblical and Wild Western precedent. Like a cross between John the Baptist and Jim Bridger, he subsists on "olives, almonds, figs, sage, carob, mint leaves [and] anything" he can get his hands on "out there in the wilderness."[36] Only the intercession of official state authority—the khaki cavalry of the IDF—prevents him from living out his dream of frontier freedom. Like a mountain man of yore, Eli associates his repatriation to Israel with the simplification of his life and the elimination of all the corrupting complexities that he wishes to put behind him. Several elements within the story offset its main characters' facile cowboys versus Indians mentality, however, and highlight their failure to understand and appreciate Israel's multiplicity and modernity. Papernick's descriptions of the Israeli soldiers whose patrols prevent Eli from leading the freewheeling life of a wandering Judean shepherd emphasize the cultural diversity of Israeli society and also call our attention to the failures of the Jewish American imagination to comprehend that diversity and its broader significance. At one point in the story, Eli bristles at his treatment at the hands of "a short Russian soldier with a bullet-shaped head in a red beret."[37] At an earlier point in the narrative, when Eli first takes to the hills, "a dark, Sephardi-looking soldier" warns him that it isn't safe for him to wander in one particular area because it is too close—"paralyzed," as the Sephardi soldier puts it—to an IDF firing range. Because he doesn't see "any Arabs" in the vicinity, Eli assumes that he is safe from all possible harm. Informed by an American popular culture and its underlying racialist ideologies, the only threat he is capable of anticipating is the one posed by the Enemy Other. He refuses to leave and makes a fool of himself in the process. When the soldier good-humoredly tries to lure him away from his rocky pastures with the promise of sex with the girls (or boys) on his IDF base, Eli asks, "What about my sheep?" "You like fuck sheep?" the Sephardi soldier asks in the spirit of bemused and ironic tolerance. "Okay, sheep okay." In the face of Eli's zealotry, Israel itself seems to be proffering "a grimace, a scowl, [and] a timeless shrug."[38]

Eli is so fully consumed by ideas about the significance of returning to "the Holy Land" that he lacks an awareness of where he actually is and who actually lives there. Ignoring the facts on the ground, Eli assures the dark soldier that he has no intention of repairing to the army base or any other place he is told to go. "The land will take care of us," he says, only weeks away from having left New York City for Judea. "I can go wherever I want," Eli tells the soldier. "I'm a Jew on Jewish land."[39] The problem with this mentality is that it revolves around the fiction that there can be such a thing as purely "Jewish" land where the rules that apply to human interaction in the modern world can be suspended. Israel may well be the Jewish homeland, or one of several Jewish homelands, but that doesn't mean that those who dwell on its land are not subject to the same sorts of contingencies and compromises that govern life everywhere else in the world. Zev, who proves to be a frequent dispenser of bad advice, assures Eli that "there are two laws in the wild West Bank: one for us and one for the Arabs."[40] This may be superficially true and may even guide the actions of the Israeli soldiers who, despite their annoyance at the Jewish American zealots who make their lives more difficult, still protect them from harm at the hands of Arabs. For Jews and Arabs alike, however, the underlying feeling on the "wild West Bank" is one of desolation and hostility. Despite their proximity to so many Jewish holy places and the freedom, or impunity, with which they heedlessly travel from one shrine or compound to the next, the story's two main characters are perpetually strangers to their surroundings. By the end of the story, their determination to act in the face of their obliviousness turns one of them into a murderer.

For better or worse, both characters' initial impulse to immigrate to Israel was inspired, at least initially, by the better angels of their Jewish American nature. Children of privilege whose companionship and idealism dated back to their first meeting in the peaceful, harmonious, and pleasantly buzzed atmosphere of a John Lennon memorial, their countercultural proclivities quickly led them both down the path of self-indulgent and self-destructive substance abuse. For his part, the machine-gun-toting Zev confesses to Eli that his reason for having come to Israel in the first place was his eagerness to be in Jerusalem, the "City of Peace." "I was into peace," Zev explains, so "I just got on a plane one day with my rucksack." However enthusiastically he may have wished, in Lennon's words, to "imagine there's no countries . . . and no religion too," the Land of Israel was hardly the place to indulge such fantasies. As Zev puts it, "You can't be into peace here": "People look at you like they want to put you away, they say, 'what do you mean, "peace"'? Reality poisons you, you just look around and everywhere there is violence and hatred and brutality. On the buses, on the street, people will kill you if you take their parking spot. Forget about the Arabs, there's nowhere else in the world where Jews are hated so much by other Jews."[41] In America, at least, Jews can imagine themselves to be outsiders and, on that basis, find common cause with not only one another but also seekers of peace worldwide. On the Wild West Bank, by contrast, such countercultural delusions are quickly and cruelly overruled. In a perverse counterpoint to their earlier communion at the John Lennon memorial, Zev and Eli try to console themselves by visiting the shrine dedicated to the memory of Baruch Goldstein, the American-born doctor who massacred twenty-nine Palestinians at the Cave of the Patriarchs in 1994. As a preliminary act to Eli's killing of the Palestinian rock-thrower, the prayer they intone there serves as the logical near-conclusion to their Jewish American pilgrimage. After all, Baruch Goldstein's particular form of martyrdom (he was killed by an Arab mob after committing his massacre) was the apotheosis of the Wild West Bank mentality.

In the face of so much cynicism, only the land itself is capable of articulating anything approaching wisdom. As Eli wanders through the desert hoping to receive further messages from the same divine counsel that inspired him to "Go to the House of Israel" in the first place, the land and its creatures display a profound indifference toward him. Eli yearns to view the land as a silent collection point for knowledge and understanding, but he fails to recognize that he is woefully incapable of reading its meanings. In a further echo of American precedent, his communion with the natural world mimics the one described by Emerson, Thoreau, Whitman, and the other mid-nineteenth-century American Transcendentalists whose ideas helped inspire the 1960s counterculture. The lethally innocent and peculiarly American viewpoint that launches Zev and Eli on their problematic quest to be free Jewish wanderers on "Jewish land" originates in this mentality, which not only assigns meaning to the elements that comprise the natural world but also assumes humans' ability to deduce those meanings responsibly. In his desert wanderings, as Papernick explains in a winking allusion to Walt Whitman's poetry, Eli Haller "would hold a single blade of grass in his hands for hours and feel its texture." Like a .38-toting, *peyas*-wearing Walt Whitman, the television-producer-cum-shepherd "discovered that all the elements of the universe existed inside of everything."[42] Like the American frontiersmen who justified acts of brutality with their imperious insistence that no law other than that of nature itself could bind them, Eli equates his intuition and physical prowess with divine license. Papernick hints strongly, however, at the tragic folly inherent in such a mentality.

As he follows his sheep around, Eli is repeatedly visited by a mute wolf who becomes the receptor for his deepest doubts and most urgent questions. At first, the wolf simply mirrors Eli's own silence, quietly sitting by his side, evincing no apparent interest in threatening his sheep. As Eli ventures deeper and deeper into the wilderness, however, and as he projects more and more of his imperial self onto the land that surrounds him, things begin to change. His superimpositions of meaning take on an autoerotic quality that hearkens back to his days as a drunken, overindulged New York television producer. He now sees the desert unfurl before him "like women . . . naked and round, lounging in the sun" with "spread legs, bare breasts, and long arched necks." Once content to offer him silent, confirming accompaniment, the wolf returns to kill one of his sheep, "leaving the carcass for him to find." A less narcissistic and more subtle and attentive observer of the natural world if not of God's judgment might at this exact point decide that the sheep's death is indicative, among other things, of the habits of ordinary wolves. Habituated as he is to interpreting the world around him as a projection of his own tiny and egocentric moral universe, however, and reading himself into an imaginary Bible, Eli decides that the sheep's killing means that he must now "atone for his sins." In a slapdash and logically clumsy attempt to replicate Abraham's time on Mount Moriah, he slaughters one of the remaining sheep as personal penance for his failures as a son and a father. As he slashes the sheep's throat, he shouts, "For the master race!"[43] Like generations of previous zealots, Jewish and otherwise, Eli has attached his own moral redemption to the triumph of his tribe and the vanquishing of its presumed enemies. Like generations of previous watchers of American movies, he also knows who the good guys are and that he is one of them.

Eli's "return" to the Land of Israel is a desperate attempt to rectify personal wrongs through grandiose, delusion-fueled action that originates in his larger-than-life heroic American fantasies as well as his certainty concerning his own greatness and innocence. After Zev arranges for him to meet his *bashert*, or chosen wife, he approaches Jerusalem "as if he [is] two thousand years old . . . [and] prepared to bring the Messiah at last to Israel and the Jewish people." When a group of Palestinian "urchins" throws rocks at his car and smashes his windshield, he becomes an avenging prophet. He reaches into the glovebox for his .38 and empties its bullets into the one he can still hit, who is riding away from him on a donkey. As he picks up the dead boy's body and carries it to the trunk of his car, he registers its weight as similar to that of the boy he abandoned in New York. While the parallel between his own son and the Arab boy isn't lost on him, he is entirely untroubled by it. Having outdone Abraham himself by sacrificing two boys instead of none, he dons his mirrored shades, throws his pistol back in the glovebox, and guns the engine hard enough to extract himself from the ditch in which he is parked. By now, the pirate radio station on his car radio is "blaring" Elvis Presley's rendition of "Blue Moon of Kentucky," whose lyrics not only resonate with Eli's state of only mildly qualified regret but whose meaning in this context are also strongly suggestive of his hubris. In the song, a sad lover forgivingly acknowledges the Kentucky moon's right to "keep on shining" on the one that "proved untrue" to him. With regard to the dead Arab boy, Eli, too, is in a forgiving mood—toward himself. "These things happen on the road to redemption," he thinks to himself, "but God forgives you for what you do."[44] It's all good, he seems to be saying. As long as Jews like him can prevail on the Wild West Bank, all will be right with the world.

Papernick's invocation of Kentucky's legacy in connection with Eli's act of violence is no less appropriate to his interest in frontier spaces. At the time of the United States' birth, after all, Kentucky was the quintessential frontier locale. Popularly believed to connote the "land of tomorrow" (in the language of the Iroquois), the area west of the Cumberland Gap drew settlers in large numbers after Daniel Boone's famous crossing of the Appalachians. Known for its long history of bloodshed as well as for its promising pastures of "blue grass," Kentucky's place in early American history mirrors that of the West Bank territories in the years since Israel's founding in 1948. Papernick's interest in exploring Jewish American expansion into and through Greater Israel is well-served by his allusion to the commonwealth that, at its founding in 1792, was widely perceived to be the main proving ground for the territorial expansion of the American empire. By common reputation, it was a place where people expected to make up their own rules.

Having once been the quintessentially American frontier environment, the Bluegrass State serves as an even more central reference point in Miller's *Welcome to Heavenly Heights*. Like the Wild West Bank, it is more of a dreamland and an abstraction than a real place. As a group of English-speaking women socializes in the *succah* that she has set up on her balcony out of three canvas sheets and "a hippie bedspread," Debra points to a pinpoint of refracted sunlight on the tabletop that she refers to as "ratbane blue." It is a color that none of her friends have heard of before, but as she explains to them, "it's the color of the flowers and the color of the sky" where she grew up in Kentucky as the daughter of a hillbilly woman and a visiting Jewish botanist who worked for the U.S. Forest Service.[45] Whatever its proper name might be, her friend Tova believes that the blue light is also unique to Judea. As Israeli military helicopters hover above their apartment complex, the women of Heavenly Heights prove to be continually unable to retain the vestiges of their American existence in a Middle Eastern war zone. They also fall short of being able to acclimate to their new home, and in the face of so many shaping memories and determinative myths, the ratbane blue of the sky proves to be nothing more than a nice idea whose qualities can never charm these characters' actual lives. It is the unattainable sky, after all, as opposed to the actual ground upon which they stand. *Welcome to Heavenly Heights* is a novel about what it means to be homeless in the exact place that is supposed to be one's home.

As a Kentucky-bred adoptive Orthodox Jew lacking any kinship ties anywhere in the world, Debra is the book's only fitting candidate for a new life on an arid and physically unwelcoming Jewish settlement. Never having experienced any other specifically Jewish geography before making aliyah, she is not drawn, as so many of the novel's other characters are, into making comparisons between Jewish America and Jewish Israel. As the product of an environment whose very landscape features molded her sense of place and her sense of self, she has also learned that the experience of place is primarily an internal one. In order to feel as if one is at home anywhere, one has to know what home feels like in the first place. Debra grew up in a place where it was impossible not to feel connected to the local geography. As the child of a Jewish parent who always grew up with the sense that she was a foreigner in such an environment, on the other hand, she also knew what it felt like to be a stranger. "Only the 'traveler' who never having left his home comes home to it," Emily Budick writes, "can declare that home as his or hers." As the legatee of a tradition that "has resisted [the] tendency toward transcendentalization and allegorization of place," but as a person who also grew up in an environment in which place also played an outsized role in shaping people's sense of their cultural identity, Debra is particularly adept at understanding how and why geography matters, or ought to matter, to Jews especially.[46]

When Debra was growing up, she heard people talking about how "blood flows thick." It made her "picture how the rain swelled Lower Back Creek and the water rushed through. The water left sediment, took sediment as it went, leaving and taking, working both ways until the water and the sediment altered each other. Nowadays [she said,] I imagine a roving Jewish soul, sailing about in the Upper World, looking for a place to come back in, reassert itself. It was all logical because of my blood. I had this Jewish soul placed in a backwoods girl."[47] Among the several American-born women of Heavenly Heights, Debra has the longest tenure of residency and possesses the most practical knowledge about how to live in Israel. Nonetheless, when she reflects upon her immediate surroundings during the *succah* gathering with her suburban-born friends, she cannot help but conjure a reference to the Kentucky sky. When those same friends want to know how a person who grew up at the foot of a landscape feature named Pinnacle Mountain could possibly be Jewish, she tells them about the mountain creek that flowed past the house where she and several generations worth of her ancestors were raised. As a character, Debra is both highly sensitive to the importance of her surrounding physical surroundings and also fully capable of being exiled from them. Debra's atypical geographical origin allows Miller to explore the implications of place within the context of current-day Jewish American geography. From the Jewish American perspective, place-making evokes homelike but also exilic feelings.

Whether Debra possesses a Jewish soul or not, she is the daughter of a botanist and a person who defines her relationship to the world through her references to one of its herbaceous products. Early in the novel, she hearkens back to the hours she spent on the porch with her grandmother, picking pits out of citrons. That act in itself was indicative of how a Jewish soul could not only arrive in the American backwoods but also attempt, at least, to take root there. While the citron[48] is not native to Kentucky, it is able to grow "in the kitchen between the stove and the wall." The citron plant had been brought as a gift to his wife's family by Debra's now long-departed father, and, as Debra herself experiences it, "was the only concrete thing she grasped of her father, besides her very self." The citron's configuration is unique. As the narrator points out, its outside wasn't the same as its inside: "The heaven smell and the thick yellow skin could fool you." On the outside, Debra, who had been raised by a grandmother who knew nothing about Judaism, was as pure a product of Appalachia as might be found anywhere. She was well-versed in its traditions, devoted to her kin, and knowledgeable about its flora and fauna. On the inside, on the other hand, where the "essence" of a citron or a Jewish soul could be found, lay a more mysterious self that was less easily demonstrable and, perhaps, less attractive or at least understandable and accessible to the outside world. For her part, Debra is well used not only to appearing to be one sort of person while embodying another but also to feeling out of place wherever she goes. Because she requires soil in which to take root but has also learned to live as "a bird in flight,"[49] she embodies the Jewish American geographical dilemma.

"An Ordinary Knob of a Hill": De-sanctifying the Promised Land

In the years between the Oslo Peace Accord of the early 1990s and the Second Intifada of the early 2000s, when the prospect of a Palestinian state seemed first imminent and then doomed to oblivion, the landscapes that comprise Israel and especially the occupied territories came under new and heightened scrutiny. Multiple parties injected new energy into debates on matters such as settlement growth, access to holy sites, rights of return, and national security. Every one of the hills, valleys, ancient cities, and newly established enclaves that dotted the landscape of Judea and Samaria was in contention. While the task of the officials and combatants was to lay claims and assert authority over particular parcels of land, honest literary treatment of the situation demanded the opposite approach. While an unrelenting attachment to (or, for that matter, a calculated willingness to relinquish) land drove policy, the job of writers like Papernick and Miller was to question the entire notion of sovereignty and homeland. Biblical and Koranic precedent, among other factors, instigated intransigence and a sense of eternal entitlement to a land that, in and of itself, resisted such facile encompassment.

While both of their books are deeply invested in exploring the meaning of place, Papernick's and Miller's work reverses the typical pattern according to which the Land of Israel has been imagined by Jewish American writers. They reduce its mythological associations. They emphasize its contiguity with the rest of the world, especially including the intensively built environments of the contemporary United States. Resisting the temptation to be swept up by what Jonathan Boyarin refers to as "the allegorical relationship between geography and memory," Papernick and Miller deliver counterintuitive readings of Israel's landscape by depriving both the ancient and the modern of their previously fixed transcendent associations. They ignore the significance of ruins and refuse to exult over the postmodernity of the contemporary built environment. On occasion, the Israel they describe is a thrilling place to be. More often it proves to be a disappointing and exasperatingly ordinary environment whose physical features highlight and mirror the troubled but hardly heroic lives of their protagonists. In Papernick's short story collection, the storied streets of Jerusalem form a typically sad backdrop for characters who have retreated there in the desperate hope of instilling meaning and purpose in their lives. Physical space plays an almost ironic role in his fiction, as if its primary purpose is to mock or at least deflate the projective impositions of human beings.

"Lucky Eighteen," the final story in Papernick's 2002 collection, depicts a pair of Jewish American misfits seeking an elusive spiritual fulfillment in the Holy Land. Like Eli and Zev, the two young men in the story are pals whose growing up, such as it was, occurred in New York City and consisted in large part of their mutual participation in antisocial behaviors. Stuart Kravetz and Shawn Silver have known one another, as Papernick explains, since "second grade in Hebrew school when Shawn dropped his pen so he could catch a peek up Miss Mikhalabani's skirt and was smacked on the head with a ruler." As is the case in "The Ascent of Eli Israel," one of the characters arrives in Israel first and purports to usher the other one into its maelstrom of cacophonous hyperactivity. Kravetz is the would-be Virgil. He has been sent to Israel by his parents, who are worried that his playing in a punk band called "Bitefinger Baby," whose drummer has just stabbed someone, is about to get him in trouble. The parents are under no illusions that their son will be "making the desert bloom," let alone helping build "a light unto all nations." Shawn Silver joins him in hopes of reliving some of the pair's earlier adventures, which included a "wild summer" of partying and traveling the length of Israel after their senior year of high school.[50] The sojourn in Israel epitomizes the scenario that Naomi Sokoloff describes, according to which "Israel . . . become[s] a haven for mixed-up young Americans."[51] Instead of redeeming them, of course, the experience intensifies not only their despair but their collective descent into bitterness, emotional deadness, and socially destructive behavior. Papernick's unsentimental depiction of a perpetually darkened, physically spare, and overcast Jerusalem landscape shapes his readers' experience throughout the story.

From the characters' initial emergence from the "subterranean gloom of Elijah's Cup" at the story's outset to its disturbing conclusion, in which Shawn brazenly photographs and sexualizes the severed corpse of a female victim among the debris of an exploded bus (Number Eighteen), Jerusalem comes across as a bleak and blighted city. Its "slick and luminous streets" play host to a motley crowd of petty, self-absorbed, and singularly unholy individuals of all nationalities and religious persuasions, including "barefoot English travelers, blond Swedish tourists, wayward rabbinical students, wild-eyed mystics, mustached Palestinian laborers, broad-shouldered U.N. troopers, [and] Russian whores."[52] While both Stuart and Shawn appear to have gone there in search of some mixture of motivation and excitement, the place itself yields little of the first and an overwhelming and bewildering quantity of the second. The juxtaposition of the characters' already considerable personal deficiencies against the backdrop of what Papernick refers to, in an allusion to Mark Twain's nineteenth-century depiction of it, as "the knobbiest town in the world" delivers a heavy dose of despair. It isn't just that Jerusalem proves to be a singularly troubled environment. The problem that Papernick's depiction highlights is that it is a troubled environment that continually tempts people with an empty promise of transcendence. As Stuart Kravetz looks out at it from the balcony of his apartment building, he cradles a copy of poems by Yehuda Amichai, the famed Israeli poet who also struggled to come to terms with what it meant to inhabit such a historically and religiously fraught landscape. The surrounding view corroborates the exact sentiments of Amichai's poetry, whose direct address Papernick quotes directly: "You are beautiful, like prophecies / And sad, like those which come true."

In contemplation of his own sad and failed romance with a young woman he left behind in New York City, Stuart sees the "crooked and countless domes" that mark the skyline of "a city where Melville had written in disgust about the Crusader church being a sickening cheat where all is glitter and nothing is gold." The narrator's reference to two classic nineteenth-century American authors in the immediate aftermath of his pointed citation of Amichai's poetry is not an arbitrary allusive touch. It is suggestive of his interest in exploring the patterns according to which Jerusalem has inspired, and often disappointed, the imaginations of writers in both the Jewish and American literary canons. With their mutual emphasis on the notion of a promised land, writers whose roots lie in both traditions cannot help but be tempted to go in search of it. For his part, the former punk rocker Stuart Kravetz fancies himself a "literary exile," even in the land whose restoration to the Jewish sovereignty was supposed to put an end to two millennia of exile. Ironically, as he looks out from his apartment balcony "toward the golden Dome of the Rock"—the very site of the ancient destroyed temple toward which Jews have looked longingly in prayer for centuries—he feels the very opposite of what a person in his situation should feel. "The winding streets and alleys" of Jerusalem offer Kravetz nothing but temporary diversion and momentary intrigue.[53] Papernick enacts the exact reversal to which Jonathan Boyarin alludes in his essay on ruins. He associates the city's most modern features with its ancient legacy of violence. He superimposes a postmodern chaos over its biblical-era shrines.

Neither of the two extremes of Israeli culture that are on display in Jerusalem stand a chance of rectifying Kravetz's despair. Elijah's Cup, the bar that the two young men frequent throughout the story, is a noisy and squalid den whose exit is defiled by "splashes of beer and vomit" and whose atmosphere is downright apocalyptic, as befitting its biblical name. On Sylvester (New Year's) Eve, a melee breaks out when a concentration camp survivor attempts to tattoo a German visitor's arm with the words "Never Forget" while the crowd laughs at the spectacle. The protagonists adjourn to another bar, The Shelter, which Papernick describes as being "decorated like a fallout shelter" and full of people dancing to the Ramones' "I Wanna Be Sedated." The dancefloor is a tangle of "swaying bodies, where soldiers' M-16s slapped against their backs" and "girls wearing gas masks and bikinis" thump around.[54] Earlier in the story, when Shawn introduces Stuart to a lively, tall, and dark-haired young woman of "maybe . . . Yemenite or Moroccan" Jewish background, readers encounter an even more stereotypical depiction of hedonistic and nihilistic Israeli secularity. Ravit has just turned eighteen and is about to begin her service in the IDF, but her aspirations lie elsewhere. "Fuck the Army . . . and fuck the crazy religious of this city . . . I'm going to Thailand next week," she says, pantomiming the act of inhaling on a joint.[55]

As for the "crazy religious," Papernick's depiction of their enclaves and influence is hardly any more uplifting than his version of the secular imprint upon the city. Thanks in large part to Shawn Silver's photographic instigations, all three of the Abrahamic religions are defiled by what goes on in Jerusalem, particularly at the city's most ancient and revered shrines. When Shawn visits the Church of the Holy Sepulcher, he convinces a young Australian woman to pose naked on the Stone of Unction while smoking a cigarette, an act which results in their both being chased out of the building by a monk "shouting 'American' and 'Fuck.'" Near the story's conclusion, Papernick describes "an old Muslim tomb" elsewhere in the city "where men trade blow jobs after dark." When he stops by the Dome of the Rock, "where the Prophet Muhamad had begun his night journey to heaven," he photographs a Swedish girl "face to the ground, dress thrown over her head, bare behind in the air."[56] In short order, he convinces two young Arab boys to sell the sacrilegious postcards he has just created out of these spectacles to passing tourists. As for the Land of Israel as the eternal focal point of Jewish existence, Shawn Silver manages to drain all meaning and value from its features as well. When the two young men visit an old bookstore near the Dome of the Rock, he flips through a book of photographs of Israel's early days whose contents, as he angrily enumerates them, suggest the bleakness of the entire Zionist enterprise:

"Man building a fucking house, street scene Tel Aviv, ugly face no shirt, ugly face sun hat, rabbi, man with gun, eyepatch, ugly, ugly, ugly." As Stuart Kravetz clings to the last vestiges of his belief in Israel's promise, his nihilistic friend utters the painful truth to him: "You are living in the land of the perennially fucked . . . a fantasy land of ghosts and fucking kooks." When two Bus Eighteens are blown up by suicide bombers within days of one another and a bystander announces that "Oslo is dead," even the romantically inclined Kravetz, surrounded as he is by so many indications of blight, can't help but agree.[57]

Where Jerusalem's darkened state extinguishes what little remains of Stuart Kravetz's fondness for Israel and belief in its future, Risa Miller's descriptions of the Jordan Valley, Mount Meron, and Hebron in *Welcome to Heavenly Heights* eliminate her characters' illusions regarding their imminent restoration to spiritual wholeness in the Holy Land. Although with considerably less dark and cynical fervor than Papernick applies to his description of Jerusalem, Miller situates her questing characters in these symbolically fraught landscapes in order to call our attention to the space that intercedes between their desire for wholeness and the disappointing, or at least neutral, truths that prevent them from achieving it. In each instance, the writer represents the surrounding landscape's ordinariness and refusal to display transcendent meaning as well as its potential for peace-shattering volatility. She highlights the sense of place, but in doing so, she empties it of any of the residual theological import that might bring her characters any closer to redemption. Places in Israel turn out to be like places in America and everywhere else in the world. As new inhabitants of these places, the novel's characters discover that their home is still shaped and defined for them by the often less-than-transformational, though occasionally harrowing, experiences they have in it.

Miller's descriptions remind us that even the most storied sites in the world are, in large part, subject to and participants in the monotonous, though painfully fleeting, passage of ordinary time. As her characters Mike and Tova lie in bed in the pension they are visiting on their family outing to Hebron, they hear "the toilet tank gurgle and the sucking noise the baby make[s] in his sleep." Noises coming from the farther distance offer still more familiarity. "Out in town," she writes, "somewhere in the direction of the Cave where, like them, the Patriarchs and Matriarchs were resting and watching, there was a siren—probably a car alarm, Mike told himself—and small explosions—probably the backfire of a truck."[58] If Mike is right, his new home in Israel is no different from his old home in Baltimore. It is a place where he will undoubtedly spend many sleepless nights thinking about things over which he has little, if any, control. If he is wrong, and the alarm and explosions are indicative of a violent future he would rather not contemplate as the father of three young children, he may decide that Baltimore is home after all. That Miller has compared the nighttime vigilance of her modern-day Jewish American characters to that of the long-dead Abraham, Sarah, Isaac, and Rebecca who were buried at Machpelah is suggestive of her interest in reducing, as opposed to magnifying, the transcendent power of the biblical landscape to change the lives of its modern-day inhabitants.

In accordance with Miller's interest in representing the Land of Israel as a place that yields a continuum of possible experiences, she narrates the trip to the Jordan Valley in such a way as to call attention to the contrast between the tranquility of its beginning and near-terror of its ending. In advance of the outbreak of summer and desperate to offer their restless children a pleasant diversion away from the isolated atmosphere of Heavenly Heights, Tova and Mike pack their minivan with supplies and leave the City of Gold behind. As the van's cassette player entertains the children with "Uncle Moishy and His Mitzvah Men," each of whose songs ends with the singer "yearning for Jerusalem," the family watches as "Jerusalem [recedes] in the rearview mirror." Everything about the adventure sounds pleasant, upbeat, and comparable in its benign innocence to a similar outing in the United States. After more than an hour's drive north, the five family members arrive at a kibbutz where a dirt road leads them to the river's shore and a kiosk where a young man named Boaz takes their money and rents them an orange and red raft. The entry point is a place "fifteen or twenty miles beneath the Banias, where the water combined with winter runoff and the natural spins and waterfalls flowed down from Mt. Hermon, the highest point in the country." Surrounded by corn- and cotton-fields "ready for the winter harvest," the family begins its river adventure in a "calm, smooth, [and] relaxing" mode that Tova associates with Sundays. The river itself provides a ride of amusement park quality, with its "bends and rocks calibrated by the Creator," as Miller puts it, to thrill the family "better than any roller coaster" might. Her resort to such a tongue-in-cheek figure reminds us once again of the strange and banal proximity that Israel forces upon its inhabitants and visitors. God may be ever-present in the land of the Bible, but if that is so, we must be not be discomfited by the fact that we can only understand and describe God by referring to Him in terms dictated to us by our seemingly petty modern-day experiences.

Likewise, tempted as Miller's characters may be to absolve God of responsibility for the disturbing and traumatic experiences that shape life and conditions in the modern world, once they have marked His presence in and impact upon the landscape history of the ancient world, He must be allowed and expected to dwell in those places forever. After taking them to within sight of the peak of Mount Hermon and the town of Kiryat Shemona, the Jordan River deposits Mike and Tova's family in a quiet spot where the "water trickle[s] and rushe[s]" and the sound "in the rest of the world [i]s turned off." Tova looks around at her contented children and imagines giving birth to several more. At that moment, the family hears several "*ka booms*" in succession, and Mike realizes that Kiryat Shemona, only "a couple of miles away," is being targeted by Hezbollah's Katyusha rockets. The family escapes mortal danger easily enough, but their peaceful

moment spent in contemplation of a long-awaited homecoming has been shattered. Once again, Miller invokes a scriptural turn of phrase to emphasize the
contiguity of day-to-day life with biblical precedent within the Land of Israel. As
Tova turns to place her body over that of her little son Avi to protect him from the
rocket-fire, she calls him "Sheffela," or "little lamb." His mother, Miller writes, had
"brought him to a slaughter."[59] When they were surrounded by the mundanity of
an American suburbia, at least, they never had to fear the wrath of Israel's God. In
fact, their lives there had been made more beautiful by the distance that separated
them from that wrath not to mention their naive longing to be closer to it.

At Mount Meron, where more than a hundred thousand observant Jews travel
annually on Lag b'Omer to visit the tomb of Shimon bar Yochai and in order to
give their three-year-old sons their first haircuts, Tova can't help but be reminded
of her American past and, at the same time, at least somewhat disappointed by
her Israeli present. On the approach to the mountain, the family encounters "a
herd of cattle and two cowboys" attempting to cross the road on their horses.
When one of the men asks his horse, "*Aht mishoogat*" ("Are you crazy?"), Mike
turns to Tova and says, "'*Mishoogat*' . . . What happened to 'Hi-ho Silver?'" The
scene resonates well with the Wild West Bank theme, but the sight of the cowboy's
tzitzit "flying back straight as the horse's tail" and his sandaled feet tells Mike and
Tova that he is "not exactly the Marlboro Man" and that they are a long way from
the familiar sights of home. Forty minutes later, Mount Meron itself appears to
them "curiously shrunken from the Meron of Tova's imagination: an ordinary
knob of a hill, green and brown." On the slopes of the mountain itself, the family
struggles through a multiplying crowd along a "blacktop sidewalk" and "through
parked cars that had installed themselves tip to tip in a rude caravan," weighed
down not only by the difficult task of transporting small children in strollers
through such chaos but also by the mundane concerns that accompany all such
ventures. Would they manage to find Rabbi Shapiro, whom Tova understands to
be a substitute figure for Mike's own father, "abandoned in Florida, six thousand
miles away"? What about the pair of scissors that Tova seems to have forgotten in
the car, the scissors that Rabbi Shapiro will need in order to cut Yoni's hair? When
the adventure is over, even though all of those concerns have been put to rest by
Mike's encounter with Shapiro and his assistant, Tova remains unsettled. All she
can think is that her little boy, like her life, has "suddenly" been transformed by
an experience, a "*cutting away* and *becoming*" into a home whose contours and
implications she will never quite understand.[60]

"Past Present Future": Perpetual Exile

The meaning of their new life is elusive. The characters who populate *Welcome
to Heavenly Heights* discover how difficult it can be to reconcile their personal
experience with their surrounding geography. To Jewish American newcomers

like Risa Miller's characters, Israel is both strange and familiar. Its landscape and its native-born residents present new arrivals with a fait accompli, and its languages challenge their abilities not only to communicate ordinary needs and ideas but also to fully understand themselves. In the aftermath of the trip to Mount Meron, for instance, Tova finds herself wondering how she will recount the experience she had there on the following day to the members of her Hebrew class. If she wants to describe to her classmates how she felt when Mike appeared out of the crowd with Rabbi Shapiro, what tense of the verb *see* would she use? More important, when the teacher asked the members of the class "*Mah hadash*, what's new?" she would have to make up her mind whether the state that she had been in was one of "becoming" or of "being."[61] From Tova's perspective, which may be similar to that of any other Jewish American who chooses to move there and adapt to its cantankerous culture and challenging landscape, Israel is a place where one must stop "being" an American and "become" an Israeli in order to fit in.

At the same time, as Jews who have already given much thought not only to Israel but also to the entire history of the Jewish people in and out of exile, the characters in both Papernick's stories and Miller's novel must also be at least somewhat adept at already "being" from Israel. To paraphrase a judgment that Irving Howe made in the 1970s, in the last several decades, Jewishness has evolved from its former status as an "experience" to its current status as an "essence."[62] Its storied, ancient landscape, though it can only be known firsthand through present-day exposure, has been a central feature of Jewish identity for millennia. This is one of the things that Mike lies awake thinking about on the night following his visit to Hebron and the Cave of Machpelah. He considers "how the Patriarch Abraham bought the cave from Efron the Hittite to bury his wife Sara. It was the first recorded real estate purchase in the world. Efron the Hittite was by some accounts smarmy, by some accounts respectful, and Abraham made a point of purchasing the Cave the field next to it in public, in front of all the Hittites. Then there was an idea that a standard of dwelling somewhere is having a burial place there. Past present future."[63] The story of this particular land has been so compelling that it never stops shaping the lives of the people who inhabit it, whoever they are and whatever relationship they may bear or believe that they bear to its central personages. *The Ascent of Eli Israel* and *Welcome to Heavenly Heights* both deliver characters and situations that call attention to the difficulties faced by people whose intense desire to be at home somewhere in the world is continually offset by the fact that the meaning of home itself can only be made palpable to them through longing. Their arrival in Israel, to borrow Sidra DeKoven Ezrahi's phrasing, "invite[s] a final epic closure that threatens the storytelling enterprise itself."[64] In both books, the longing itself is made more complex by the fact that it originates from an initial dislocation in America, of all places. Having been raised in a country that has long been the world's object of unfulfillable desire, they have gone in search of home in an even more elusive resting place.

MYSTICAL ENCOUNTERS AND ORDINARY PLACES

The Gomez Mill House is the oldest Jewish house in North America. It is sheltered in a quiet, wooded corner along the western shore of the Hudson River, just outside Newburgh, New York. Several years after I'd first read about the place, my wife, Janice, and I stumbled upon the tiny sign on route 9W that announced our nearness to it. We happened to be passing through the area on an overcast June evening during a weekend trip in the Hudson Valley. Over the years, I've developed three ways of encountering historical markers. I pass the ones that are located near my home without even registering them. When I'm traveling away from home, I usually notice historical markers only as I go whizzing past them—if I feel an occasional impulse to turn around in order to look at them, I rarely act upon it. I do pay attention, though, when I see a sign that resonates mystically with a condition of my soul. As I happened on that June evening to be in the thick of writing a book about Jewish American literature and the sense of place, the sign that pointed out the turn for the Gomez Mill House felt particularly momentous. How many such sites even exist in the United States? How likely had we been to happen upon one of them on an evening when all we were trying to do was get an inexpensive dinner on the road? We followed the directions and stopped to take a look around the house and grounds. I couldn't suppress my feeling of surprise at the ordinariness of the circumstances that had led us to such an unanticipated juncture.

As the essays in this book attempt to show, the Jewish encounter with the American landscape has both quotidian and mystical aspects. Luis Moses Gomez, a Sephardic merchant who arrived in New York in 1703, purchased the land where the house now stands in 1714 in his bid to establish himself there as a fur trader and timber merchant. Gomez conducted business downriver with New York merchants and upriver with Native Americans. He built a house that he knew would last, out of fieldstone (red brick was added later), and his sons continued on as its proprietors well past his death. In certain respects, there was nothing terribly remarkable about any of this. The modernization of Europe, the expansion of Atlantic trade networks, and the loosening of Old World religious restrictions had been under way for some time by the time the Gomezes built their house by the Hudson. Jews began settling in the Americas in the early seventeenth century, and by the early 1700s, considerably larger communities of Jewish landholders in places like Surinam as well as on several islands in the Caribbean had already been established.

Nonetheless, that a Jewish family owned and cultivated more than three thousand acres in the middle of what was at that time the great western wilderness was novel. On the assumption that these Jews had come to stay, the Gomezes' neighbors began referring to the tributary of the Hudson that flowed past their house as Jews Creek. After centuries of insecurity and itinerancy, of caution and calculation, this family felt sufficiently assured of its place in the social hierarchy to establish a fixed home in a place that few Europeans, let alone Jews, would ever set eyes on. The very idea that Jews might be not only able but also eager to settle in one place, that they would attach their fortunes and future prospects to the resources and contours of a strange land, was largely untested. It is no wonder, given such circumstances, that the place where the Gomezes came in 1714 has been singled out for special attention by historians of the Jewish American experience. The house is on the National Register of Historic Places and has been maintained as a historical site by the Gomez Foundation for Mill House since 1979.

Like many other people who came to North America from Europe during the colonial period, the Gomezes did not remain in the same place; their house passed out of Jewish hands long ago, in 1772. Their having left the place behind was of a piece with the general trend, however. The Hudson Valley, like several other regions of the northeastern interior, has witnessed great demographic shifts since migrants from the Old World first came there in the seventeenth century. Jews have not lived continuously in the Gomez Mill House, but it is just as true that people of Dutch descent no longer dominate Lower Manhattan. While Jews have been continuously invested in the inhabitation of North America, their presence and direct impact upon the landscape has often been difficult to delineate. That there are very few Gomez Mill Houses to be visited in the United States does not reflect any lack of interest on the part of Jews in being meaningfully connected to the land, however. The sense of place is a condition of the mind. In the end, it is not the places themselves but the ways in which they have been imagined and represented that shape their influences upon us and their presence in our collective imagination. Like everyone else, Jews have cultivated a relationship to the landscape of North America not just by inhabiting it but also by thinking about its meanings.

As a touchstone to the imagination, the Gomez Mill House is unique because it is one of the few identifiable physical traces we can find that speaks to this long-standing relationship. Its fieldstone and red brick solidity reifies the notion of America as a Jewish homeland. At the same time, in its relative obscurity and, for that matter, in its complete congruity with the surrounding landscape, it reminds us that while Jews have been making their presence known in America for centuries, their means of doing so have rarely been physically evident. In this book, I have tried, as Ellen Mordecai did in her 1880s recollection of Spring Farm, to give voice and shape to a different type of relationship to the land, according to which place forms its impressions as a subject and inspiration point for literature. The essays in the book represent my best attempt to explore the role that the geography of North America has played in shaping the Jewish American literary imagination. If a place like the Gomez Mill House is important in the context of a study like this one, it is because its mere physicality serves as a reminder of the place-ness of place. My unexpected encounter with it on that June evening got me thinking about the much more elusive topographical record of Jewish inhabitation that the land itself embodies. Someone has yet to write a book about that subject. Every corner of the nation bears some record or remnant of an early, if not continuous, Jewish presence, but the physical manifestations of that presence are not nearly as obvious or readable to most of us as the words of generations worth of writers. Building a house or a synagogue, or even just crossing a desert or a river, is an expressive act, but not necessarily a reflective one.

To create literature, on the other hand, is to think out loud, to speak for the sake of speaking. Each chapter of *A Hundred Acres of America* addresses a history not so much of physical encounters as of the broader cultural implications of those encounters. Whether the authors about whom I have written have been inspired (or appalled, for that matter) by the snow-capped peaks of the Rockies, the irrigated lawns of New Jersey suburbs, or the stony pastures of the Jerusalem hills, their work attempts to make meaning out of their experiences in those places and to square those experiences with their sense of what it means to be a Jewish person in America. Their approach to the subject entails extended consideration not only of their own individual relationships to places but also of pre-existing tendencies within American literature. To write about landscapes, they must not only be familiar with them firsthand but also through their prior exposure to and knowledge of the literature, or at least the contemporary mythology, of place. Few witnesses to the geography of the Far West can ever see it without conjuring their memories of Western movies. Jewish writers like Edna Ferber couldn't write about small-town Wisconsin without thinking about how other writers, particularly non-Jewish writers, had already developed a habit of writing about it. For the most part, writing about place has enabled Jewish American writers to participate in and, more often than not, challenge or at least interrogate canonically established trends within American literature. When they attend to this task, to borrow from a recent article by Adam Gopnik, they show us "how to savor American history without sentimentalizing it, and how to claim an American identity without ceasing to inquire into how strangely identities are made."[1]

In five of the six instances about which I have written in *A Hundred Acres of America*, the authors in question engage these sorts of trends and motifs from the outside. The writers' critique or elision of dominant patterns is louder than their endorsement of them. Carvalho and Benjamin rehistoricize the frontier by ignoring its traditional treatment as an arena for heroic human conduct. The Jewish colonial revivalists challenge the myth of America's rural heritage by calling attention to the nation's founding as an urban and commercial enterprise. Rather than exult in or lament the abandonment of small-town America, Leiser and Ferber remind their readers of its dynamism. Even when Jewish American writers weigh in on the troubling implications of their own post–World War II embourgeoisement, they do so without relying on preexisting formulas for doing so. Roth and Goodman don't equate exurban landscapes with the extinction of the self or the sect but with the disturbing results that follow from their exaltation and isolation. Our own age's newfound privileging of multicultural perspectives also fails, at a certain level, to resonate with Jewish writers like Rebecca Goldstein and Jonathan Safran Foer. Constrained by their troubling estrangement from the nation's most fraught and narrative-rich historical landscapes, they must situate their attempts to reconstruct a Jewish past in an imagined, impossible Eastern European landscape where the Holocaust lingers as the only meaningful legacy.

Only the final chapter of this book promulgates, or at least feints in the direction of promulgating, a dominant motif in American literature—the immigrant narrative. This is an ironic result, for two reasons. First of all, the rise of the immigrant narrative represents the one instance in which Jewish American authors, albeit of an earlier era, were among the inventors of a motif that later shaped and even evolved into a mainstream literary movement. Second, in Jonathan Papernick's and Risa Miller's fiction, the immigration in question represents the abandonment, rather than the reinvention or reinhabitation, of Jewish America. That these two Jewish American writers enact their most characteristically American gestures in the very act of describing their protagonists' repatriation to a land other than America should serve as a reminder that the literature of place and the experience of place are distinct entities. Papernick and Miller write about Israel in order to reflect on their protagonists' American identities, which were forged in relationship to North America. Moreover, that these two writers' resort to a quintessentially American device as a vehicle for facilitating their characters' removal from America suggests that the immigrant motif itself contains the seeds of its own dissolution.

In broader terms, American literature itself has encompassed its own undoing from its very founding and origin. It is by definition a literature of alienation—from old places, from bygone traditions, often from America itself. Sidra DeKoven Ezrahi addresses this subject as she tries to account for why Jews, among America's many literary constituencies, have been unable "to inscribe on the American landscape a truly deterritorialized, 'minor' literature." Because they have longed to belong, Jewish American writers have been reluctant to carve out separate spaces for themselves in the way that writers from several other minority traditions have. The arc of Jewish American literary history, Ezrahi points out, doesn't "so much articulate a subversive or revolutionary alternative to the major or dominant culture as seek a place in it."[2] Its practitioners' very eagerness to meet conventional standards, however, places them on the margins of a canon whose defining works, with notable exceptions, have highlighted the individual's rebellion against and estrangement from the collective. By and large, Jewish writers have achieved their greatest heights of critical acclaim in the instances in which they have mastered the narrative of alienation that has for so long defined the mainstream. Because their writing about place generally runs contrary to this tendency, on the other hand—because it both rejoices in an end to exile and laments the willful embrace of fragmentation that seems to define the contemporary era's relationship to place—it has often escaped widespread critical and literary historical notice. By being at odds with being at odds, it courts obscurity.

Ironically, in posing an alternative to the trends that dominate within American literature of place, geographically inspired Jewish American writing functions as a stay against fragmentation and as an appeal to unity not only among Jews but also across all manner of cultural divides. It seems in this way to constitute a fitting commentary on the one thing that has always distinguished place as a subject for literature—its existence as a topological arena that, by its very nature, connects people to one another and forces them into mutual proximity. New York has many neighborhoods and a diverse population, but only one Hudson River and only one Brooklyn Bridge. For all of our differences of opinion as to the exact location of the Midwest, its vast fields, thick woodlands, and sprawling towns remain steadfastly sure of themselves. For all of our disagreement about what it means and who it belongs to, the land itself insists on being gracefully indifferent to our worst offenses and most glorious achievements.

Like so many other historical shrines on the American landscape, the Gomez Mill House feels like an oasis of stolid tranquility and order, especially on a quiet summer evening when no one else is around. Since it is surrounded by high trees and is located in a slight hollow, it is easy to be there and forget that the highway that connects it to New York, Albany, and the rest of the world— the highway along which trucks pass noisily and shopping centers, fast food restaurants, and gas stations are posted every few hundred yards—is worlds away. Our appreciation of such places only confirms the existence of an urgent present from which we often feel the need to seek shelter. It should also remind us that while place can be a font of meaning, a source of identity, and a means to

ACKNOWLEDGMENTS

I have received more editorial help in the completion of this book than I have for any writing project I have undertaken. At each stage in its development, generous and talented people have offered critical insight, scholarly expertise, practical advice, and logistical, as well as moral, support. The book has benefitted greatly from this input, and I am grateful to my many benefactors.

No one has lent me more thorough assistance than my editor Elisabeth Maselli, whose guidance, editorial advice, and encouragement aided enormously in the book's development. I can't fully express my appreciation for her reliable, timely, and carefully considered responses to my many questions along the way. Though they will never know the extent of her many contributions to the shaping of this book, my readers are sure to derive the greatest benefits from Elisabeth's hard work and professionalism.

The members of my online writing group, Laura Leibman, Julia Lieberman, and Hilit Surowitz-Israel, all advised me in my development of the book proposal. So too did Marlie Wasserman and the two anonymous peer reviewers from Rutgers University Press who read and critiqued the first version of the proposal. I also received valuable input from the peer reviewers (also from Rutgers University Press) who read preliminary versions of the first two chapters and also reviewed the entire manuscript upon its completion. A little later in the process, two anonymous peer reviewers from the journal *American Jewish History* (which published a version of chapter 1 in its April 2018 edition) offered helpful insight toward the completion of that particular section of the book.

Once I had drafted the book's central essays, the following people aided me in revising, polishing, and cutting their length: Jules Chametzky, Marwood Larson-Harris, Lori Harrison-Kahan, Ben Railton, and Rachel Rubinstein. My wife, Janice Sorensen, offered incisive assistance with the book's introduction and preface. She has also lent her aesthetic and design insight into the conception of the book's cover. My son, Langston Hoberman, worked painstakingly on the index. In the course of doing so, he also called my attention to several errors that I missed earlier. More important, he has engaged me in several substantive conversations about the book as a whole that have done more than merely affirm its achievements. His inquiries have gotten me thinking about some of its troubling implications.

The staffs of the W. E. B. DuBois Library at UMASS Amherst, the Robert Frost Library at Amherst College, the Nelson Library at Smith College, and the Amelia Gallucci-Cirio Library at Fitchburg State University all lent me invaluable material support by supplying me with many of the primary and secondary sources that form the basis for the book.

I wish as well to acknowledge the support that I was afforded during the fall 2017 semester at Fitchburg State University in the form of a much-needed course release that enabled me to draft the book's final chapter, introduction, and conclusion. Accordingly, I wish to thank both my department chair, Lisa Gim, and Alberto Cardelle, the provost and vice president for academic affairs at Fitchburg State University, for their wholehearted support of my research and writing.

NOTES

INTRODUCTION

1. Ellen Mordecai (1790–1884) was an educator and writer. Her 1845 book, *History of a Heart*, described her conversion to Christianity. Ellen Mordecai, "Spring Farm" (unpublished typescript dictated to Annie Morel), published in 1907, American Jewish Archives, SC8428.

2. Philip Roth, "I Have Fallen in Love with American Names" (adapted from a speech given on November 20, 2002), *New Yorker*, June 5 and 12, 2017, 46–47.

3. Arnold Eisen, *The Chosen People in America: A Study in Jewish Religious Ideology* (Bloomington: Indiana University Press, 1983), 15.

4. Brooke Fredericksen, "Home Is Where the Text Is: Exile, Homecoming, and Jewish American Writing," *Studies in American Jewish Literature* 11, no. 1 (Spring 1992): 37.

5. Anna Lipphardt, Julia Brauch, and Alexandra Nocke, "Exploring Jewish Space: An Approach," in *Jewish Topographies: Visions of Space, Traditions of Place* (Aldershot: Ashgate, 2008), 1.

6. James D. Bloom, "For the Yankee Dead: Mukherjee, Roth, and the Diasporan Seizure of New England," *Studies in American Jewish Literature* 17 (1998): 43.

7. Sarah Phillips Casteel, "Landscapes: America and the Americas," in *The Cambridge History of Jewish American Literature*, ed. Hana Wirth-Nesher (New York: Cambridge University Press, 2016), 414.

8. Joseph Amato, *Rethinking Home: A Case for Writing Local History* (Berkeley: University of California Press, 2002), 4.

9. Sidra DeKoven Ezrahi, *Booking Passage: Exile and Homecoming in the Modern Jewish Imagination* (Berkeley: University of California Press, 2000), 19.

10. Benjamin Schreier, *The Impossible Jew: Identity and the Reconstruction of Jewish American Literary History* (New York: New York University Press, 2015), 8.

11. Michael Kramer, "The Wretched Refuse of Jewish American Literary History," *Studies in American Jewish Literature* 31, no. 1 (2012): 62.

12. Patricia Nelson Limerick, "Region and Reason," in *All Over the Map: Rethinking American Regions*, ed. Edward L. Ayers, Patricia Nelson Limerick, Stephen Nissenbaum, and Peter S. Onuf (Baltimore: Johns Hopkins University Press, 1996), 84.

13. Emily Bingham, *Mordecai: An Early American Family* (New York: Hill and Wang, 2003), 84.

14. Casteel, "Landscapes," 428.

CHAPTER 1 — "IN THIS VESTIBULE OF GOD'S HOLY TEMPLE"

1. Solomon Nunes Carvalho, *Incidents of Travel and Adventure in the Far West*, ed. Bertram Korn (Philadelphia: Jewish Publication Society of America, 1954), 127, 130.

2. Rachel Rubinstein, *Members of the Tribe: Native America in the Jewish Imagination* (Detroit: Wayne State University Press, 2010), 35.

3. James Fenimore Cooper, *The Last of the Mohicans* (1826) (New York: Dover, 2003), 21.

4. Richard Slotkin, *Gunfighter Nation: The Myth of the Frontier in Twentieth-Century America* (1992) (Norman: University of Oklahoma Press, 1998), 13.

5. Dalia Kandiyoti, *Migrant Sites: America, Place, and Diaspora Literatures* (Hanover, N.H.: University Press of New England, 2009), 26.

6. Israel Joseph Benjamin, *Three Years in America, 1859–1862* (originally published in Hanover in 1862), ed. Oscar Handlin (New York: Arno Press, 1975), 301.

7. Kandiyoti, *Migrant Sites*, 25, 27.

8. The classic text on this movement in American literature is Henry Nash Smith's *Virgin Land: The American West as Symbol and Myth* (Cambridge: Harvard University Press, 1950).

9. Scholarly treatments of nineteenth-century American folk heroes and legends date back to the founding of American Studies in the mid-twentieth century. Among other works, Constance Rourke's *American Humor: A Study of the National Character* (1931), Walter Blair's *Half-Horse, Half Alligator: The Growth of the Mike Fink Legend* (1960), and Carolyn Brown's *The Tall Tale in American Folklore and Literature* (1989) all offer useful insight into the use of hyperbole within the context of western literature.

10. John Livingston, "Introduction," in *Jews of the American West*, ed. Moses Rischin and John Livingston (Detroit: Wayne State University Press, 1991), 16.

11. Thomas Bangs Thorpe, "The Big Bear of Arkansas," in *The Big Bear of Arkansas and Other Tales*, ed. William T. Porter (Philadelphia: T. B. Peterson, 1843), 17.

12. Earl Pomeroy, "On Becoming a Westerner: Immigrants and Other Migrants," in *Jews of the American West*, ed. Moses Rischin and John Livingston (Detroit: Wayne State University Press, 1991), 194.

13. Pomeroy, 26.

14. Sander Gilman, "Introduction," in *Jewries at the Frontier: Accommodation, Identity, Conflict*, ed. Sander Gilman and Gilbert Shain (Urbana-Champaign: University of Illinois Press, 1999), 3.

15. Barbara Mann, *Space and Place in Jewish Studies* (New Brunswick: Rutgers University Press, 2012), 110.

16. One of the most detailed Puritan eschatological speculations regarding the Jewish origins of Native Americans can be found in Thomas Thorowgood's *Iewes in the Americas* (1650). The subject is treated in detail in Richard Cogley's "The Ancestry of American Indians: Thomas Thorowgood's *Iewes in America* (1650) and *Jews in America* (1660)," *English Literary History* 35 (Fall 2005): 304–330.

17. Moses Rischin, "The Jewish Experience in America: A View from the West," in *Jews of the American West*, ed. Moses Rischin and John Livingston (Detroit: Wayne State University Press, 1991), 32.

18. Bryan Stone, *The Chosen Folks: Jews on the Frontiers of Texas* (Austin: University of Texas Press, 2010), 12.

19. Mary Louise Pratt, *Imperial Eyes: Travel Writing and Transculturation* (New York: Routledge, 2008), 3.

20. In 2015, filmmaker Steve Rivo produced a highly acclaimed documentary entitled *Carvalho's Journey*. Focusing primarily on Carvalho's artistic career, his appointed role as the expedition's daguerreotypist, as well as his background as a product of Charleston, South Carolina's dynamic Jewish community, the filmmaker includes considerable visual footage taken at various sites in Kansas, Colorado, and Utah that Carvalho was known to have photographed. See http://carvalhosjourney.com.

21. Frémont began his career as an explorer as an army engineer in 1838 and conducted several major expeditions along the route of the Oregon Trail, across the Great Basin, and through the Sierra Nevada through the 1840s. In the early 1850s, he served briefly as a U.S. senator from California and, in 1856, was the first Republican to be nominated for the presidency. See Richard Morris, *The Encyclopedia of American History* (New York: Harper, 1953), 661–662. The trip that Carvalho's book described was Frémont's fifth (and final) expedition across the Rockies. As a prominent abolitionist in league with his father-in-law, Thomas Hart Benton, Frémont attached great importance to the fashioning of a "central" route across the continent—that is, one that would encourage the westward migration of settlers from the free states. Other statesmen, notably including Jefferson Davis, were strong advocates of a southern route.

22. Despite his apparent reluctance to broach the subject of his Jewishness in *Incidents* (interestingly, the closest he comes to doing so occurs in connection with his descriptions of animal butchery along the journey, when he can't help but convey his revulsion at the prospect of blood-drinking and game-consumption), the contours of his biography show that Carvalho was a committed Jew and an "ardent and outspoken character in the nineteenth century Jewish community." See Elizabeth Kessin Berman, "Transcendentalism and Tradition: The Art of Solomon Nunes Carvalho," *Jewish Art* 16/17 (1990/1991): 66. He was an active participant in Jewish congregations in Charleston, Philadelphia, and New York, and even lent some assistance to the burgeoning Jewish community of Los Angeles at the end of his journey to California. See also Dale Rosengarten, "Portrait of Two Painters: The Work of Theodore Sidney Moïse and Solomon Nunes Carvalho," in *By Dawn's Early Light: Jewish Contributions to American Culture from the Nation's Founding to the Civil War* (Princeton: Princeton University Press, 2016), 140.

23. M. L. Marks, *Jews among the Indians* (Chicago: Benison Books, 1992), 127.

24. Robert Shlaer, *Sights Once Seen: Daguerreotyping Frémont's Last Expedition through the Rockies* (Santa Fe: Museum of New Mexico Press, 2000), 41.

25. Rubinstein, *Members of the Tribe*, 35.

26. In 1856, John Bigelow prepared a campaign biography to accompany Frémont's bid for the presidency. Pages 432–442 of *Memoir of the Life and Public Services of John Charles Frémont* were composed of an extended excerpt from the journal upon which Carvalho based his *Incidents*.

27. Sarah Phillips Casteel, "Landscapes: America and the Americas," in *The Cambridge History of Jewish American Literature*, ed. Hana Wirth-Nesher (New York: Cambridge University Press, 2016), 428.

28. Carvalho, *Incidents of Travel*, 90.

29. Bertram Korn's introduction to the Carvalho narrative includes several reproductions of the artist's work.

30. Carvalho, *Incidents of Travel*, 90–91.

31. Emerson's famous "transparent eyeball" passage reads as follows: "Standing on the bare ground,—my head bathed by the blithe air, and uplifted into infinite space,—all mean egotism vanishes. I become a transparent eye-ball; I am nothing; I see all; the currents of the Universal Being circulate through me; I am part or particle of God." Ralph Waldo Emerson, *Nature* (1836) (Boston: James Monroe, 1849), 7; Carvalho, *Incidents of Travel*, 143–145.

32. For further discussion of Carvalho's resonance with Transcendentalism, see both Berman, "Transcendentalism and Tradition," and Rosengarten, "Portrait of Two Painters."

33. Carvalho, *Incidents of Travel*, 207–208.

34. Carvalho, 86. It is worth noting, however, that despite his apparent inexperience as an outdoorsman, Carvalho had indeed acted the part of the hero in an earlier phase of his life. Caught in a shipwreck on the return journey from Barbados to the mainland, he managed to reach the shore with a rope in hand, which he then used in order to rescue his fellow passengers and the vessel's crew members. See Rosengarten, "Portrait of Two Painters," 165.

35. Rosengarten, 165.
36. Rosengarten, 97.
37. Rosengarten, 201.
38. Rosengarten, 201.
39. Rosengarten, 300.
40. Rosengarten, 111–112.
41. Rosengarten, 115.
42. Rischin, "Jewish Experience in America," 31.
43. Rischin, 31.
44. Oscar Handlin, in Benjamin, *Three Years in America*, 5.
45. Benjamin, 41.
46. Benjamin, 130.
47. Oscar Handlin points out that Benjamin's extensive borrowings from the works of others "was one of the usual practices of the travelers of his day." Handlin, in Benjamin, *Three Years in America*, 8.
48. Benjamin, 205.
49. Benjamin, 213.
50. Benjamin, 215.
51. Benjamin, 130.
52. Benjamin, 158.
53. Benjamin, 143.
54. Benjamin, 143.
55. Rischin, "Jewish Experience in America," 32.
56. Benjamin, *Three Years in America*, 121.
57. Benjamin, 300, 301.
58. Benjamin, 298.
59. Benjamin.
60. Benjamin.
61. Benjamin, 130–131.

CHAPTER 2 — COLONIAL REVIVAL IN THE IMMIGRANT CITY

1. Isaac Markens, *The Hebrews in America: A Series of Historical Sketches* (New York: self-pub., 1888), 2.
2. Markens, 21.
3. Markens, 1, 18.
4. Deborah Dash Moore, *Urban Origins of American Judaism* (Athens: University of Georgia Press, 2014), 152.
5. Susan Reynolds Williams, *Alice Morse Earle and the Domestic History of Early America* (Amherst: University of Massachusetts Press, 2013), 88.
6. Williams, 3.
7. Dalia Kandiyoti, *Migrant Sites: America, Place, and Diaspora Literatures* (Hanover, N.H.: University Press of New England, 2009), 55.
8. Charles Daly, *The Settlement of the Jews in North America*, ed. Max Kohler (New York: Philip Cowan, 1893), vii.
9. If people of Anglo Saxon heritage had viewed themselves as the members of an ethnic group, of course, then a great many of the nation's historical societies might well have asserted the same about themselves much earlier.
10. Daly, *Settlement of the Jews*, viii.
11. Among these books, Hyman Polock Rosenbach's *Jews in Philadelphia Prior to 1800* (1883), Isaac Markens's *The Hebrews in America* (1888), Max Kohler's revision of Judge Charles Daly's *The Settlement of the Jews in North America* (the original work had been published by *The*

Jewish Times in 1872; Kohler's edition was published in 1893), Henry Samuel Morais's *The Jews of Philadelphia* (1894), Simon Wolf's *The American Jew as Patriot, Soldier, and Citizen* (1895), Barnett Elzas's *The Jews of South Carolina*, and Samuel Oppenheimer's *The Early History of the Jews of New York, 1654–1664* (1909) constituted the revivalists' concerted effort to assert the importance of Jews to the founding and sustained prosperity of the nation's oldest cities.

12. Michael Kramer, "The Wretched Refuse of Jewish American Literary History," *Studies in American Jewish Literature* 31, no. 2 (Spring 2012): 64.

13. Moore, *Urban Origins*, 14.

14. Gerald Sorin, *The Jewish People in America. A Time for Building: The Third Migration, 1880–1920* (Baltimore: Johns Hopkins University Press, 1992), 10.

15. Kramer, "Wretched Refuse," 66.

16. Barbara Mann, *Space and Place in Jewish Studies* (New Brunswick: Rutgers University Press, 2012), 129.

17. Mann, 93.

18. Kandiyoti, *Migrant Sites*, 76.

19. Lila Corwin Berman, *The Jewish Romance with the Modern City: Loving, Leaving, and Reforming* (Ann Arbor: Jean and Samuel Frankel Center for Judaic Studies, 2016), 12.

20. Henry James, *Collected Travel Writings: Great Britain and America: English Hours, The American Scene, Other Travels*, ed. Richard Howard (New York: Library of America, 1993), 466–467.

21. Jacob Riis, *How the Other Half Lives* (New York: Charles Scribner's Sons, 1890), 7.

22. Williams, *Alice Morse Earle*, 89–90.

23. Sarah Orne Jewett, *The Country of the Pointed Firs* (1896), in *Short Fiction of Sarah Orne Jewett and Mary Wilkins Freeman*, ed. Barbara Solomon (New York: New American Library, 1979), 123.

24. Jules Chametzky, *Our Decentralized Literature: Cultural Mediations in Selected Jewish and Southern Writers* (Amherst: University of Massachusetts Press, 1986).

25. Kandiyoti, *Migrant Sites*, 49.

26. Kandiyoti, 52.

27. Annie Pollard and Daniel Soyer, *Emerging Metropolis: New York Jews in the Age of Immigration, 1840–1920* (New York: New York University Press, 2015), 145.

28. Abraham Cahan, *Yekl: A Tale of the New York Ghetto* (1896) (New York: Dover, 1970), 14.

29. Murray Baumgarten, "Their New York: Possessing the 'Capital of Words,'" in *The Cambridge History of Jewish American Literature*, ed. Hana Wirth-Nesher (New York: Cambridge University Press, 2016), 380.

30. Hana Wirth-Nesher and Michael Kramer, "Introduction: Jewish American Literatures in the Making," in *The Cambridge Companion to Jewish American Literature* (Cambridge: Cambridge University Press, 2003), 3.

31. Daly, *Settlement of the Jews*, ix.

32. Henry Morais, *The Jews of Philadelphia: Their History from the Earliest Times to the Present Time* (Philadelphia: Levytype Company, 1894), 6.

33. Morais, 6.

34. One of the most prominent works of literature to do so was Emma Lazarus's sonnet "1492" (1888), which referred to its eponymous subject as a "two-faced year." Ande Manners notes that in 1892, on the four hundredth anniversary of Columbus's landfall, the prominent attorney and statesman Oscar Straus corresponded with a Jewish historian on this exact subject. Straus wished his addressee, Dr. Moritz Keyserling, to undertake a study of "the role Jews may have played in the discovery of America." Straus drew a direct connection between the topic of America's discovery and the "large Russian [Jewish] immigration to our country": "You can well understand," he wrote, "what an important result it would have if it were historically shown that our race have had a direct part in the discovery of America." Ande Manners, *Poor Cousins* (New York: Coward, McGann, and Geoghegan, 1972), 61.

35. Michael Kramer, "The Origins of Jewish American Literary History," in *The Cambridge Companion to Jewish American Literature*, ed. Hannah Wirth-Nesher and Michael Kramer (Cambridge: Cambridge University Press, 2003), 28.

36. Samuel Oppenheimer, *The Early History of the Jews in New York, 1654–1664* (New York: American Jewish Historical Society, 1909), 16.

37. Daly, *Settlement of the Jews*, xv.

38. Markens, *The Hebrews in America*, 12.

39. Barnett Elzas, *The Jews of South Carolina from the Earliest Times to the Present Day* (Philadelphia: Lippincott, 1905), 120.

40. Morais, *The Jews of Philadelphia*, 18.

41. Markens, *The Hebrews in America*, 9.

42. Markens, 14.

43. Markens, 15.

44. Moore, *Urban Origins*, 9.

45. Markens, *The Hebrews in America*, 19–20.

46. Morais, *The Jews of Philadelphia*, 13–14.

47. Markens, *The Hebrews in America*, 38.

48. Henry Wadsworth Longfellow, "The Jewish Cemetery at Newport," in *The Poetical Works of Henry Wadsworth Longfellow* (Boston: Houghton Mifflin, 1888), 3:33–36.

49. Morais, *The Jews of Philadelphia*, 14.

50. Elzas, *The Jews of South Carolina*, 122.

51. Moore, *Urban Origins*, 39.

52. Benjamin Carp, *Rebels Rising: Cities and the American Revolution* (Oxford: Oxford University Press, 2007), 5.

53. Morais, *The Jews of Philadelphia*, 31.

54. Simon Wolf, *The American Jew as Patriot, Soldier, and Citizen*, ed. Louis Edward Levy (Philadelphia: Levytype Company, 1895), 12.

55. Markens, *The Hebrews in America*, 40.

56. Wolf, *American Jew*, 13.

57. Hyman Polack Rosenbach, *The Jews in Philadelphia Prior to 1800* (Philadelphia: Edward Stern, 1883), 13.

58. Rosenbach, 17.

59. Morais, *The Jews of Philadelphia*, 22.

60. Morais, 22.

61. Morais, 21.

62. Markens, *The Hebrews in America*, 67.

63. Beth Wenger, "Sculpting an American Jewish Hero: The Monuments, Myths, and Legends of Haym Solomon," in *Divergent Jewish Cultures: Israel and America*, ed. Deborah Dash Moore and S. Ilan Troen (New Haven: Yale University Press, 2001), 127.

64. Morais, *The Jews of Philadelphia*, 25.

65. Elzas, *The Jews of South Carolina*, 87.

66. Laura Leibman, *Messianism, Secrecy, and Mysticism: A New Interpretation of Early American Jewish Life* (Portland: Vallentine Mitchell, 2012), 2.

67. Rosenbach, *The Jews in Philadelphia*, 27.

68. Markens, *The Hebrews in America*, 75.

69. Markens, 75.

70. Markens, 76.

71. Markens, 77.

72. Markens, 76.

73. Elzas, *The Jews of South Carolina*, 119.

74. Elzas, 132.

75. Elzas, 145.

76. Daly, *Settlement of the Jews*, vi.

77. Sorin, *The Jewish People in America*, 10.

78. Esther Panitz, "The Polarity of American Jewish Attitudes towards Immigration," *American Jewish Historical Quarterly* 53 (1953): 118.

79. Kramer, "Wretched Refuse," 64.

80. Sorin, *The Jewish People in America*, 39.

81. Markens, *The Hebrews in America*, 2.

82. Wolf, *American Jew*, 544.

83. Wolf, viii.

84. Morais, *The Jews of Philadelphia*, 208.

85. Morais, vi–vii.

86. Wolf, *American Jew*, 566.

87. Wolf, 546.

88. Moore, *Urban Origins*, 3.

CHAPTER 3 — "A RARE GOOD FORTUNE TO ANYONE"

1. Edna Ferber, *A Peculiar Treasure* (New York: Garden City Publishing Company, 1940), 10.

2. Joyce Antler, *The Journey Home: Jewish Women and the American Century* (New York: Free Press, 1997), 160.

3. With regard to the figure of 150,000 small-town Jews, Lee Levinger cites a 1937 census of American Jews that was conducted by Harry S. Linfield. See Lee Levinger, "The Disappearing Small-Town Jew," *Commentary* 14 (August 1952): 157. For a much greater level of detail on the demography of small-town Jewry, including exact population figures for dozens of "three-digit" small-town Jewish communities across the United States, see the appendix of tables in Lee Shai Weissbach, *Jewish Life in Small-Town America: A History* (New Haven: Yale University Press, 2005), 338–357.

4. Ewa Morawska, *Insecure Prosperity: Small-Town Jews in Industrial America, 1890–1940* (Princeton: Princeton University Press, 1997), xiv.

5. Morawska, xiv.

6. Weissbach, *Jewish Life in Small-Town America*, 5.

7. Earl Raab, "Report from the Farm," *Commentary* 8 (December 1949): 577.

8. Adam Mendelsohn, *The Rag Race: How Jews Sewed Their Way to Success in America and the British Empire* (New York: New York University Press, 2015), 59.

9. Gerald M. Phillips, "Jews in Rural America," *Commentary* 29 (February 1960): 163.

10. Leonard Rogoff, *Homelands: Southern Jewish Identity in Durham and Chapel Hill, North Carolina* (Tuscaloosa: University of Alabama Press, 2001), 1.

11. While this chapter focuses its efforts on two writers whose work was coincident with the "classic era" of small-town Jewish life, there is, in fact, a long-standing literature of the rural Jewish experience in the United States, most of which was produced in the period's long aftermath. The sociologist Peter Rose made an inaccurate claim in 1976 when he said that the literature of small-town Jewish life "is limited to sketchy life histories, journalistic descriptions, and anecdotal recollections of the experiences of individuals" (see note 35). By far the most unique full-length literary account of rural Jewish life is I. J. Schwartz's *Kentucky*, a long poem that was originally published in book form in 1925—in Yiddish. See I. J. Schwartz, *Kentucky*, trans. and ed. Gertrude Dubrovsky (Tuscaloosa: University of Alabama Press, 1990). This fascinating work has warranted exploration by several scholars, including Hasia Diner (in *Roads Taken*) and Eric Goldstein (in *The Price of Whiteness: Jews, Race, and American Identity* [Princeton: Princeton University Press, 2006]). I have omitted it from consideration here in keeping with this chapter's focus on assimilated Jewish American authors who wrote in English for English-speaking audiences. Among the several backward-glancing autobiographies and memoirs of rural Jewish life that were written and

published in the post–World War II period by men and women who were recalling either their own childhoods or memorializing their parents' and grandparents' small-town experiences (or both), some of the most noteworthy include Julian Feibelman's *The Making of a Rabbi* (1980), Faye Moskowitz's *A Leak in the Heart* (1985), Brenda Weisberg Meckler's *Papa Was a Farmer* (1988), Julie Salamon's *The Net of Dreams* (1996), Stella Suberman's *The Jew Store* (1998), and Edward Cohen's *The Peddler's Grandson: Growing Up Jewish in Mississippi* (1999), as well as Eli Evans's highly acclaimed *The Provincials* (1976).

12. Morawska, *Insecure Prosperity*, 230.

13. Janet Galligani Casey, *A New Heartland: Modernity and the Agrarian Ideal in America* (Oxford: Oxford University Press, 2009), 4.

14. Ferber, *A Peculiar Treasure*, 13.

15. Schwartz, *Kentucky*, 7 (see note 11).

16. Ferber, *A Peculiar Treasure*, 10–11.

17. Ferber, 15.

18. Lori Harrison-Kahan, *The White Negress: Literature, Minstrelsy, and the Black-Jewish Imaginary* (New Brunswick: Rutgers University Press, 2011), 62.

19. Weissbach, *Jewish Life in Small-Town America*, 105.

20. Ferber, *A Peculiar Treasure*, 18.

21. Ferber, 19.

22. Ferber, 20.

23. Levinger, "The Disappearing Small-Town Jew," 161.

24. Ferber, *A Peculiar Treasure*, 31.

25. Ferber, 31.

26. Ferber, 40.

27. Steven Horowitz and Miriam Landsman, "The Americanization of Edna: A Study of Ms. Ferber's Jewish American Identity," *Studies in American Jewish Literature* 2 (1982): 72.

28. Ferber, *A Peculiar Treasure*, 41–42.

29. Ferber, 36.

30. Ferber, 31–32.

31. Ferber, 41.

32. In calling attention to this point, Lee Shai Weissbach refers to Anthony Channell Hilfer's *The Revolt from the Village: 1915–1930* (Chapel Hill: University of North Carolina Press, 1969). See Weissbach, *Jewish Life in Small-Town America*, 5.

33. William Barilas, *The Midwestern Pastoral: Place and Landscape in the Literature of the American Heartland* (Athens: Ohio University Press, 2006), 24.

34. Hilfer, *The Revolt from the Village*, 17.

35. Hilfer, 31.

36. Barilas, *The Midwestern Pastoral*, 21.

37. Casey, *A New Heartland*, 7.

38. Commercial activities that took place in rural communities were integral to the urbanizing economy, as Lee Shai Weissbach points out. While the rest of the nation hurtled "toward greater urbanization . . . smaller cities and towns retained their roles as crucial elements in America's urban network," owing in part to the proliferation of Jewish retailers who moved back and forth between the two environments. See Weissbach, *Jewish Life in Small-Town America*, 50.

39. Hasia Diner, "Entering the Mainstream of Modern Jewish History: Peddlers and the American Jewish South," *Southern Jewish History* 8 (2005): 2.

40. Toby Shafter, "The Fleshpots of Maine: Portrait of a Downeast Community," *Commentary* 7 (January 1949): 65.

41. Diner, "Entering the Mainstream," 2.

42. Mendelsohn, *The Rag Race*, 59.

43. Hasia Diner, *Roads Taken: The Great Jewish Migrations to the New World and the Peddlers Who Forged the Way* (New Haven: Yale University Press, 2015), 159.

44. Mark Bauman, *The Southerner as American: Jewish Style* (Cincinnati: American Jewish Archives, 1996), 16.

45. Levinger, "The Disappearing Small-Town Jew," 161.

46. Weissbach, *Jewish Life in Small-Town America*, 5.

47. Wallace Nutting, *Massachusetts Beautiful* (Framingham: Old America Company, 1923), 208.

48. Cyrus Adler, ed., *The American Jewish Year Book 5661* (September 24, 1900, to September 13, 1901) (Philadelphia: Jewish Publication Society of America, 1901), 2:71.

49. Foster was referring not only to Jews but also to a host of other Eastern European immigrants who had begun buying up agricultural land throughout southern New England. Quoted in Mary M. Donohue and Kenneth Libo, "Hebrew Tillers of the Soil: Connecticut's Jewish Farms," *Hog River Journal*, Spring 2006, 4.

50. Raab, "Report from the Farm," 578.

51. Ferber, *A Peculiar Treasure*, 10.

52. Two such accounts are Abraham Kohn's diary of his years as a peddler in pre–Civil War New England (see http://americanjewisharchives.org/publications/journal/PDF/1951 _03_03_00_doc_kohn_goodman.pdf) and Haiman Philip Spitz's 1886 autobiography, which is available through the Documenting Maine Jewry project.

53. Joseph Leiser, *American Judaism: The Religion and Religious Institutions of the Jewish People in the United States* (New York: Bloch, 1925), 86. It is worth noting that, shortly after arriving in Rochester, this same grandfather actually returned to Europe for several years!

54. Joseph Leiser, *Canaway and the Lustigs* (Cincinnati: Cincinnati Young Israel, 1909—reissued in 2015 by Forgotten Books, London), 15.

55. Leiser, 15.

56. Leiser, 21.

57. Leiser, 31.

58. Leiser, 30.

59. Leiser, *American Judaism: The Religion and Religious Institutions of the Jewish People in the Unites States, A Historical Survey* (New York: Bloch, 1925), 70–74.

60. Leiser, *Canaway and the Lustigs*, 13.

61. Diner, *Roads Taken*, 181. Diner points out that when Jewish retailers named their stores after various cities (the idea of a "Rochester Clothing Store" being located in Canaway was a fairly modest proposition; Paris and New York were among the more popular names among Jewish storeowners), they promoted the idea that their establishments were outposts of urban fashion. See also Weissbach, *Jewish Life in Small-Town America*, 191.

62. Leiser, *Canaway and the Lustigs*, 35.

63. Leiser, 70–73.

64. Leiser, *American Judaism*, 70.

65. Weissbach, *Jewish Life in Small-Town America*, 141.

66. Leiser, *Canaway and the Lustigs*, 130–134.

67. Ferber, *A Peculiar Treasure*, 35.

68. Ferber, 35.

69. Ferber, 49.

70. Ferber, 38.

71. Ferber did not indicate the race of the lynching victim. At least three *attempted* lynchings took place in Ottumwa during the seven years that Edna Ferber and her family lived there. A 1914 survey of these and other incidents of mob violence in the state of Iowa offers no insight into the race of the men who were attacked. See State Historical Society of Iowa, "Attempted Lynchings," *Annals of the State of Iowa* 11, no. 4 (1914): 260–285.

72. Diner, "Entering the Mainstream," 20; *Roads Taken*, 172.

73. Helene Gerard, "Yankees in Yarmulkes: Small-Town Jewish Life in Eastern Long Island," *American Jewish Archives* 38 (April 1986): 44.

74. Ferber, *A Peculiar Treasure*, 33–34.

75. Ferber, 45–46.

76. Ferber, 50.

77. Ferber, 58.

78. Antler, *The Journey Home*, 163.

79. Antler, 161.

80. Ferber, *A Peculiar Treasure*, 57.

81. See Barilas, *The Midwestern Pastoral*, 12. The critic's use of the concept is borrowed from Leo Marx, *The Machine in the Garden: Technology and the Pastoral Ideal in America* (Oxford: Oxford University Press, 1964). As Barilas explains, the complex pastoral is an ironic mode that "emphasizes social forms such as war, technology, and urbanization" as it represents the changing conditions of rural life.

82. Ferber, *A Peculiar Treasure*, 58.

83. Ferber, 59.

84. Antler, *The Journey Home*, 165.

85. Ferber, *A Peculiar Treasure*, 11.

86. Horowitz and Landsman, "The Americanization of Edna," 70.

87. Ferber, *A Peculiar Treasure*, 65.

88. Edna Ferber, *Fanny Herself* (New York: Frederick Stokes, 1917), 24.

89. Leiser, *Canaway and the Lustigs*, 24–25.

90. Ferber, *Fanny Herself*, 25.

91. Antler, *The Journey Home*, 164.

92. Harrison-Kahan, *The White Negress*, 68.

93. Horowitz and Landsman, "The Americanization of Edna," 70.

94. Ferber, *Fanny Herself*, 25.

95. Harrison-Kahan, *The White Negress*, 65.

96. Antler, *The Journey Home*, 136.

97. Antler, 151.

98. Ferber, *Fanny Herself*, 181.

99. Morawska, *Insecure Prosperity*, 226.

100. Ferber, *Fanny Herself*, 182.

101. See note 11 for a partial list of these post–World War II small-town memoirs.

102. Shafter, "Fleshpots of Maine," 67.

CHAPTER 4 — "THE LONGED-FOR PASTORAL"

1. Michael Galchinsky, "Scattered Seeds: A Dialogue of Diaspora," in *Insider/Outsider: American Jews and Multiculturalism*, ed. David Biale, Michael Galchinsky, and Susannah Heschel (Berkeley: University of California Press, 1998), 196.

2. Edward Shapiro, *We Are Many: Reflections of American Jewish History and Identity* (Syracuse: Syracuse University Press, 2005), 103.

3. The period immediately following World War II was profoundly transformational for Jewish Americans. Between 1940 and 1957, the number of Jewish Americans who held white-collar jobs grew from 10 percent to 55 percent. Fully a third of the nation's Jewish population moved to suburban communities between 1945 and 1965. See Samuel Freeman, *Jew vs. Jew: The Struggle for the Soul of American Jewry* (New York: Simon and Schuster, 2000), 40.

4. Marshall Sklare (and Joseph Greenbaum), *Jewish Identity on the Suburban Frontier* (New York: Basic Books, 1967), x.

5. Hana Wirth-Nesher, *Call It English: The Languages of Jewish American Literature* (Princeton: Princeton University Press, 2006), 54.

6. Ranen Omer-Sherman, *Diaspora and Zionism in Jewish American Literature* (Hanover, N.H.: Brandeis University Press, 2002), 227.

7. Deborah Dash Moore, "Introduction," in *American Jewish Identity Politics*, ed. Deborah Dash Moore (Ann Arbor: University of Michigan Press, 2008), 5.

8. For a contemporary account of an Orthodox community in conflict with mainstream America, see, for instance, Stephen G. Bloom, *Postville: A Clash of Cultures in Heartland America* (San Diego: Harcourt, 2000), which describes the establishment of a kosher chicken slaughterhouse in rural Iowa.

9. George Lipsitz, "The Possessive Investment in Whiteness: Racialized Social Democracy and the 'White' Problem in American Studies," *American Quarterly* 47, no. 3 (1995): 369–387. The two federal programs for which Lipsitz assigns responsibility for this result are the Federal Housing Authority (the FHA act was initiated in 1934) and the postwar "urban renewal" movement.

10. Kenneth Jackson, *Crabgrass Frontier: The Suburbanization of the United States* (New York: Oxford University Press, 1985), 4.

11. Steven M. Cohen and Arnold M. Eisen, *The Jew Within: Self, Family, and Community in America* (Bloomington: Indiana University Press, 2000), 2.

12. Philip Roth, *American Pastoral* (New York: Vintage, 1997), 85, 307.

13. Andrew Furman, *Contemporary Jewish American Writers and the Multicultural Dilemma: Return of the Exiled* (Syracuse: Syracuse University Press, 2000), 36.

14. Furman, 307.

15. Arnold Eisen, *The Chosen People in America: A Study in Jewish Religious Ideology* (Bloomington: Indiana University Press, 1983), 136.

16. Omer-Sherman, *Diaspora and Zionism*, 195.

17. Evelyn Avery, "Allegra Goodman's Fiction: From the Suburbs to Gan Eden," *Studies in American Jewish Literature* 22 (2003): 41; and Ruth Wisse, "The Joy of Limits" (review of *Kaaterskill Falls*), *Commentary* 106, no. 6 (1998): 67–70.

18. See Vincent Brook, ed., *You Should See Yourself: Jewish Identity in Postmodern American Culture* (New Brunswick: Rutgers University Press, 2006), 5.

19. Jackson, *Crabgrass Frontier*, 4.

20. Robert Beuka, "Cue the Sun: Soundings from Millennial Suburbia," *Iowa Journal of Cultural Studies* 3 (Fall 2003): 154–162. Reprinted in Nicolaides and Wiese, eds., *The Suburb Reader* (New York: Routledge, 2006), 333; Tom Martinson, *American Dreamscape: The Pursuit of Happiness in Postwar Suburbia* (New York: Carroll and Graf, 2000), 179.

21. John Cheever, "The Five-Forty-Eight," *New Yorker*, April 10, 1954.

22. Don DeLillo, *White Noise* (New York: Penguin, 1985), 59.

23. Beuka, "Cue the Sun," 334.

24. Thomas Pynchon, *The Crying of Lot 49* (New York: Penguin, 2012), 7.

25. Dolores Hayden, *Building Suburbia: Green Fields and Urban Growth* (New York: Vintage, 2003), 1.

26. Omer-Sherman, *Diaspora and Zionism*, 266.

27. Allegra Goodman, *Kaaterskill Falls* (New York: Dial Press, 1998), 271.

28. Omer-Sherman, *Diaspora and Zionism*, 224.

29. Cohen and Eisen, *The Jew Within*, 7.

30. Roth, *American Pastoral*, 89.

31. David Brauer, "American Anti-pastoral: Incontinence and Impurity in *American Pastoral* and *The Human Stain*," *Studies in American Jewish Literature* 23 (2004): 70.

32. Roth, *American Pastoral*, 28. The resonance between Zuckerman's assertion and the opening sentence of *Walden* is unmistakable: "When I wrote the following pages," Thoreau announced in 1854, "I lived alone, in the woods, a mile from any neighbor . . . on the shore of Walden Pond." Henry David Thoreau, *Walden* (1854) (New York: Thomas Crowell, 1910), 1.

33. Roth, 14.

34. Brian McDonald, "The Real American Crazy Shit: On Adamism and Democratic Individuality in *American Pastoral*," *Studies in American Jewish Literature* 23 (2004): 36.

35. Derek Parker-Royal, "Fictional Realms of Possibility: Reimagining the Ethnic Subject in Philip Roth's *American Pastoral*," *Studies in American Jewish Literature* 20 (2001): 7.

36. Roth, *American Pastoral*, 301.

37. Roth, 302.

38. Sarah Phillips Casteel, "Landscapes: America and the Americas," in *The Cambridge History of Jewish American Literature*, ed. Hana Wirth-Nesher (New York: Cambridge University Press, 2016), 423.

39. Omer-Sherman, *Diaspora and Zionism*, 52.

40. Roth, *American Pastoral*, 303–309.

41. Roth, 302–303.

42. Roth, 86–87.

43. Goodman, *Kaaterskill Falls*, 5.

44. Goodman, 106.

45. Dean Franco, *Race, Rights, and Recognition: Jewish American Literature Since 1969* (Ithaca: Cornell University Press, 2012), 62.

46. Goodman, *Kaaterskill Falls*, 218–219.

47. Avery, "Allegra Goodman's Fiction," 41.

48. Eileen Watts, "Fault Lines: Surveying the Boundary between Sacred and Secular in Allegra Goodman's *Kaaterskill Falls*," *Studies in American Jewish Literature* 19 (2000): 97.

49. Goodman, *Kaaterskill Falls*, 98.

50. Franco, *Race, Rights, and Recognition*, 96.

51. Thoreau, *Walden*, 110.

52. See chapter 3. The history of Jews in the Catskills is represented in Abraham Lavender and Clarence Steinberg, *Jewish Farmers of the Catskills: A Century of Survival* (Gainesville: University Press of Florida, 1995).

53. Goodman, *Kaaterskill Falls*, 20–21.

54. Washington Irving, *The Sketch Book* (New York: Signet, 1961).

55. Goodman, *Kaaterskill Falls*, 53.

56. Goodman, 6–7.

57. James D. Bloom, "For the Yankee Dead: Mukherjee, Roth, and the Diasporan Seizure of New England," *Studies in American Jewish Literature* 17 (1998): 43.

58. Lene Schoett-Kristensen, "Allegra Goodman's *Kaaterskill Falls*: A Liturgical Novel," *Studies in American Jewish Literature* 24 (2005): 29.

59. Goodman, *Kaaterskill Falls*, 82–83.

60. Goodman, 13.

61. Omer-Sherman, *Diaspora and Zionism*, 93.

62. David Myers, *American Paradox: Spiritual Hunger in an Age of Plenty* (New Haven: Yale University Press, 2000), 7–8.

63. Omer-Sherman, *Diaspora and Zionism*, 202.

64. Grace Paley, "The Used Boy Raisers," in *The Little Disturbances of Man* (New York: Viking, 1959), 132. See also Omer-Sherman, *Diaspora and Zionism*, 3.

65. Charles Olson, *Call Me Ishmael* (San Francisco: City Lights Books, 1947), 11.

66. Eric Goldstein, *The Price of Whiteness: Jews, Race, and American Identity* (Princeton: Princeton University Press, 2006), 208.

67. Sidra DeKoven Ezrahi, "State and Real Estate: Territoriality and the Modern Jewish Imagination," *Studies in Contemporary Jewry* 8 (1992): 57.

68. Casteel, "Landscapes," 414.

69. Casteel, 415.

CHAPTER 5 — RETURN TO THE SHTETL

1. Rabbi Max Wall, personal interview (Burlington, Vermont), October 18, 2004.

2. Michael Rothberg, *Multidirectional Memory: Remembering the Holocaust in the Age of Decolonization* (Stanford: Stanford University Press, 2009), 3.

3. Dan Miron, "The Literary Image of the Shtetl," *Jewish Social Studies* 1, no. 3 (Spring 1995): 3; and Jeffrey Shandler, *Shtetl: A Vernacular Intellectual History* (New Brunswick: Rutgers University Press, 2014), 130.

4. The shtetl as it has been commonly imagined dates back to the latter half of the eighteenth century, when the Polish nobility invited large numbers of Jews to settle the countryside as the administrators of market towns and the Jewish population of what was then Poland grew from 175,000 to 750,000. Samuel Kassow, "Introduction," in *The Shtetl: New Evaluations*, ed. Steven Katz (New York: New York University Press, 2007), 4.

5. Eric Goldstein, *The Price of Whiteness: Jews, Race, and American Identity* (Princeton: Princeton University Press, 2006), 236.

6. Jeremy Shere, "Imagined Diaspora: The Shtetl in Allen Hoffman's *Small Worlds* and Jonathan Safran Foer's *Everything Is Illuminated*," *Polin* 22 (2010): 455.

7. Steven Zipperstein, *Imagining Russian Jewry: Memory, History, Identity* (Seattle: University of Washington Press, 1999), 94.

8. Shere, "Imagined Diaspora," 454.

9. Alan Berger, *Children of Job: American Second-Generations Witnesses to the Holocaust* (Albany: State University of New York Press, 1997), 2.

10. Michael Chabon, "The Language of Lost History," *Harper's Magazine*, October 1997, 33.

11. William Boelhower, "Ethnographic Politics," in *Memory and Cultural Politics: New Approaches to American Ethnic Literature*, ed. Amritjit Singh, Joseph Skerrett, and Robert E. Hogan (Boston: Northeastern University Press, 1996), 38.

12. Anna Ronelle, "Three American Jewish Writers Imagine Eastern Europe," *Polin* 19 (2007): 380.

13. Boelhower, "Ethnographic Politics," 27.

14. Ronelle, "Three American Jewish Writers," 373.

15. Boelhower, "Ethnographic Politics," 36.

16. If there were a possible exception to this rule, it lay in the work of the colonial revivalists of the late nineteenth century (see chapter 2), who had labored to inscribe a historical and Jewish presence onto the cities of the Eastern Seaboard. For all of their interest in establishing the facts of early Jewish American history and attaching the history of the Jews to the history of America, however, the revivalists were too invested in their own Jewish identity and tradition to associate such episodes with any notion of true antiquity. Whatever stake that Jews might have had in the development of the American nation, it bore little significance within the wider context of their history as a people, whose recorded episodes stretched back to biblical times.

17. Goldstein, *The Price of Whiteness*, 213.

18. Merle Bachman, *Recovering "Yiddishland": Threshold Moments in American Literature* (Syracuse: Syracuse University Press, 2008), 9.

19. See especially Merle Bachman's *Recovering Yiddishland* and Jeffrey Shandler's *Adventures in Yiddishland: Postvernacular Language and Culture* (Berkeley: University of California Press, 2006).

20. Boelhower, "Ethnographic Politics," 39.

21. Leslie Marmon Silko, *Ceremony* (New York: Penguin, 1977), 187, 191.

22. Gloria Naylor, *Mama Day* (New York: Vintage, 1988), 3–4.

23. Boelhower, "Ethnographic Politics," 27.

24. Sidra DeKoven Ezrahi, *Booking Passage: Exile and Homecoming in the Modern Jewish Imagination* (Berkeley: University of California Press, 2000), 19.

25. Jennifer Glaser, "The Politics of Difference and the Future(s) of American Jewish Literary Studies," in "The Jewish Mystical Text as Literature," special issue, *Prooftexts* 29, no. 3 (Fall 2009): 476.

26. Amy Hungerford, "How Jonathan Safran Foer Made Love," *American Literary History* 25, no. 3 (Fall 2013): 611.

27. Sandor Gilman, *Multiculturalism and the Jews* (New York: Routledge, 2006), 186.

28. Andrew Furman, *Contemporary Jewish American Writing and the Multicultural Dilemma* (Syracuse: Syracuse University Press, 2000), 100.

29. As a child growing up in Schluftchev, Sasha is called Sorel. For the duration of this chapter, however, I refer to her by her adoptive adult name.

30. Murray Baumgarten, "Their New York: Possessing the 'Capital of Words,'" in *The Cambridge History of Jewish American Literature*, ed. Hana Wirth-Nesher (New York: Cambridge University Press, 2016), 96.

31. Rebecca Goldstein, *Mazel* (New York: Viking, 1995), 5.

32. Goldstein, 5.

33. Goldstein, 333.

34. Baumgarten, "Their New York," 91.

35. Shere, "Imagined Diaspora," 459.

36. Shandler, *Shtetl*, 48, 135.

37. Ronelle, "Three American Jewish Writers," 382.

38. Since Goldstein seems at pains to show us that Phoebe, Sasha's American-born granddaughter, is quite content with her life in the latter-day shtetl of Lipton, readers are less likely to share Sasha's contempt for shtetl life.

39. Goldstein makes the latter comparison twice in the novel.

40. Goldstein, *Mazel*, 67.

41. Goldstein, 63.

42. Israel Bartal, "Imagined Geography: The Shtetl, Myth, and Reality," in *The Shtetl: New Evaluations*, ed. Steven Katz (New York: New York University Press, 2007), 191.

43. Goldstein, *Mazel*, 106.

44. Goldstein.

45. Goldstein, 125–126.

46. Goldstein, 336.

47. Goldstein, 354–356, 108.

48. Baumgarten, "Their New York," 81.

49. Helene Meyers, "Homelands and Homemaking: Rebecca Goldstein's *Mazel*," *Journal of Modern Literature* 33, no. 3 (Spring 2010): 139.

50. Jonathan Boyarin, *Storm from Paradise: The Politics of Jewish Memory* (Minneapolis: University of Minnesota Press, 1992), xvi.

51. Avrom Bendavid-Val, *The Heavens Are Empty: Discovering the Lost Town of Trochenbrod* (New York: Pegasus, 2010).

52. Jonathan Safran Foer, "Foreword," in *The Heavens Are Empty*, by Avrom Bendavid-Val (New York: Pegasus Books, 2011), xiv.

53. Elaine Safer, "Illuminating the Ineffable: Jonathan Safran Foer's Novels," *Studies in American Jewish Literature* 25 (2006): 113.

54. Shere, "Imagined Diaspora," 463.

55. Jonathan Foer, *Everything Is Illuminated* (New York: Harper Perennial, 2003), 59.

56. Foer, 3.

57. Shere, "Imagined Diaspora," 458.

58. Foer, *Everything Is Illuminated*, 8.

59. Foer, 270.

60. Shandler, *Shtetl*, 46.

61. Foer, "Foreword," xiv.

62. Chabon, "The Language of Lost History," 33.

63. Boelhower, "Ethnographic Politics," 38.

64. Michael Galchinsky, "Scattered Seeds: A Dialogue of Diaspora," in *Insider/Outsider: American Jews and Multiculturalism*, ed. David Biale, Michael Galchinsky, and Susannah Heschel (Berkeley: University of California Press, 1998), 9.

65. Shandler, *Adventures in Yiddishland*, 49.

66. Chabon, "The Language of Lost History," 33.

CHAPTER 6 — TURNING DREAMSCAPES INTO LANDSCAPES
ON THE "WILD WEST BANK" FRONTIER

1. Jon Papernick, *The Ascent of Eli Israel and Other Stories* (New York: Arcade, 2002), 83.

2. Risa Miller, *Welcome to Heavenly Heights* (New York: St. Martin's Press, 2003), 6.

3. Stephen Cohen and Arnold Eisen, *The Jew Within: Self, Family, and Community in America* (Bloomington: Indiana University Press, 2000), 8.

4. Sidra DeKoven Ezrahi, "State and Real Estate: Territoriality and the Modern Jewish Imagination," *Studies in Contemporary Jewry* 8 (1992): 59.

5. Matti Friedman, "Distant Cousins," *Jewish Review of Books*, Fall 2017, 51.

6. Sidra DeKoven Ezrahi, "Our Homeland the Text . . . Our Text the Homeland: Exile and Homecoming in the Modern Jewish Imagination," *Michigan Quarterly Review* 31, no. 4 (Fall 1992): 477.

7. Ezrahi, 477.

8. Bernard Malamud, "Bernard Malamud: A Writer's Experience," interview by Celia Betsky, *Harvard Crimson*, January 22, 1973, http://www.thecrimson.com/article/1973/1/22/bernard-malamud-a-writers-experience-pbibn/.

9. Moshe Davis and Alvin Rosenfeld, "Promised Land(s): Zion, America, and American Jewish Writers," *Jewish Social Studies* 3, no. 3 (Spring–Summer 1997): 122.

10. Andrew Furman, *Israel through the Jewish American Imagination* (New York: State University of New York Press, 1997), 2.

11. Michael Kramer, "Balancing Acts" (unpublished essay, used by permission from the author), 7.

12. Sidra DeKoven Ezrahi, *Booking Passage: Exile and Homecoming in the Modern Jewish Imagination* (Berkeley: University of California Press, 2000), 230.

13. Tresa Grauer, "'A Drastically Bifurcated Legacy': Homeland and Jewish Identity in Contemporary Jewish-American Literature," in *Divergent Jewish Cultures: Israel and America*, ed. Deborah Dash Moore and S. Ilan Troen (New Haven: Yale University Press, 2001), 245.

14. Philip Roth, *Portnoy's Complaint* (New York: Random House, 1969), 253.

15. Grauer, "'A Drastically Bifurcated Legacy,'" 244–245.

16. Papernick and Miller are by no means the only contemporary Jewish American writers whose work features Israel prominently. Since 2000, works by Nathan Englander, Jonathan Safran Foer, Naama Goldstein, Michael Lavigne, and Harvey Pekar, among others, have significantly expanded the canon of Jewish American fiction about Israel. See Naomi Sokoloff, "Israel in the Jewish American Imagination," in *Cambridge History of Jewish American Literature*, ed. Hana Wirth-Nesher (Cambridge: Cambridge University Press, 2016), 362–379.

17. Ezrahi, "Our Homeland," 482.

18. See Jeffrey Shandler and Beth Wenger, eds., *Encounters with the Holy Land: Place, Past, and Future in American Jewish Culture* (Philadelphia: National Museum of American Jewish History/University of Pennsylvania, 1998).

19. See Grauer, "'A Drastically Bifurcated Legacy.'"

20. Laurence Silberstein, "Mapping, Not Tracing: Opening Reflection," in *Mapping Jewish Identities*, ed. Laurence Silberstein (New York: New York University Press, 2000), 15.

21. Anzia Yezierska, *Bread Givers* (New York: Doubleday, 1925), 209.

22. Edwidge Danticat, *Breath, Eyes, Memory* (New York: Vintage, 1994), 48.

23. Nessa Rapoport, quoted in Richard Siegel and Tamar Sofer, *The Writer in the Jewish Community: An Israeli-American Dialogue* (Rutherford: Fairleigh Dickinson University Press, 1993), 44.

24. Naomi Sokoloff, "Imagining Israel in American Jewish Fiction: Anne Roiphe's *Lovingkindness* and Philip Roth's *The Counterlife*," *Studies in American Jewish Literature* 10, no. 1 (1991): 66.

25. Michael Galchinsky, "Scattered Seeds: A Dialogue of Diaspora," in *Insider/Outsider: American Jews and Multiculturalism*, ed. David Biale, Michael Galchinsky, and Susannah Heschel (Berkeley: University of California Press, 1998), 200.

26. Jerold Auerbach, *Are We One? Jewish Identity in the United States and Israel* (New Brunswick: Rutgers University Press, 2001), 13.

27. Miller, *Welcome to Heavenly Heights*, 24.

28. Jonathan Boyarin, *Palestine and Jewish History: Criticism at the Borders of Ethnography* (Minneapolis: University of Minnesota Press, 1996), 325.

29. Papernick, *The Ascent of Eli Israel*, 114.

30. Miller, *Welcome to Heavenly Heights*, 207.

31. See, for instance, Joe Charlaff, "Right of Reply: US Airport Security—Israeli Style," *Jerusalem Post*, April 1, 2009, http://www.jpost.com/Opinion/Op-Ed-Contributors/Right-of-Reply-US-airport-security-Israeli-style.

32. Papernick, *The Ascent of Eli Israel*, 83.

33. Papernick, 93–94.

34. Papernick, 98.

35. Papernick, 99.

36. Papernick, 87.

37. Papernick, 99–100.

38. Papernick, 89.

39. Papernick, 87–89.

40. Papernick, 99.

41. Papernick, 105–106.

42. Papernick, 80.

43. Papernick, 101–102.

44. Papernick, 113–115.

45. Miller, *Welcome to Heavenly Heights*, 25, 69.

46. Emily Miller Budick, "Exodus, Discovery, and Coming Home to the Promised Land," in *People of the Book: Thirty Scholars Reflect on Their Jewish Identity*, ed. Jeffrey Rubin-Dorsky and Shelley Fisher Fishkin (Madison: University of Wisconsin Press, 1996), 217, 227.

47. Miller, *Welcome to Heavenly Heights*, 73.

48. Used in the Jewish ritual observation of Sukkoth, the citron is called an *Etrog* in Hebrew.

49. Miller, *Welcome to Heavenly Heights*, 20, 24–25.

50. Papernick, *The Ascent of Eli Israel*, 147.

51. Sokoloff, "Imagining Israel," 71.

52. Papernick, *The Ascent of Eli Israel*, 145, 158.

53. Papernick, 151.

54. Papernick, 166–167.

55. Papernick, 153–155.

56. Papernick, 157–158.

57. Papernick, 160, 182.

58. Miller, *Welcome to Heavenly Heights*, 212.

59. Miller, 137–141.

60. Miller, 193–201.

61. Miller, 203.

62. See Richard Siegel and Tamar Sofer, *The Writer in the Jewish Community: An Israeli-American Dialogue* (Rutherford: Fairleigh Dickinson University Press, 1993), 70.

63. Miller, *Welcome to Heavenly Heights*, 211–212.

64. Ezrahi, *Booking Passage*, 14.

CONCLUSION

1. Adam Gopnik, "The Patriot: The Collected Non-fiction of Philip Roth," *New Yorker*, November 13, 2017, 75.

2. Sidra DeKoven Ezrahi, "State and Real Estate: Territoriality and the Modern Jewish Imagination," *Studies in Contemporary Jewry* 8 (1992): 59.

INDEX

Abraham, 137, 142, 152. *See also* Isaac; Moriah, Mount
Abrahams, Emanuel, 44
Adamic myth, 90–91, 94–95, 98. *See also* innocence, myth of American
African Americans, 7, 108, 111
Aleichem, Sholem, 125
American Dream, 95, 96
American Jewish Historical Society, 34
Amichai, Yehuda, 147
Amsterdam, 14, 42, 44, 50
Anderson, Sherwood, 78, 80; *Winesburg, Ohio*, 62–63, 65
anti-Semitism, 53, 61, 65, 79–80, 106
Appalachia, 145. *See also* Kentucky
Appalachians (mountain range), 143. *See also* Kentucky
Appleton, Wisconsin, 60–61, 73–76, 78, 80
Arabs, 130, 137–138, 140–141. *See also* Palestinians
Ashkenazim, 5, 32, 34–36. *See also* Eastern European Jews; German Jews; Russian Jews

Baltimore, 14, 130, 149
Barbados, 14, 42
Bellow, Saul, 132
Ben-Gurion, David, 99
Benjamin, Israel Joseph, 11–14; *Five Years of Travel in the Orient, 1846–1851*, 23; *Three Years in America*, 11, 13–14, 23–31
Benjamin, Walter, 122
Berkshires (region in western Massachusetts), 90
Bible, 13, 90
Blake, William, 95

Boone, Daniel, 91
Boston, 18, 37, 50
Bridger, Jim, 13, 139
Bryant, William Cullen, 16
buffalo, 21–22
Burlington, Vermont, 105

Cahan, Abraham, 131, 134; *Yekl*, 39
California, 11, 14–15, 19, 21, 23–28
Canandaigua, New York, 59, 67
Captain Wolff (Delaware scout), 22
Carson, Kit, 13
Carvalho, David, 14
Carvalho, Solomon Nunes, 9–25, 29–31, 156; *Incidents of Travel and Adventure in the Far West*, 10–11, 13–23, 30–31
Cascades (mountain range), 24
Catskills (region in New York State), 99–101
Cave of the Patriarchs, 141, 149–150, 152. *See also* Israel: Hebron
Chabon, Michael, 107
Charleston, South Carolina, 9, 14, 40, 43, 46, 49–52. *See also* South Carolina
Cheever, John, 86–87
Chelm tales, 125
Cheyenne (Native American tribe), 9, 22
Chicago, 60, 73, 79
Church, Frederic, 101
Church of the Holy Sepulcher, 148
Civil War, 13, 24, 29, 31, 62, 64
Cloisters, 99
Cold War, 84
Cole, Thomas, 16; "Falls of the Kaaterskill," 101–102
colonial revival, 6, 32–56
Colorado, 18, 80

ABOUT THE AUTHOR

MICHAEL HOBERMAN teaches American literature at Fitchburg State University. His books include *New Israel/New England: Jews and Puritans in Early America* and *Yankee Moderns: Folk Regional Identity in the Sawmill Valley of Western Massachusetts*. He has held an NEH Long-Term Fellowship and a Fulbright Senior Scholar Fellowship at Utrecht University.